Made in the USA
San Bernardino, CA
06 April 2015

In the name of Allah, the Most Gracious, the Most Merciful

PREFACE

Praise be to Allah, the Lord of the Worlds, Who has said in His Noble Book,

كِتَابٌ أَنْزَلْنَاهُ إِلَيْكَ مُبَارَكٌ لِيَدَّبَّرُوا آيَاتِهِ وَلِيَتَذَكَّرَ أُولُو الْأَلْبَابِ ﴿٢٩﴾

*"(This is) a blessed Book which **We** have revealed to you, that they may ponder over its Verses and those of understanding would be reminded."* [Al-Quran 38:29];

أَفَلَا يَتَدَبَّرُونَ الْقُرْآنَ أَمْ عَلَىٰ قُلُوبٍ أَقْفَالُهَا ﴿٢٤﴾

"Then do they not ponder upon the Quran, or are there locks upon their hearts." [Al-Quran 47:24].

وَأَنْ أَتْلُوَ الْقُرْآنَ ۖ فَمَنِ اهْتَدَىٰ فَإِنَّمَا يَهْتَدِي لِنَفْسِهِ

"And to recite the Quran, and whoever is guided is only guided for (the benefit of) his own soul." [Al-Quran 27:92].

And may peace and blessings of Allah be upon the Prophet, Muhammad (SAWS), who said: *"The best among you is he who learns the Quran and then teaches it (to others)."* [Bukhari].

Obligations of the Quran on every Muslim

Based on the Quran and Hadith, it can be said that every Muslim has the following obligations towards the Quran

- To believe in the Quran;
- To read it and recite it daily;
- To understand its commandments;
- To act upon its teachings; and
- To convey its teachings to others

It is obvious that most of these obligations cannot be fully discharged unless the understanding of the Quran is acquired! When those who were given the book of Allah could no longer prove themselves to be its worthy bearers, they were described as donkeys laden with books. Allah (SWT) says,

مَثَلُ الَّذِينَ حُمِّلُوا التَّوْرَاةَ ثُمَّ لَمْ يَحْمِلُوهَا كَمَثَلِ الْحِمَارِ يَحْمِلُ أَسْفَارًا

"The likeness of those who were entrusted with the Taurat then they did not bore it (i.e., failed in the obligations), is like the donkey who carries volumes (of books but understands nothing from them)." [Al-Quran 62:5].

On the Day of Judgment our beloved Prophet (SAWS) will say:

$$\text{وَقَالَ الرَّسُولُ يَٰرَبِّ إِنَّ قَوْمِي اتَّخَذُوا هَٰذَا الْقُرْآنَ مَهْجُورًا}$$

"And the Messenger will say, 'O my Lord! Indeed, my people treated this Quran as a forsaken thing.'"
[Al-Quran 25:30].

Most of us devote a precious part of our lives to build our careers. We study a number of books, most of them in detail, in our schools, colleges, and universities. All these hardships are made to achieve the worldly gains. Do we devote at least a small percentage of our lifetime to the study of the Quran, which contains true guidance for achieving the success in this life and in the eternal life hereafter?

We want newspaper as soon as we get up in the morning and we read books and magazines of our fancy. It is indeed very sad that we have plenty of time at our disposal for everything except for studying the Quran.

Only if we could regularly recite the Quran with understanding, it would not only strengthen our faith but revolutionize our true relationship with Allah.

Importance of Understanding the Quran via the Arabic Text

The Quran is revealed in Arabic. It is neither prose nor poetry but a unique combination of both. It is simply inimitable and untranslatable. However, in spite of the limitations of translation, a sincere reader of the Quran will not be deprived of guidance. The message of the Quran is so powerful that it will have its due effect on the reader even if one reads the 'translation' only. But to feel the real charm of its originality by one's heart, mind, and reason, and ultimately by the soul, one should understand the Quran via the Arabic text.

We are linked with the Quran through one or all of the following sources: one's own recitation, listening to it in individual/congregational prayers, and audio and video channels. However, it is essential that we understand the full message of our Creator.

Easy to learn

It may be emphasized here that there are around 80,000 words in the Quran but the actual words are only around 2000!!! This could also be termed as one of the many miracles of the Quran. Accordingly, if a reader decides to learn only 10 new words everyday, he can understand the basic message of the Quran within a period of seven months! So it is indeed very easy to understand the Quran, provided one is willing to learn it.

$$\text{وَلَقَدْ يَسَّرْنَا الْقُرْآنَ لِلذِّكْرِ فَهَلْ مِن مُّدَّكِرٍ}$$

"And We have certainly made the Quran easy to understand and remember, so is there any who will remember (or receive admonition)?" [Al-Quran 54:17, 22, 32, 40].

See the video of a student of Al-Muminah School, Mumbai, India, titled "Even children can learn the Quran word-for-word" at http://www.youtube.com/watch?v=UL7gYBb1CBc

This present work may not be termed as an addition to the existing translations, but an attempt to equip the reader to understand the revelation directly from the text; thus it will Insha-Allah be a very useful tool for those who are willing to study the Quran and try to understand it. A beginner can bear in mind the meanings of each Arabic word provided right below it. Since many words are repeated in the Quran, the student will find for himself that within a few months of regular study, he is indeed able to understand the Quran through the text itself.

It may also be pointed out that a beginner does not have to, in the start itself, be worried about learning extensive grammar or how to speak the Arabic language. In fact, one has to develop vocabulary **before** learning grammar for the following reasons:

- A child first learns words and then starts linking them together. We speak our mother tongue fluently without ever learning the grammatical rules. That is to say, we learn it by repeatedly listening to the words.
- Learning extensive grammar before improving vocabulary is like putting the cart before the horse. Or it is like learning different styles of swimming by moving hands in the air inside a swimming pool without water. One has to fill the swimming pool with water (i.e., increase vocabulary) and then learn to swim (i.e., to connect the words with grammatical rules).

Importance of daily recitation

إِنَّ الَّذِينَ يَتْلُونَ كِتَابَ اللَّهِ وَأَقَامُوا الصَّلَوٰةَ وَأَنفَقُوا مِمَّا رَزَقْنَٰهُمْ سِرًّا وَعَلَانِيَةً يَرْجُونَ تِجَٰرَةً لَّن تَبُورَ ﴿٢٩﴾

"Indeed, those who recite the Book of Allah, and establish prayer, and spend out of what We have provided them secretly and openly, they hope for a transaction (profit) that will never perish." [Al-Quran 35:29].

We should therefore make it binding upon ourselves, among others, to recite the Quran everyday along with an effort to understand it via the Arabic text. If we recite one Ju'z (para) everyday, we can complete the Quran once every month. This will not only strengthen our faith but also revolutionize our relationship with Allah.

Some features of this work:

Even though there are many translations of the meanings of the Quran, they do not help the reader in linking the Arabic words to their meanings. The only purpose of this word-for-word translation is to facilitate learning the language of the Quran. Even though a few word-for-word translations exist but the format of the present work is different from them.

- The meaning of each word is given right below it.
- The translation provided in the left column is kept close to the Arabic and not literal. The objective of the whole exercise is to enable the reader understand directly from Arabic.
- Last, but not the least, the layout is such that it can also be used for regular recitation enabling constant revision.

Also, please note:

- The square brackets [ ] is placed on such words which are necessary in Arabic sentence structure but are not used in the English sentence structure. For example, look at **[the]** below:

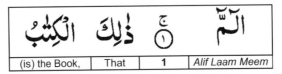

- Parentheses ( ) are placed on those words which are not there explicitly in the Arabic text but the structure of the complete Arabic sentence conveys the meanings which include those words. For example, look at **(is)** below:

In translating the words, every effort is made to choose the English word from the existing authentic Quran translations. Among others, we have benefited from the translations of Saheeh International, Abdullah Yusuf Ali, Pickthall, Shakir, Muhammad Mohar Ali, Muhammad Asad, Muhammad Taqi-ud-din Al-Hilali and Muhammad Muhsin Khan extensively. The compilers will be grateful to those who can spare some time and communicate the errors, if any, to them. Insha-Allah, they will be corrected in future editions of this work.

Acknowledgements

Up to the fourth Juz (para) Shaikh Abdul Ghafoor Parekh and up to the first Juz (para) and a part of second Juz (para) Dr. Abdulazeez Abdulraheem and Mr. Mohammad Abdulazeez Saadi were extensively involved in this work. However, after that they could not continue because of their busy schedules. Dr. Abdul-Moiz, graduate Jamia Nizamia, Ph.D., Osmania University, Hyderabad; Lecturer, Department of Arabic, Delhi University has reviewed this work.

A number of other people have helped in accomplishing this huge task. We are indebted to them for all their help. May Allah reward them abundantly, Dr. Mohammed Rafiqul Awal (Ph.D.) and Mr. Faisal Mujtaba Ahmed (M.S.) for developing macros and other programs for facilitating this work; Mr. Nazeeruddin (M.S.), Mr. Raziuddin (M.S.), Mr. Tariq Maghrabi (M.S.) Mr. Jehangir Pasha (M.S.), Mr. Mir Ali Shajee (M.S.), Mr. Mujtaba Shareef (M.S.), Mr. Arifus Salam Shaikh (M.S.), and Mr. Abul Bashar (M.S.) for their help in providing different translations in a format that was easily accessible for cross checking.

The compilers
Dr. Shehnaz Shaikh (M.B.B.S., M.D.)
Ms. Kausar Khatri (B.Com., B.Ed.)
July 2007

For feedback and suggestions contact Dr Shehnaz Shaikh, Founder, Al-Muminah School (www.almuminahschool.org) Cell: 91-9322266035, email: dr.shehnaz@gmail.com

All rights reserved. No part of this publication may be reproduced or transmitted in any form or by any means, electronic, mechanical, photocopying, recording, or otherwise, without the prior written permission of the compilers.

PDF version of this work is available for free download for personal use at www.emuslim.com
Mobile software of this work is available at www.guidedways.com

QPS Setting & Printing by: Alhuda Publications, Darya Ganj, New Delhi-110002, Tel: 011-64536120
E-mail: alhudapublications@yahoo.com

Juz (Para) Index

Juz Number	Surah name	Ayah number	Page number
Juz 1	Al-Fatiha	1: [1- 7]	1
	Al-Baqarah	2: [1-141]	2
Juz 2	Al-Baqarah	2: [142-253]	28
Juz 3	Al-Baqarah	2: [254-286]	55
	Al-e-Imran	3: [1-91]	65
Juz 4	Al-e-Imran	3:[92-200]	82
	An-Nisa	4: [1-23]	103
Juz 5	An-Nisa	4: [24-147]	110
Juz 6	An-Nisa	4: [148-176]	137
	Al-Maidah	5: [1-82]	143
Juz 7	Al-Maidah	5: [83-120]	165
	Al-Anam	6: [1-110]	173
Juz 8	Al-Anam	6: [111-165]	194
	Al-Araf	7: [1-87]	206
Juz 9	Al-Araf	7: [88-206]	222
	Al-Anfal	8: [1-40]	242
Juz 10	Al-Anfal	8: [41-75]	249
	At-Taubah	9: [1-93]	255

Surah Al-Fatiha

① الرَّحِيْمِ	الرَّحْمٰنِ	اللّٰهِ	بِسْمِ	
1 the Most Merciful.	the Most Gracious,	(of) Allah,	In (the) name	

1. In the name of Allah, the Most Gracious, the Most Merciful.

② الْعٰلَمِيْنَ	رَبِّ	لِلّٰهِ	اَلْحَمْدُ
2 of the universe	the Lord	(be) to Allah,	All praises and thanks

2. All praises and thanks be to Allah, the Lord of the universe.

مٰلِكِ	③ الرَّحِيْمِ	الرَّحْمٰنِ
(The) Master	3 the Most Merciful.	The Most Gracious,

3. The Most Gracious, the Most Merciful.

اِيَّاكَ	④ الدِّيْنِ	يَوْمِ
You Alone	4 (of the) Judgment.	(of the) Day

4. The Master of the Day of Judgment.

⑤ نَسْتَعِيْنُ	وَاِيَّاكَ	نَعْبُدُ
5 we ask for help.	and You Alone	we worship,

5. You Alone we worship, and You Alone we ask for help.

⑥ الْمُسْتَقِيْمَ	الصِّرَاطَ	اِهْدِنَا
6 the straight.	(to) the path,	Guide us

6. Guide us to the straight path.

اَنْعَمْتَ	الَّذِيْنَ	صِرَاطَ
You have bestowed (Your) Favors	(of) those	(The) path

الْمَغْضُوْبِ	غَيْرِ	عَلَيْهِمْ
those who earned (Your) wrath,	not (of)	on them,

⑦ الضَّآلِّيْنَ	وَلَا	عَلَيْهِمْ
7 (of) those who go astray.	and not	on themselves

7. The path of those on whom You have bestowed Your Favors, not the path of those who earned Your wrath, and not of those who go astray.

Surah Al-Baqarah

In the name of Allah, the Most Gracious, the Most Merciful.

1. *Alif Laam Meem*

2. This is the Book, there is no doubt in it, a Guidance for the God-conscious.

3. Those who believe in the unseen, and establish the prayer, and spend out of what **We** have provided them.

4. And those who believe in what is revealed to you (O Muhammad SAWS!), and what was revealed before you, and in the Hereafter they firmly believe.

5. Those are on Guidance from their Lord, and it is those who are the successful ones.

Surah 2: The cow (v. 1-5)

Part - 1

البقرة - 2 | الٓمٓ - 1

أَمۡ	ءَأَنذَرۡتَهُمۡ	عَلَيۡهِمۡ	سَوَآءٌ	كَفَرُواْ	ٱلَّذِينَ	إِنَّ
or	whether you warn them	to them	(it) is same	disbelieve[d],	those who	Indeed,

عَلَىٰ	خَتَمَ ٱللَّهُ	٦	يُؤۡمِنُونَ	لَا	تُنذِرۡهُمۡ	لَمۡ
on	Allah has set a seal	6	they believe.	not	you warn them,	not

وَلَهُمۡ	غِشَاوَةٌۖ	أَبۡصَـٰرِهِمۡ	وَعَلَىٰٓ	سَمۡعِهِمۡۖ	وَعَلَىٰ	قُلُوبِهِمۡ
And for them	(is) a veil.	their vision	and on	their hearing,	and on	their hearts

يَقُولُ	مَن	ٱلنَّاسِ	وَمِنَ	٧	عَظِيمٌ	عَذَابٌ
say,	(are some) who	the people	And of	7	great.	(is) a punishment

بِمُؤۡمِنِينَ	هُم	وَمَا	ٱلۡأٓخِرِ	وَبِٱلۡيَوۡمِ	بِٱللَّهِ	ءَامَنَّا
(are) believers (at all).	they	but not	[the] Last,"	and in the Day	in Allah	"We believed

يَخۡدَعُونَ	وَمَا	ءَامَنُواْ	وَٱلَّذِينَ	يُخَـٰدِعُونَ ٱللَّهَ	٨
they deceive	and not	believe[d],	and those who	They seek to deceive Allah	8

إِلَّآ	أَنفُسَهُمۡ	وَمَا	يَشۡعُرُونَ	٩	فِى	قُلُوبِهِم
except	themselves,	and not	they realize (it).	9	In	their hearts

عَذَابٌ	وَلَهُمۡ	مَّرَضٗا	فَزَادَهُمُ ٱللَّهُ	مَّرَضٞ
(is) a punishment	and for them	(in) disease;	so Allah increased them	(is) a disease,

لَهُمۡ	قِيلَ	وَإِذَا	١٠	يَكۡذِبُونَ	كَانُواْ	بِمَا	أَلِيمُۢ
to them,	it is said	And when	10	[they] lie.	they used to	because	painful

مُصۡلِحُونَ	نَحۡنُ	إِنَّمَا	قَالُوٓاْ	فِى ٱلۡأَرۡضِ	تُفۡسِدُواْ	لَا
(are) reformers."	we	"Only	they say,	the earth,"	spread corruption	"(Do) not

ٱلۡمُفۡسِدُونَ	هُمُ	إِنَّهُمۡ	أَلَآ	١١
(are) the ones who spread corruption,	themselves	indeed they	Beware,	11

ءَامِنُواْ	لَهُمۡ	قِيلَ	وَإِذَا	١٢	يَشۡعُرُونَ	لَا	وَلَـٰكِن
"Believe	to them,	it is said	And when	12	they realize (it).	not	[and] but

ٱلسُّفَهَآءُۗ	ءَامَنَ	كَمَآ	أَنُؤۡمِنُ	قَالُوٓاْ	ٱلنَّاسُ	ءَامَنَ	كَمَآ
the fools?"	believed	as	"Should we believe	they say,	the people,	believed	as

يَعۡلَمُونَ	لَا	وَلَـٰكِن	ٱلسُّفَهَآءُ	هُمُ	إِنَّهُمۡ	أَلَآ	١٣
they know.	not	[and] but	(are) the fools	themselves	certainly they	Beware,	13

وَإِذَا	ءَامَنَّا	قَالُوٓاْ	ٱلَّذِينَ	لَقُواْ	وَإِذَا
But when	"We believe[d]."	they say,	believe[d],	those who	they meet	And when

Surah 2: The cow (v. 6-14) — **Part - 1**

6. Indeed, those who disbelieve, it is same to them whether you warn them or do not warn them, they will not believe.

7. Allah has set a seal on their hearts and on their hearing, and on their vision is a veil. And for them is a great punishment.

8. And among the people there are some who say, "We believe in Allah and in the Last Day," but they are not believers (at all).

9. They seek to deceive Allah and those who believe, but they do not deceive except themselves and they do not realize it.

10. In their hearts is a disease, so Allah has increased their disease, and for them is a painful punishment because they used to lie.

11. And when it is said to them, "Do not spread corruption on the earth," they say, "We are only reformers."

12. Indeed, they are the ones who spread corruption, but they do not realize it.

13. And when it is said to them, "Believe as the people have believed," they say, "Should we believe as the fools have believed?" Indeed, they themselves are the fools, but they do not know.

14. And when they meet those who believe, they say, "We believe." But when

البقرة-٢ — الم-١

4

we	only	(are) with you,	"Indeed, we	they say,	their evil ones,	with	they are alone

in	and prolongs them	at them,	mocks	Allah	14	(are) mockers."

bought	(are) the ones who	Those	15	they wander blindly.	their transgression,

were they	and not	their commerce	profited	So not	for [the] guidance.	[the] astraying

kindled	(of) the one who	(is) like (the) example	Their example	16	guided-ones.

their light	Allah took away	his surroundings,	it lighted	then, when	a fire,

blind,	dumb,	Deaf,	17	(so) they (do) not see.	darkness[es],	in	and left them

in it (are)	the sky	from	like a rainstorm	Or	18	[they] will not return.	so they

from	their ears	in	their fingers	They put	and lightning.	and thunder,	darkness[es],

(is) the One Who encompasses	And Allah	[the] death.	(in) fear (of)	the thunderclaps

Whenever	their sight.	snatches away	the lightning	Almost	19	the disbelievers.

they stand (still).	on them	it darkens	and when	in it,	they walk	for them	it flashes

and their sight.	their hearing,	He would certainly have taken away	Allah had willed,	And if

O mankind!	20	All-Powerful.	thing	every	(is) on	Allah	Indeed,

before you,	and those [who]	created you	the One Who	your Lord,	worship

---

they are alone with their evil ones, they say, "Indeed, we are with you, we are only mocking."

15. Allah mocks at them, and prolongs them in their transgression (while) they wander blindly.

16. Those are the ones who have bought astraying (in exchange) for guidance. So their commerce did not profit them, nor were they guided.

17. Their example is like the example of one who kindled a fire; then, when it lighted all around him, Allah took away their light and left them in darkness, so they do not see.

18. Deaf, dumb, and blind - so they will not return (to the right path).

19. Or like a rainstorm from the sky in which is darkness, thunder, and lightning. They put their fingers in their ears to keep out the stunning thunderclaps in fear of death. And Allah encompasses the disbelievers.

20. The lightning almost snatches away their sight. Whenever it flashes for them, they walk therein, and when darkness covers them, they stand (still). And if Allah had willed, He would certainly have taken away their hearing and their sight. Indeed, Allah has power over everything.

21. O mankind! Worship your Lord, the **One Who** created you and those before you,

Surah 2: The cow (v. 15-21) — **Part - 1**

Surah 2: The cow (v. 22-26)

22. (He) Who has made the earth a resting place for you, and the sky a canopy, and sent down rain from the sky, and brought forth therewith fruits as provision for you. So do not set up rivals to Allah while you know (the truth).

23. And if you are in doubt about what We have revealed to Our slave (Muhammad SAWS), then produce a chapter like it, and call your witnesses other than Allah, if you are truthful.

24. But if you do not do (it), and you will never be able to do (it), then fear the Fire whose fuel is men and stones, prepared for the disbelievers.

25. And give good news (O Muhammad SAWS!) to those who believe and do righteous deeds that for them will be Gardens under which rivers flow. Whenever they are provided with a provision of fruit therefrom, they will say, "This is what we were provided with before." And they will be given things in resemblance; and they will have therein purified spouses, and they will abide therein forever.

26. Indeed, Allah is not ashamed to set forth an example even of a mosquito

27. Those who break the Covenant of Allah after its ratification, and cut what Allah has ordered to be joined, and spread corruption on the earth. It is those who are the losers.

28. How can you disbelieve in Allah? When you were dead (lifeless), and He gave you life. Then He will cause you to die, then (again) He will bring you (back) to life, and then to Him you will be returned.

29. He is the One Who created for you all that is in the earth. Moreover, He turned to the heaven and fashioned them seven heavens. And He is the All-Knower of everything.

30. And when your Lord said to the angels, "Indeed, I am going to place a vicegerent on the earth." They said, "Will You place therein one who will spread corruption and shed blood, while we glorify You with Your praises

Surah 2: The cow (v. 27-30)

Surah 2: The cow (v. 31-36)

Arabic (right-to-left)	English word-by-word
وَنُقَدِّسُ لَكَ ۖ قَالَ إِنِّي أَعْلَمُ مَا لَا تَعْلَمُونَ	and we sanctify [to] You." He said, "Indeed, I know what you (do) not know."
(30) وَعَلَّمَ ءَادَمَ الْأَسْمَآءَ كُلَّهَا ثُمَّ عَرَضَهُمْ	30 And He taught Adam the names - all of them. Then He displayed them
عَلَى الْمَلَٰٓئِكَةِ فَقَالَ أَنۢبِـُٔونِي بِأَسْمَآءِ هَٰٓؤُلَآءِ إِن	to the angels, then He said, "Inform Me of (the) names of these, if
كُنتُمْ صَٰدِقِينَ (31) قَالُوا۟ سُبْحَٰنَكَ لَا عِلْمَ لَنَآ	you are truthful." 31 They said, "Glory be to You! No knowledge (is) for us
إِلَّا مَا عَلَّمْتَنَآ ۖ إِنَّكَ أَنتَ الْعَلِيمُ	except what You have taught us. Indeed You! You (are) the All-Knowing,
الْحَكِيمُ (32) قَالَ يَٰٓـَٔادَمُ أَنۢبِئْهُم بِأَسْمَآئِهِمْ ۖ فَلَمَّآ	the All-Wise. 32 He said, "O Adam! Inform them of their names." And when
أَنۢبَأَهُم بِأَسْمَآئِهِمْ قَالَ أَلَمْ أَقُل لَّكُمْ إِنِّىٓ	he had informed them of their names, He said, "Did not I say to you, Indeed, I
أَعْلَمُ غَيْبَ السَّمَٰوَٰتِ وَالْأَرْضِ وَأَعْلَمُ مَا تُبْدُونَ	[I] know (the) unseen (of) the heavens and the earth, and I know what you reveal
وَمَا كُنتُمْ تَكْتُمُونَ (33) وَإِذْ قُلْنَا لِلْمَلَٰٓئِكَةِ	and what you [were] conceal." 33 And when We said to the angels,
ٱسْجُدُوا۟ لِءَادَمَ فَسَجَدُوٓا۟ إِلَّآ إِبْلِيسَ أَبَىٰ	"Prostrate to Adam," [so] they prostrated, except Iblees. He refused
وَٱسْتَكْبَرَ وَكَانَ مِنَ ٱلْكَٰفِرِينَ (34) وَقُلْنَا	and was arrogant and became of the disbelievers. 34 And We said,
يَٰٓـَٔادَمُ ٱسْكُنْ أَنتَ وَزَوْجُكَ ٱلْجَنَّةَ وَكُلَا مِنْهَا	"O Adam! Dwell you and your spouse (in) Paradise, and [you both] eat from it
رَغَدًا حَيْثُ شِئْتُمَا وَلَا تَقْرَبَا هَٰذِهِ	freely (from) wherever you [both] wish. But do not [you two] approach this
ٱلشَّجَرَةَ فَتَكُونَا مِنَ ٱلظَّٰلِمِينَ (35) فَأَزَلَّهُمَا	[the] tree, lest you [both] be of the wrongdoers." 35 Then made [both of] them slip
ٱلشَّيْطَٰنُ عَنْهَا فَأَخْرَجَهُمَا مِمَّا	the Shaitaan from it, and he got [both of] them out from what

---

and sanctify **You**?" He said, "Indeed, **I** know that which you do not know."

31. And **He** taught Adam all the names. Then **He** displayed them to the angels and said, "Inform **Me** the names of these, if you are truthful."

32. They said, "Glory be to **You**! We have no knowledge except what **You** have taught us. Indeed, it is **You** who are the All-Knowing, the All-Wise."

33. **He** said, "O Adam! Inform them of their names." And when he had informed them of their names, **He** said, "Did **I** not tell you that **I** know the unseen of the heavens and the earth? And **I** know what you reveal and what you conceal."

34. And when **We** said to the angels, "Prostrate to Adam," they prostrated, except Iblees. He refused and was arrogant and became of the disbelievers.

35. And **We** said, "O Adam! Dwell you and your wife in Paradise, and eat freely from wherever you wish, but do not approach this tree, lest you be among the wrongdoers."

36. Then Shaitaan made them slip out of it and got them out from that

in which they were. And **We** said, "Go down, as enemies to one another; and on the earth will be your dwelling place and a provision for a period."

37. Then Adam received (some) words from his Lord, and **He** turned towards him (in mercy). Indeed, it is **He** Who is Oft-returning (to mercy), the Most Merciful.

38. **We** said, "Go down from it, all of you. And when there comes to you Guidance from **Me**, then whoever follows **My** Guidance, they will have no fear, nor will they grieve.

39. And those who disbelieve and deny **Our** Signs, they are the companions of the Fire; they will abide in it forever."

40. O Children of Israel! Remember **My** favor which **I** bestowed upon you, and fulfill **My** Covenant (upon you), **I** will fulfill your covenant (from Me), and fear **Me** and **Me** alone.

41. And believe in what **I** have sent down confirming that which is (already) with you, and be not the first to disbelieve in it. And do not exchange **My** Signs for a small price, and fear **Me** and **Me** Alone.

42. And do not mix the truth with falsehood or conceal the truth while you know (it).

43. And establish the prayer and give *zakah* and bow down with those who bow down.

44. Do you order

Surah 2: The cow (v. 37-44)   **Part - 1**

تَتْلُونَ	وَأَنْتُمْ	أَنْفُسَكُمْ	وَتَنْسَوْنَ	بِالْبِرِّ	النَّاسَ	
[you] recite	while you	yourselves,	and you forget	[the] righteousness	[the] people	
بِالصَّبْرِ	وَاسْتَعِينُوا	﴿٤٤﴾	تَعْقِلُونَ	أَفَلَا	الْكِتَابَ	
through patience	And seek help	44	you use reason?	Then, will not	the Book?	
وَالصَّلَاةِ		إِلَّا عَلَى الْخَاشِعِينَ		لَكَبِيرَةٌ	وَإِنَّهَا	
45	the humble ones,	on	except	(is) surely difficult	and indeed, it	and the prayer;
الَّذِينَ	يَظُنُّونَ	أَنَّهُمْ	مُلَاقُو	رَبِّهِمْ	وَأَنَّهُمْ	إِلَيْهِ رَاجِعُونَ
will return.	to Him	and that they	their Lord	will meet	that they	believe- Those who
يَا بَنِي	إِسْرَائِيلَ	اذْكُرُوا	نِعْمَتِيَ	الَّتِي	أَنْعَمْتُ	عَلَيْكُمْ
upon you	I bestowed	which	My Favor	Remember	(of) Israel!	O Children 46
وَأَنِّي	فَضَّلْتُكُمْ	عَلَى الْعَالَمِينَ	﴿٤٧﴾	وَاتَّقُوا	يَوْمًا	لَا
(will) not	a day,	And fear	47	the worlds.	over	[I] preferred you	and that I
تَجْزِي	نَفْسٌ	عَنْ نَفْسٍ	شَيْئًا	وَلَا	يُقْبَلُ	مِنْهَا
from it	will be accepted	and not	anything,	(another) soul	any soul	avail
شَفَاعَةٌ	وَلَا	يُؤْخَذُ	مِنْهَا	عَدْلٌ	وَلَا	هُمْ
they	and not	a compensation,	from it	will be taken	and not	any intercession,
يُنْصَرُونَ	﴿٤٨﴾	وَإِذْ	نَجَّيْنَاكُمْ	مِنْ	آلِ فِرْعَوْنَ	
(the) people of Firaun	from	We saved you	And when	48	will be helped.	
يَسُومُونَكُمْ	سُوءَ الْعَذَابِ	يُذَبِّحُونَ	أَبْنَاءَكُمْ	وَيَسْتَحْيُونَ		
and letting live	your sons	slaughtering	torment,	horrible	(who were) afflicting you (with)	
نِسَاءَكُمْ	وَفِي	ذَلِكُمْ	بَلَاءٌ	مِنْ	رَبِّكُمْ	عَظِيمٌ ﴿٤٩﴾
49	great.	your Lord	from	(was) a trial	that	And in	your women.
وَإِذْ	فَرَقْنَا	بِكُمُ	الْبَحْرَ	فَأَنْجَيْنَاكُمْ	وَأَغْرَقْنَا	
and We drowned	then We saved you,	the sea,	for you	We parted	And when	
آلَ فِرْعَوْنَ	وَأَنْتُمْ	تَنْظُرُونَ	﴿٥٠﴾	وَإِذْ	وَاعَدْنَا	
We appointed	And when	50	(were) looking.	while you	(the) people of Firaun	
مُوسَى	أَرْبَعِينَ	لَيْلَةً	ثُمَّ	اتَّخَذْتُمُ	الْعِجْلَ	مِنْ بَعْدِهِ وَأَنْتُمْ
and you	after him	the calf	you took	Then	nights.	forty	(for) Musa
ظَالِمُونَ	﴿٥١﴾	ثُمَّ	عَفَوْنَا	عَنْكُمْ	مِنْ بَعْدِ	ذَلِكَ
that,	after	you	We forgave	Then	51	(were) wrongdoers.

Surah 2: The cow (v. 45-52)

people to be righteous and you forget (to practice it) yourselves, while you recite the Book? Then will you not use reason (intellect)?

45. And seek help through patience and prayer; and indeed, it is difficult except for the humble ones,

46. (They are those) who believe that they will meet their Lord and that they will return to **Him**.

47. O Children of Israel! Remember **My** Favor which **I** bestowed upon you, and that **I** preferred you over the worlds.

48. And fear a day when no soul will avail another in the least, nor will intercession be accepted from it, nor will compensation be taken from it, nor will they be helped.

49. And (recall) when **We** saved you from the people of Firaun, who were afflicting you with a horrible torment, slaughtering your sons and letting your women live. And in that was a great trial from your Lord.

50. And (recall) when **We** parted the sea for you and saved you and drowned the people of Firaun while you were looking on.

51. And (recall) when **We** made an appointment with Musa for forty nights. Then you took the calf (for worship) after him (i.e., his departure) and you were wrongdoers.

52. Then, even after that, **We** forgave you

so that you may be grateful.

53. And (recall) when **We** gave Musa the Book (Taurat) and the Criterion (of right and wrong) that perhaps you would be guided.

54. And (recall) when Musa said to his people, "O my people! Indeed you have wronged yourselves by taking the calf (for worship). So turn in repentance to your Creator and kill yourselves. That is best for you in the sight of your Creator." Then **He** accepted your repentance. Indeed, **He** is the Oft-returning (to mercy), the Most Merciful.

55. And when you said, "O Musa! We will never believe you until we see Allah manifestly," so the thunderbolt seized you while you were looking on.

56. Then **We** revived you after your death, so that you might be grateful.

57. And **We** shaded you with clouds and sent down to you *manna* and quails. Eat from the good things, which **We** have provided you. And they did not wrong **Us**, but they were doing wrong to themselves.

58. And when **We** said, "Enter this town and eat abundantly from wherever you wish, and enter the gate bowing humbly and say, 'Repentance,' **We** will forgive your sins for you. And **We** will increase

Surah 2: The cow (v. 53-58)   Part - 1

the good-doers (in reward)."

59. But those who wronged changed the words from that which had been said to them for another; so **We** sent down upon the wrongdoers a punishment from the sky because they were defiantly disobeying.

60. And when Musa asked for water for his people, **We** said, "Strike the stone with your staff." Then twelve springs gushed forth from it. All the people (of the twelve tribes) knew their drinking place. "Eat and drink from the provision of Allah, and do not act wickedly on the earth spreading corruption."

61. And when you said, "O Musa! We can never endure one (kind of) food. So pray to your Lord to bring forth for us out of what the earth grows, its herbs, its cucumbers, its garlic, its lentils, and its onions." He said, "Would you exchange that which is better for that which is inferior? Go down to (any) city and indeed you will have what you have asked for." And humiliation and misery were struck upon them and they drew on themselves the wrath of Allah. That was because they used to disbelieve in the Signs of Allah

الٓمّٓ - ١   البقرة - ٢

and kill the Prophets without any right. That was because they disobeyed and they were transgressing.

62. Indeed, those who believed, and those who became Jews, and the Christians, and the Sabians - who believed in Allah and the Last Day and did righteous deeds, will have their reward with their Lord; they will have no fear, nor will they grieve.

63. And when We took your covenant, and We raised above you the mount (saying), "Hold firmly that which We have given you, and remember what is in it, perhaps you would become righteous."

64. Then even after that you turned away. Had it not been for the Grace and Mercy of Allah upon you, surely you would have been among the losers.

65. And indeed, you knew those amongst you who transgressed in the matter of the Sabbath. So We said to them, "Be apes, despised."

66. And We made it a deterrent punishment for those who were present and those who succeeded them and an admonition for those who fear Allah.

67. And when Musa said to his people, "Indeed, Allah commands you to slaughter a cow," they said, "Do you take us in ridicule?" He said,

وَيَقْتُلُونَ	النَّبِيِّنَ	بِغَيْرِ	الْحَقِّ ۗ	ذَٰلِكَ	بِمَا	
and kill	the Prophets	without (any)	[the] right.	That	(was) because	
عَصَوا	وَّكَانُوا	يَعْتَدُونَ ۝٦١	إِنَّ	الَّذِينَ	ءَامَنُوا	
they disobeyed	and they were	transgressing. 61	Indeed,	those who	believed	
وَالَّذِينَ	هَادُوا	وَالنَّصَارَىٰ	وَالصَّابِئِينَ	مَنْ	ءَامَنَ	
and those who	became Jews	and the Christians	and the Sabians -	who	believed	
بِاللَّهِ	وَالْيَوْمِ	الْءَاخِرِ	وَعَمِلَ	صَالِحًا	فَلَهُمْ	أَجْرُهُمْ
in Allah	and the Day	[the] Last	and did	righteous deeds,	so for them	(is) their reward
عِنْدَ	رَبِّهِمْ	وَلَا	خَوْفٌ	عَلَيْهِمْ	وَلَا	هُمْ يَحْزَنُونَ ۝٦٢
with	their Lord	and no	fear	on them	and not	they will grieve. 62
وَإِذْ	أَخَذْنَا	مِيثَاقَكُمْ	وَرَفَعْنَا	فَوْقَكُمُ	الطُّورَ	خُذُوا
And when	We took	your covenant	and We raised	over you	the mount,	"Hold
مَا	ءَاتَيْنَاكُم	بِقُوَّةٍ	وَاذْكُرُوا	مَا	فِيهِ	لَعَلَّكُمْ
what	We have given you	with strength,	and remember	what	(is) in it,	perhaps you
تَتَّقُونَ ۝٦٣	ثُمَّ	تَوَلَّيْتُم	مِّنْ بَعْدِ			
(would become) righteous." 63	Then	you turned away	after			
ذَٰلِكَ ۖ	فَلَوْلَا	فَضْلُ اللَّهِ	عَلَيْكُمْ	وَرَحْمَتُهُ		
that.	So if not	(for the) Grace of Allah	upon you	and His Mercy,		
لَكُنتُم	مِّنَ	الْخَاسِرِينَ ۝٦٤	وَلَقَدْ	عَلِمْتُمُ		
surely you would have been	of	the losers. 64	And indeed,	you knew		
الَّذِينَ	اعْتَدَوْا	مِنكُمْ	فِي السَّبْتِ	فَقُلْنَا	لَهُمْ	
those who	transgressed	among you	in the (matter of) Sabbath.	So We said	to them,	
كُونُوا	قِرَدَةً	خَاسِئِينَ ۝٦٥	فَجَعَلْنَاهَا	نَكَالًا	لِّمَا	
"Be	apes,	despised." 65	So We made it	a deterrent punishment	for those	
بَيْنَ يَدَيْهَا	وَمَا خَلْفَهَا	وَمَوْعِظَةً	لِّلْمُتَّقِينَ ۝٦٦			
(in) front of them	and those after them	and an admonition	for those who fear (Allah).			
وَإِذْ	قَالَ مُوسَىٰ	لِقَوْمِهِ	إِنَّ اللَّهَ	يَأْمُرُكُمْ		
And when	Musa said	to his people,	"Indeed, Allah	commands you		
أَن	تَذْبَحُوا	بَقَرَةً ۖ	قَالُوا	أَتَتَّخِذُنَا	هُزُوًا ۖ	قَالَ
that	you slaughter	a cow."	They said,	"Do you take us	(in) ridicule."	He said,

Surah 2: The cow (v. 62-67)   **Part - 1**

"I seek refuge in Allah from being among the ignorant."

68. They said, "Pray to your Lord to make clear to us what it is." He (Musa) said, "**He** says, 'It is a cow neither old nor young, but of middle age,' so do what you are commanded."

69. They said, "Pray to your Lord to make clear to us its color." He (Musa) said, "**He** says, 'It is a yellow cow, bright in color, pleasing to those who see it.'"

70. They said, "Pray to your Lord to make clear to us what it is. Indeed, all cows look alike to us. And indeed, if Allah wills, we will surely be guided."

71. He (Musa) said, "**He** says, it is a cow neither trained to plough the earth nor water the field; sound, with no blemish on it." They said, "Now you have come with the truth." So they slaughtered it, though they were near to not doing it.

72. And (recall) when you killed a man and disputed concerning it, but Allah brought forth that which you were concealing.

73. So We said, "Strike him with a part of it." Thus Allah revives the dead,

Surah 2: The cow (v. 68-73) Part - 1

Surah 2: The cow (v. 74-78)

73. and shows you **His** Signs, perhaps you may use your intellect.

74. Then (even after that) your hearts hardened like stones or even worse in hardness. And indeed, there are stones from which rivers gush forth, and indeed, there are some of them (i.e., the stones) which split asunder and water flows from them, and indeed, there are some of them (i.e., the stones) which fall down because of fear of Allah. And Allah is not unaware of what you do.

75. Do you hope (O believers!) that they would believe you while indeed a party of them used to hear the words of Allah and then distort it after they had understood it, knowingly?

76. And when they meet those who believe, they say, "We have believed." But when they are alone with one another, they say, "Do you tell them what Allah has revealed to you so that they (might) use it in argument against you before your Lord? Then do you not understand?"

77. Do they not know that Allah knows what they conceal and what they declare?

78. And among them are unlettered (i.e., illiterate) people

79. So woe to those who write the book with their own hands, then say, "This is from Allah," to exchange it for a little price. So woe to them for what their hands have written and woe to them for what they earn.

80. And they say, "Never will the Fire touch us except for a few days." Say, "Have you taken a covenant from Allah, so that Allah will never break **His** Covenant? Or do you say against Allah that which you do not know?"

81. Yes, (on the contrary) whoever earns evil and his sins have surrounded him - those are the companions of the Fire; they will abide in it forever.

82. And those who believe and do righteous deeds, those are the companions of Paradise; they will abide in it forever.

83. And (recall) when **We** took the covenant from the Children of Israel (saying), "Do not worship except Allah, and be good to parents, relatives, orphans and the needy, and speak good to people and establish the prayer

and give the *zakah*." Then you turned away, except a few of you, and you were refusing.

84. And when **We** took your covenant, "Do not shed your (i.e., each other's) blood or evict yourselves (one another) from your homes." Then you ratified while you were witnessing.

85. Then you are those (same ones) who kill one another and evict a party of you from their homes, support one another against them in sin and transgression. And if they come to you as captives, you ransom them; while their eviction (itself) was forbidden to you. So do you believe in part of the Book and disbelieve in (another) part? Then what should be the recompense for those who do so among you except disgrace in worldly life; and on the Day of Resurrection they will be sent back to the most severe punishment? And Allah is not unaware of what you do.

86. Those are the ones who have bought the life of this world (in exchange) for the Hereafter; so the punishment will not be lightened for them, nor will they be helped.

87. And indeed **We** gave Musa the Book and **We** followed him up with (a succession of)

Surah 2: The cow (v. 84-87) Part - 1

Messengers. And **We** gave Isa, the son of Maryam, clear signs and supported him with the Holy Spirit. Is it not so, that whenever there came to you a Messenger with what you yourselves did not desire, you acted arrogantly? So a party (of Messengers) you denied and another party you killed.

88. And they said, "Our hearts are wrapped." Nay, Allah has cursed them for their disbelief; so little is that which they believe.

89. And when there came to them a Book (Qur'an) from Allah confirming what was with them, though before that they used to pray for victory over disbelievers - then when there came to them that which they recognized, they disbelieved in it. So the curse of Allah is on the disbelievers.

90. Evil is that for which they have sold themselves, that they disbelieved in what Allah has revealed, grudging that Allah sends down of **His** Grace upon whom **He** wills from among **His** servants. So they have drawn on themselves wrath upon wrath. And for the disbelievers is a humiliating punishment.

91. And when it is said to them, "Believe in what Allah has revealed," they say, "We believe (only) in what was revealed to us." And they disbelieve in what came after it, while it is the truth confirming that which is with them. Say, "Then why did you kill the Prophets of Allah before, if you were believers?"

92. And indeed Moses came to you with clear signs, then you took the calf (in worship) after he left, and you were wrongdoers.

93. And when We took your covenant and We raised above you the mount, "Hold firmly what We gave you and listen," they said, "We heard and we disobeyed." And they were made to imbibe (the love of) the calf into their hearts because of their disbelief. Say, "Evil is that which your faith orders you, if you are believers."

94. Say, "If the home of the Hereafter with Allah is exclusively for you and not for others of mankind, then wish for death, if you are truthful."

95. And they will never wish for it, ever, because of what their hands have sent ahead (i.e., their deeds). And Allah knows the wrongdoers.

96. And you will surely find them the most greedy of mankind for life, and (even greedier) than those who associate partners with Allah. Each one of them loves

Surah 2: The cow (v. 92-96) — Part - 1

97. Say, "Whoever is an enemy to Jibreel - for indeed he has brought it (i.e., Quran) down upon your heart (O Muhammad!) by the permission of Allah, confirming what came before it and a guidance and glad tidings for the believers."

98. Whoever is an enemy to Allah and **His** Angels, and **His** Messengers, and Jibreel and Meekael, then indeed Allah is an enemy to the disbelievers.

99. And indeed **We** revealed to you clear Verses, and none disbelieve in them except the defiantly disobedient.

100. Is it (not the case that) whenever they made a covenant, a party of them threw it away? Nay, most of them do not believe.

101. And when a Messenger of Allah came to them confirming that which was with them, a party of those who were given the Book threw away the Book of Allah behind their backs as if they did not know.

102. And they followed what the devils had recited over the kingdom of Sulaiman. It was not Sulaiman who disbelieved, but the devils disbelieved, teaching

Surah 2: The cow (v. 97-102)   Part - 1

people magic and that which was sent down to the two angels, Harut and Marut in Babylon. But neither of these two taught anyone unless they had said, "We are only a trial, so do not disbelieve (by practicing magic)." And (yet) they learnt from those two that by which they cause separation between a man and his wife. But they could not harm anyone with it except by Allah's permission. And they learn that which harms them and does not profit them. And indeed they knew that whoever purchased it (i.e., magic) would not have any share in the Hereafter. And surely evil is that for which they sold themselves, if they only knew.

103. And if they had believed (the truth) and feared Allah, then indeed the reward from Allah would have been better, if they only knew.

104. O you who believe! Do not say 'Raina,' but say 'Unzurna' and listen. And for the disbelievers is a painful punishment.

105. Neither those who disbelieve among the People of the Book, nor those who associate partners with Allah like (it at all) that any good should be sent down to you from your Lord. But Allah chooses for **His** Mercy

Surah 2: The cow (v. 103-105)   Part - 1

whom **He** wills. And Allah is the Possessor of Great Bounty.

106. Whatever **We** abrogate of a sign or cause it to be forgotten, **We** bring a better one or similar to it. Do you not know that Allah has power over everything?

107. Do you not know that to Allah belongs the Kingdom of the heavens and the earth? And you do not have, besides Allah, any protector or any helper.

108. Or do you intend to ask your Messenger as Musa was asked before? And whoever exchanges faith for disbelief has certainly strayed from the right path.

109. Many of the People of the Book wish they could turn you back to disbelief after you have believed, out of jealousy from themselves, (even) after the truth has become clear to them. So forgive them and overlook until Allah brings **His** Command. Indeed, Allah has power over everything.

110. And establish prayer and give *zakah*. And whatever good you send forth for yourselves, you will find it with Allah. Indeed, Allah is All-Seer of what you do.

111. And they say, "None will enter Paradise except one who is a Jew or a Christian." That is their wishful thinking. Say, "Bring your proof if you are truthful."

112. Yes, whoever submits his face (i.e., himself) to Allah and is a good-doer, then his reward is with his Lord. And no fear will be on them, nor will they grieve.

113. The Jews say, "The Christians have nothing (true to stand) upon." And the Christians say, "The Jews have nothing (true to stand) upon," although they both recite the Book. Thus say those who do not know (the Book, making) similar statements. Allah will judge between them on the Day of Resurrection in (all those matters over) which they were differing (between themselves).

114. And who are more unjust than those who prevent the name of Allah from being mentioned in **His** masajid and strive for their destruction? (As for) those, it is not for them that they enter them (i.e., masajid) except in fear. For them, there is disgrace in this world and a great punishment in the Hereafter.

115. And to Allah belongs the east and the west, so wherever you turn, there is the face of Allah. Indeed, Allah is All-Encompassing, All-Knowing.

Surah 2: The cow (v. 111-115)

مَا	لَّهُۥ	بَل	سُبْحَٰنَهُۥ	وَلَدًا	ٱتَّخَذَ ٱللَّهُ	وَقَالُوا۟	
(is) what	for Him	Nay,	Glory be to Him!	a son."	"Allah has taken	And they said,	
۞	قَٰنِتُونَ	كُلٌّ	وَٱلْأَرْضِ	ٱلسَّمَٰوَٰتِ	فِى		
116	(are) humbly obedient.	All	and the earth.	the heavens	(is) in		
أَمْرًا	قَضَىٰٓ	وَإِذَا	وَٱلْأَرْضِ	ٱلسَّمَٰوَٰتِ	بَدِيعُ		
a matter,	He decrees	And when	and the earth!	(of) the heavens	(The) Originator		
لَا	ٱلَّذِينَ	وَقَالَ	۞	فَيَكُونُ	كُن	لَهُۥ	فَإِنَّمَا يَقُولُ
(do) not	those who	And said	117	and it becomes.	"Be,"	to it	[so] only He says
قَالَ	كَذَٰلِكَ	ءَايَةٌ	تَأْتِينَآ	أَوْ	يُكَلِّمُنَا ٱللَّهُ	لَوْلَا	يَعْلَمُونَ
said	Like that	a sign?	comes to us	or	Allah speaks to us	"Why not	know,
قَد	قُلُوبُهُمْ	تَشَٰبَهَتْ	قَوْلِهِمْ	مِّثْلَ	مِن قَبْلِهِم	ٱلَّذِينَ	
Indeed,	their hearts.	Became alike	their saying.	similar	before them	those	
إِنَّا	۞	يُوقِنُونَ	لِقَوْمٍ	ٱلْءَايَٰتِ	بَيَّنَّا		
Indeed We!	118	(who) firmly believe.	for people	the signs	We have made clear		
وَنَذِيرًا		بَشِيرًا		بِٱلْحَقِّ		أَرْسَلْنَٰكَ	
and (as) a warner.		(as) a bearer of good news		with the truth,		[We] have sent you	
وَلَن	۞	ٱلْجَحِيمِ	أَصْحَٰبِ	عَنْ	تُسْـَٔلُ		وَلَا
And never	119	(of) the blazing Fire.	(the) companions	about	you will be asked		And not
تَتَّبِعَ	حَتَّىٰ	ٱلنَّصَٰرَىٰ	وَلَا	ٱلْيَهُودُ	عَنكَ		تَرْضَىٰ
you follow	until	the Christians	and [not]	the Jews	with you		will be pleased
وَلَئِنِ		ٱلْهُدَىٰ	هُوَ	هُدَى ٱللَّهِ	إِنَّ	قُلْ	مِلَّتَهُمْ
And if		(is) the Guidance."	it	(the) Guidance of Allah,	"Indeed,	Say,	their religion.
مَا	ٱلْعِلْمِ	مِنَ	جَآءَكَ	ٱلَّذِى	بَعْدَ	أَهْوَآءَهُم	ٱتَّبَعْتَ
not	the knowledge,	of	has come to you	what	after	their desires	you follow
ٱلَّذِينَ	۞	نَصِيرٍ	وَلَا	وَلِىٍّ	مِنْ	مِنَ ٱللَّهِ	لَكَ
Those,	120	any helper.	and not	protector	any	Allah from	for you
تِلَاوَتِهِۦٓ		حَقَّ		يَتْلُونَهُۥ		ٱلْكِتَٰبَ	ءَاتَيْنَٰهُمُ
(of) its recitation.		(as it has) right		recite it		the Book	We have given them
هُمْ	فَأُو۟لَٰٓئِكَ	بِهِۦ	يَكْفُرْ	وَمَن	بِهِۦ	يُؤْمِنُونَ	أُو۟لَٰٓئِكَ
they	then those,	in it,	disbelieves	And whoever	in it.	believe	Those (people)

116. And they say, "Allah has taken a son." Glory be to **Him**! Nay, to **Him** belongs whatever is in the heavens and the earth. All are humbly obedient to **Him**.

117. The Originator of the heavens and the earth! When **He** decrees a matter, **He** only says to it, "Be," and it becomes.

118. And those who do not know say, "Why does Allah not speak to us or a sign come to us?" Thus said those before them, (uttering) similar statements. Their hearts resemble each other. **We** have indeed made the signs clear for the people who firmly believe.

119. Indeed, **We** have sent you (O Muhammad SAWS!) with the truth, as a bearer of good news and a warner. And you will not be asked about the companions of the blazing Fire.

120. And the Jews and the Christians will never be pleased with you until you follow their religion. Say, "Indeed, the Guidance of Allah is the (only) Guidance." And if you follow their desires after what has come to you of the knowledge, you will have neither any protector from Allah nor any helper.

121. Those to whom **We** have given the Book, recite it as it should be recited. They believe in it. And whoever disbelieves in it - it is those who

Surah 2: The cow (v. 116-121)

Surah 2: The cow (v. 122-126)

122. O Children of Israel! Remember **My** Favor which **I** bestowed upon you and **I** preferred you over the worlds.

123. And fear a Day when no soul will avail another in the least, and no compensation will be accepted from it, nor will any intercession benefit it, nor will they be helped.

124. And (remember) when his Lord tried Ibrahim with words (i.e., commandments) and he fulfilled them, **He** said, "Indeed **I** will make you a leader for mankind." He (Ibrahim) said, "And of my offspring?" **He** said, "**My** Covenant does not include the wrongdoers."

125. And (remember) When **We** made the House (Kabah) a place of (frequent) return (i.e., pilgrimage) for mankind and a place of security and said, "Take the standing place of Ibrahim as a place of prayer." And **We** made a covenant with Ibrahim and Ismail, (saying), "Purify **My** House for those who circumambulate it, and those who seclude themselves for devotion and prayer and those who bow down and prostrate."

126. And when Ibrahim said, "My Lord, make this a secure city and provide its people with fruits - whoever of them believes in Allah and the Last Day," He said,

"And whoever disbelieves - I will grant him enjoyment for a little; then I will force him to the punishment of the Fire, and evil is the destination."

127. And when Ibrahim was raising the foundations of the House (i.e., Kabah) together with Ismail, (they prayed), "Our Lord! Accept (this service) from us. Indeed, You Alone are the All-Hearing, the All-Knowing.

128. Our Lord! Make us submissive (i.e., Muslim) to You and from our offspring a community submissive to You. And show us our ways of worship and turn to us (in Mercy). Indeed, You Alone are the Oft-returning, the Most Merciful.

129. Our Lord! Raise up in their midst a Messenger, who will recite to them Your Verses and teach them the Book and wisdom and purify them. Indeed, You Alone are the All-Mighty, the All-Wise.

130. And who will turn away from the religion of Ibrahim except the one who fools himself? And indeed We chose him (i.e., Ibrahim) in this world, and in the Hereafter he surely will be among the righteous.

131. When his Lord said to him, "Submit (yourself)," he said, "I have submitted myself to the Lord of the worlds."

132. And Ibrahim enjoined upon his sons and so did Yaqub (saying), "O my sons! Indeed, Allah has chosen

Surah 2: The cow (v. 127-132) — Part - 1

for you the (true) religion, so do not die except while you are submissive (to **Him**)."

133. Or were you witnesses when death came to Yaqub, when he said to his sons, "What will you worship after me?" They said, "We will worship your God and the God of your forefathers, Ibrahim and Ismail and Ishaq - One God. And we are submissive to **Him**."

134. That was a community which has passed away. It will have what (deeds) it earned and you will have what you have earned. And you will not be asked about what they used to do.

135. And they said, "Be Jews or Christians, then you will be guided." Say, "Nay, (we follow) the religion of Ibrahim, the upright; and he was not of those who associated partners with Allah."

136. Say, "We have believed in Allah and what is revealed to us and what was revealed to Ibrahim and Ismail and Ishaq and Yaqub and the descendants, and what was given to Musa and Isa and what was given to the Prophets from their Lord. We make no distinction between any of them. And to **Him** we are submissive (i.e., Muslims)."

137. So if they believe in the like of what you believe,

(are) submissive."	while you	except	so you should not die	the religion,	for you
when	[the] death,	Yaqub	came to	when	witnesses	were you	Or	132
"We will worship	They said,	after me?"	will you worship	"What	to his sons,	he said
and Ishaq -	and Ismail	Ibrahim	(of) your forefathers,	and (the) God	your God
(was) a community	This	133	(are) submissive."	to **Him**	And we	One.	God
you earned.	what	and for you	what it earned	for it	(which) has passed away,
And they said,	134	do.	they used to	about what	you will be asked	And not
"Nay,	Say,	(then) you will be guided."	Christians,	or	Jews	"Be
of	he was	and not	(the) upright;	(of) Ibrahim,	(the) religion
in Allah	"We have believed	Say,	135	those who associated partners (with Allah)."
and Ismail	Ibrahim	to	was revealed	and what	to us	(is) revealed	and what
(to) Musa	was given	and what	and the descendants,	and Yaqub	and Ishaq
Not	their Lord.	from	(to) the Prophets	was given	and what	and Isa
(are) submissive."	to **Him**	And we	of them.	any	between	we make distinction
in [it],	you have believed	(of) what	in (the) like	they believe [d]	So if	136

Surah 2: The cow (v. 133-137)

then indeed, they are rightly guided. But if they turn away, then they are only in dissension. So Allah will suffice you against them, and **He** is the All-Hearing, the All-Knowing.

138. (Ours is) the color (religion) of Allah! And who is better than Allah at coloring (ordaining religion)? And we are **His** worshippers.

139. Say, "Do you argue with us about Allah while **He** is our Lord and your Lord? For us are our deeds, and for you are your deeds. And we are sincere (in intentions and deeds) to **Him**.

140. Or do you say that Ibrahim and Ismail and Ishaq and Yaqub and the descendants were Jews or Christians?" Say, "Are you better knowing or is Allah?" And who is more unjust than the one who conceals a testimony that he has from Allah? And Allah is not unaware of what you do.

141. That was a community, which has passed away. It will have what (deeds) it earned and you will have what you have earned. And you will not be asked about what they used to do.

Surah 2: The cow (v. 138-141) — Part - 1

142. The foolish among the people will say, "What has turned them from the direction of prayer which they used to (face)." Say, "To Allah belong the east and the west. He guides whom He wills to the straight path."

143. And thus We have made you a community of the middle way so that you will be witnesses over mankind and the Messenger will be a witness over you. And We appointed the direction of the prayer which you used to face in order to make evident he who follows the Messenger from he who turns back on his heels. And indeed, it was a great test except for those whom Allah guided. And Allah would not let go waste your faith. Indeed, Allah is Full of Kindness towards mankind, the Most Merciful.

144. Indeed, We see the turning of your face (O Muhammad SAWS!), towards the heaven. Surely We will turn you to a direction of prayer that pleases you. So turn your face towards the direction of Al-Masjid Al-Haraam (Kabah). And wherever you (believers) are, turn your faces towards its direction. And indeed, those who were given the Book, know well that it is the truth from their Lord. And Allah is not

Surah 2: The cow (v. 142-144) — Part - 2

unaware of what they do.

145. And even if you bring to those who were given the Book all the signs, they would not follow your direction of prayer, nor will you follow their direction of prayer. And nor would they be followers of each other's direction of prayer. And if you follow their desires after knowledge has come to you, then surely you will be among the wrongdoers.

146. Those to whom We gave the Book, recognize it like they recognize their sons. But indeed, a group of them knowingly conceal the Truth.

147. The Truth is from your Lord, so do not be among the doubters.

148. And for everyone is a direction towards which he turns, so race towards good. Wherever you will be, Allah will bring you together. Indeed, Allah has power over everything.

149. And from wherever you start forth (for prayers) turn your face in the direction of Al-Masjid Al-Haraam (Kabah). And indeed, it is the truth from your Lord. And Allah is not unaware of what you do.

150. And from wherever you start forth (for prayer) turn your face in the direction

Surah 2: The cow (v. 145-150)

of Al-Masjid Al-Haraam (Kabah). And wherever you are, turn your faces towards it, so that people will not have any argument against you except the wrongdoers among them, so do not fear them but fear **Me**, so that **I** may complete **My** favor upon you, perhaps you may be guided.

151. Similarly **We** sent among you a Messenger from among you, who recites to you **Our** verses and purifies you and teaches you the Book and the wisdom, and teaches you what you were not knowing.

152. So remember **Me**, **I** will remember you. And be grateful to **Me** and do not be ungrateful to **Me**.

153. O you who believe! Seek help through patience and prayer. Indeed, Allah is with the patient ones.

154. And do not say about those who are slain in the way of Allah, "They are dead." Nay, they are alive, but you do not perceive.

155. And surely **We** will test you with something of fear, hunger, loss of wealth, lives and fruits; but give good news to the patient ones.

156. Who, when misfortune strikes them, they say, "Indeed, we belong to Allah and indeed to **Him** we

157. Those are the ones on whom are blessings from their Lord and Mercy. And they are the guided ones.

158. Indeed, the *Safa* and the *Marwah* are symbols of Allah. So whoever performs *Hajj* or *Umrah*, there is no blame on him for walking between them. And whoever does good voluntarily, then indeed, Allah is All-Appreciative, All-Knowing.

159. Indeed, those who conceal the clear proofs We revealed, and the Guidance, after We made it clear for the people in the Book - they are cursed by Allah and cursed by those who curse.

160. Except those who repent and reform themselves and openly declare, then from those, I will accept repentance, and I am the Acceptor of Repentance, the Most Merciful.

161. Indeed, those who disbelieve and die as disbelievers, upon them is the curse of Allah, the Angels and the mankind all together.

162. (They will) abide in it forever. The punishment will not be lightened for them, nor will they be reprieved.

163. And your God is one God; there is no god except **Him**, the Most Gracious, the Most Merciful.

Surah 2: The cow (v. 157-163)   Part - 2

164. Indeed, in the creation of the heavens and the earth and the alternation of the night and the day, and the ships which sail in the sea with that which benefits people, and what Allah has sent down from the sky of rain, giving life thereby to the earth after its death, and dispersing therein of all kinds of moving creatures, and directing the winds and the clouds controlled between the sky and the earth, surely are signs for people who use their intellect.

165. And (yet) among mankind are some who take for worship others besides Allah as equals to **Him**. They love them as they should love Allah. But those who believe are stronger in their love for Allah. And if only those who wronged could see, when they will see the punishment, that all power belongs to Allah and Allah is severe in punishment.

166. When those who were followed disown those who followed them, and they will see the punishment and all their ties will be cut off.

167. And those who followed will say, "If only we had (one more chance) to return (to the world), we would disown them as they have disowned us." Thus Allah will show them their deeds as regrets for them. They will never come out of the Fire.

Surah 2: The cow (v. 164-167)

168. O mankind! Eat from whatever is on the earth - lawful and good and do not follow the footsteps of Shaitaan. Indeed, he is your clear enemy.

169. He (Shaitaan) only commands you to do evil and shameful deeds and to say about Allah what you do not know.

170. And when it is said to them, "Follow what Allah has revealed," they said, "Nay, we will follow what we found our forefathers following." Even though their forefathers understood nothing, nor were they guided?

171. And the example of those who disbelieve is like the one (shepherd) who shouts at that which hears nothing but calls and cries - deaf, dumb, and blind, they do not understand.

172. O you who believe! Eat from the good things which **We** have provided you and be grateful to Allah if you worship **Him** alone.

173. He has only forbidden to you dead animals, blood, the flesh of swine, and that which has been dedicated to other than Allah. But whoever is compelled (by necessity), without (willful) disobedience nor transgressing (the limits) then there is no sin on him. Indeed, Allah is Oft-Forgiving, and Most Merciful.

Surah 2: The cow (v. 1648-173) Part - 2

174. Indeed, those who conceal what Allah has revealed of the Book, and purchase a small gain therewith, they eat nothing except Fire in their bellies. And Allah will not speak to them on the Day of Judgment, nor will He purify them, and they will have a painful punishment.

175. Those are the ones who buy astraying in place of Guidance and punishment in place of forgiveness. So what is their endurance on the Fire!

176. That is because Allah has sent down the Book in Truth. And indeed, those who differ over the Book are in extreme dissension.

177. It is not righteousness that you turn your faces towards the east or the west but righteous is he who believes in Allah, the Last Day, the Angels, the Book, and the Prophets and gives wealth in spite of love for it to the near relatives, the orphans, the needy, the wayfarer, and those who ask, and in freeing the slaves; and who establishes prayer and gives *zakah* and he who fulfils the covenant when he makes it; and he who is patient in suffering, hardship,

Surah 2: The cow (v. 174-177) — Part - 2

and periods of stress. Those are the ones who are true and it is those who are the righteous.

178. O you who believe! Legal retribution is prescribed for you in cases of murder, the freeman for the freeman, and the slave for the slave, and the female for the female. But whoever is pardoned in any way by his brother then a suitable payment should be made to him in fairness. This is a concession and mercy from your Lord. But whoever transgresses after that, will have a painful punishment.

179. And in legal retribution there is (saving of) life for you, O men of understanding! So that you may become righteous.

180. Prescribed for you when death approaches any of you, if he leaves good, that he should make a will for the parents and near relatives with due fairness - a duty on the righteous.

181. Then whoever changes it after he has heard it - the sin is only upon those who alter it. Indeed, Allah is All-Hearing, All-Knowing.

182. But if one fears from the testator any error or sin, and brings about a reconciliation between them, then there is no sin on him. Indeed, Allah

Surah 2: The cow (v. 178-182) Part - 2

البقرة-٢

is Oft-Forgiving, Most Merciful.

183. O you who believe! Fasting is prescribed to you as it was prescribed to those before you, so that you may become righteous.

184. (Fasting is for) a limited number of days. So whoever among you is sick or on a journey, then an equal number of days (are to be made up) later. And upon those who can afford it - a ransom of feeding a poor. And whoever volunteers good then it is better for him. And if you fast, it is better for you, if you only knew.

185. Ramadhaan is the month in which the Quran was revealed as a Guidance for mankind and clear proofs of Guidance and the Criterion (of right and wrong). So whoever among you witnesses the month (of Ramadhaan) should fast in it; and whoever is sick or on a journey, then the prescribed number of days (should be made up) from other days. Allah intends for you ease and does not intend for you hardship, so that you complete the prescribed period and that you magnify Allah for having guided you, so that you may be grateful.

186. And when **My** servants ask you concerning **Me**, then indeed **I** am near. **I** respect to the invocation of the supplicant

Surah 2: The cow (v. 183-186)   **Part - 2**

when he calls **Me**. So let them respond to **Me** and believe in **Me**, so that they may be led aright.

187. It is permitted for you in the nights of fasting to have sexual relations with your wives. They are your garments and you are their garments. Allah knows that you used to deceive yourselves, so **He** turned towards you and **He** forgave you. So now you may have relations with your wives and seek what Allah has ordained for you. And eat and drink until the white thread of dawn becomes distinct to you from the black thread of dawn. Then complete the fast till the night (i.e., sunset). And do not have relations with them when you are secluded in the masajid. These are the limits (set by) Allah, so do not approach them. Thus Allah makes clear **His** verses for the people, so that they may become righteous.

188. And do not consume your properties among yourselves wrongfully, nor render it before the authorities so that sinfully you may consume a portion of the wealth of the people, while you know.

189. They ask you about the new moons. Say, "They are indicators of periods for people and for Hajj (pilgrimage)." And it is not

Surah 2: The cow (v. 187-189)　　　　　　　　　**Part - 2**

وَلَٰكِنَّ	ظُهُورِهَا	مِن	الْبُيُوتَ	تَأْتُوا	بِأَن	الْبِرُّ
[and] but	their backs,	from	(to) the houses	you come	that	[the] righteousness
أَبْوَابِهَا	مِنْ	الْبُيُوتَ	وَأْتُوا	اتَّقَىٰ	مَنِ	الْبِرَّ
their doors.	from	(to) the houses	And come	fears (Allah).	(is one) who	[the] righteous
سَبِيلِ	فِي	وَقَاتِلُوا	۱۸۹	تُفْلِحُونَ	لَعَلَّكُمْ	اللَّهَ	وَاتَّقُوا
(the) way	in	And fight	189	(be) successful.	so that you may	Allah	And fear
اللَّهَ	إِنَّ	تَعْتَدُوا	وَلَا	يُقَاتِلُونَكُمْ	الَّذِينَ	اللَّهِ
Allah	Indeed,	and (do) not transgress.		fight you	those who	(of) Allah
حَيْثُ	وَاقْتُلُوهُمْ	۱۹۰	الْمُعْتَدِينَ	يُحِبُّ	لَا
wherever	And kill them	190	the transgressors.	(does) not like	
أَخْرَجُوكُمْ	حَيْثُ	مِنْ	وَأَخْرِجُوهُمْ	ثَقِفْتُمُوهُمْ
they drove you out,	wherever	from	and drive them out	you find them,
عِندَ	تُقَاتِلُوهُمْ	وَلَا	الْقَتْلِ	مِنَ	أَشَدُّ	وَالْفِتْنَةُ
near	fight them	And (do) not	[the] killing.	than	(is) worse	and [the] oppression
قَاتَلُوكُمْ	فَإِن	فِيهِ	يُقَاتِلُوكُمْ	حَتَّىٰ	الْمَسْجِدِ الْحَرَامِ
they fight you,	Then if	in it.	they fight you	until	Al-Masjid Al-Haraam
فَإِنِ	۱۹۱	الْكَافِرِينَ	جَزَاءُ	كَذَٰلِكَ	فَاقْتُلُوهُمْ
Then if	191	(of) the disbelievers.	(is the) reward	Such	then kill them.
رَحِيمٌ	غَفُورٌ	اللَّهَ	فَإِنَّ	انتَهَوْا
192	Most Merciful.	(is) Oft-Forgiving,	Allah	then indeed,	they cease,
الدِّينُ	وَيَكُونَ	فِتْنَةٌ	تَكُونَ	لَا	حَتَّىٰ	وَقَاتِلُوهُمْ
the religion	and becomes	oppression,	(there) is no	until	And fight (against) them
عَلَى	إِلَّا	عُدْوَانَ	فَلَا	انتَهَوْا	فَإِنِ	لِلَّهِ
against	except	hostility	then (let there be) no	they cease	Then if	for Allah
الْحَرَامُ	بِالشَّهْرِ	الْحَرَامُ	الشَّهْرُ	۱۹۳	الظَّالِمِينَ
[the] sacred,	(is) for the month	[the] sacred	The month	193	the oppressors.
عَلَيْكُمْ	اعْتَدَىٰ	فَمَنِ	قِصَاصٌ	وَالْحُرُمَاتُ
upon you	transgressed	Then whoever	(is) legal retribution.	and for all the violations
عَلَيْكُم	مَا	بِمِثْلِ	عَلَيْهِ	فَاعْتَدُوا
upon you.	he transgressed	(as)	in (the) same manner	on him	then you transgress

righteousness that you enter the houses from their back, but the righteous is one who fears Allah. And enter the houses from their doors. And fear Allah so that you may be successful.

190. And fight in the way of Allah those who fight against you, but do not transgress. Indeed, Allah does not like the transgressors.

191. And kill them wherever you find them and drive them out from wherever they drove you out, and oppression is worse than killing. And do not fight them near Al-Masjid Al-Haraam (Kabah) until they fight you there. But if they fight you, then kill them. Such is the reward of the disbelievers.

192. And if they cease, then indeed, Allah is Oft-Forgiving, Most Merciful.

193. And fight against them until there is no more oppression, and all worship is devoted to Allah alone. But if they cease, then let there be no hostility except against the oppressors.

194. The sacred month is for the sacred month, and for violations of sanctity there is legal retribution. Then whoever transgressed against you, then you transgress against him in the same manner as he transgressed against you.

Surah 2: The cow (v. 190-194)

۱۹٤	الْمُتَّقِيْنَ	مَعَ	اللّٰهَ	اَنَّ	وَاعْلَمُوْٓا	اللّٰهَ	وَاتَّقُوا
194	those who fear (Him).	(is) with	Allah	that	and know	Allah	And fear

بِاَيْدِيْكُمْ	تُلْقُوْا	وَلَا	اللّٰهِ	سَبِيْلِ	فِيْ	وَاَنْفِقُوْا
[with your hands]	throw (yourselves)	and (do) not	(of) Allah	(the) way	in	And spend

۱۹۵	الْمُحْسِنِيْنَ	يُحِبُّ	اللّٰهَ	اِنَّ	وَاَحْسِنُوْا ۛ	اِلَى التَّهْلُكَةِ ۛ
195	the good-doers.	loves	Allah	indeed,	And do good;	[the] destruction. into

وَاَتِمُّوا	أُحْصِرْتُمْ	فَاِنْ	لِلّٰهِ ۚ	وَالْعُمْرَةَ	الْحَجَّ	
you are held back	And if	for Allah.	and the Umrah	the Hajj	And complete	

وَلَا	الْهَدْيِ ۚ	مِنَ	اسْتَيْسَرَ	فَمَا
And (do) not	the sacrificial animal.	of	(can be) obtained with ease	then (offer) whatever

مَحِلَّهٗ ؕ	الْهَدْيُ	يَبْلُغَ	حَتّٰى	تَحْلِقُوْا رُءُوْسَكُمْ
(to) its destination.	the sacrificial animal	reaches	until	shave your heads

مِّنْ رَّأْسِهٖ	اَذًى	بِهٖٓ	اَوْ	مَرِيْضًا	فَمَنْ كَانَ مِنْكُمْ
his head	of an ailment	he (has)	or	ill	Then whoever is among you

اَمِنْتُمْ ۙ	فَاِذَآ	نُسُكٍ ۚ	اَوْ	صَدَقَةٍ	فَفِدْيَةٌ مِّنْ صِيَامٍ اَوْ
you are secure,	Then when	sacrifice.	or	charity	then a ransom of fasting or

فَمَا	اِلَى الْحَجِّ	بِالْعُمْرَةِ	تَمَتَّعَ	فَمَنْ
then (offer) whatever	(by) the Hajj,	followed of the Umrah	took advantage	then whoever

لَمْ يَجِدْ	فَمَنْ	الْهَدْيِ ۚ	مِنَ	اسْتَيْسَرَ
(can) not find -	But whoever	the sacrificial animal.	of	(can be) obtained with ease

تِلْكَ	اِذَا رَجَعْتُمْ ؕ	وَسَبْعَةٍ	فِي الْحَجِّ	اَيَّامٍ	فَصِيَامُ ثَلٰثَةِ
This	you return. when	and seven (days)	the Hajj during	days	then a fast (of) three

حَاضِرِي	اَهْلُهٗ	يَكُنْ	لَمْ	لِمَنْ	ذٰلِكَ	عَشَرَةٌ كَامِلَةٌ ؕ
present	his family	is	not	(is) for (the one) whose,	That	in all. (is) ten (days)

شَدِيْدُ	اللّٰهَ	اَنَّ	وَاعْلَمُوْٓا	وَاتَّقُوا اللّٰهَ	الْمَسْجِدِ الْحَرَامِ ؕ
(is) severe	Allah	that	and know	And fear Allah	(near) Al-Masjid Al-Haraam.

فَمَنْ	مَّعْلُوْمٰتٌ ۚ	اَشْهُرٌ	الْحَجُّ	الْعِقَابِ ؕ
then whoever	well known,	(are) months	(For) the Hajj	(in) retribution.

وَلَا	فُسُوْقَ	وَلَا	رَفَثَ	فَلَا	فَرَضَ فِيْهِنَّ الْحَجَّ
and no	wickedness	and no	sexual relations	then no	undertakes therein the Hajj

Surah 2: The cow (v. 195-197)

And fear Allah and know that Allah is with those who fear **Him**.

195. And spend in the way of Allah and let not your own hands throw yourselves into destruction. And do good; indeed, Allah loves the good-doers.

196. And complete Hajj and Umrah for Allah, but if you are held back, then offer whatever you can obtain with ease of the sacrificial animal. And do not shave your head until the sacrificial animal reaches its destination. Then whoever among you is ill or has an ailment of the scalp he must offer a ransom of fasting or charity or sacrifice. Then when you feel secure, perform Umrah followed by Hajj and offer whatever can be obtained with ease of the sacrificial animal. And whoever cannot afford it should fast for three days during Hajj and seven days after returning, making ten (days) in all. This is for those whose family does not live near Al-Masjid Al-Haraam (i.e., Kabah). And fear Allah and know that Allah is severe in retribution.

197. For Hajj there are months well known, so whoever undertakes (to perform) Hajj (in that period), should not indulge in sexual relations, nor wickedness, nor

quarrelling during Hajj. And whatever good you do - Allah is aware of it. And take provision for Hajj, but indeed, the best provision is righteousness. And fear **Me**, O men of understanding!

198. There is no sin upon you for seeking bounty from your Lord. And when you depart from Mount Arafat, remember Allah at the Sacred Monument (Mashari-l-Haram). And remember **Him** as **He** has guided you, even though, before that, you were surely among those who went astray.

199. Then depart from wherever the people depart and ask forgiveness of Allah. Indeed, Allah is Oft-Forgiving, Most Merciful.

200. Then when you complete your acts of worship, remember Allah as you remember your forefathers or (rather) with greater remembrance. Of the people there are some who say, "Our Lord! Give us in this world." They will have no share in the Hereafter.

201. And there are some who say, "Our Lord, grant us good in this world and good in the Hereafter, and save us from the punishment of the Fire."

202. Those will have a share of what they have earned, and Allah is swift

quarrelling	during	the Hajj.	And whatever	you do	of	good	Allah knows it.
			And take provision,	(but) indeed,	(the) best	provision	(is) righteousness.
And fear **Me**,	O men	(of) understanding!	197	Not is	on you
any sin	that	you seek	bounty	from	your Lord.	And when	you depart
from	(Mount) Arafat	then remember	Allah	near	the Monument	[the] Sacred.
And remember **Him**	as	**He** (has) guided you,	[and] though	you were	[from]
before [it],	surely among	those who went astray.	198	Then	depart	from
wherever	depart	the people	and ask forgiveness	(of) Allah.	Indeed,	Allah
(is) Oft-Forgiving,	Most Merciful	199	Then when	you complete[d]	your acts of worship
then remember	Allah	as you remember	your forefathers	or	(with) greater
remembrance.	And from	the people	who	say,	"Our Lord!	Grant us	in
the world."	And not	for him	in	the Hereafter	[of]	any share.	200
And from those	who	say,	"Our Lord!"	Grant us	in	the world	good	and in
the Hereafter	good,	and save us	(from the) punishment	(of) the Fire."	201
Those -	for them	(is) a share	of what	they earned,	and Allah	(is) swift

Surah 2: The cow (v. 198-202)   **Part - 2**

Surah 2: The cow (v. 203-209)

203. And remember Allah during the numbered days. Then he who hurries in two days there is no sin upon him and whoever delays, there is no sin for the one who fears (Allah). And fear Allah and know that unto **Him** you will be gathered.

204. And of the people is he whose speech pleases you in worldly life, he calls Allah to witness as to what is in his heart, and he is the most quarrelsome of opponents.

205. And when he turns away, he strives to spread corruption in the earth and destroys the crops and progeny. And Allah does not love corruption.

206. And whenever it is said to him, "Fear Allah," his (false) pride drives him to sins. Then enough for him is Hell - surely an evil resting-place.

207. And of the people is he who sells his own self seeking the pleasure of Allah. And Allah is full of Kindness to **His** servants.

208. O you who believe! Enter in Islam completely, and do not follow the footsteps of Shaitaan. Indeed, he is your open enemy.

209. Then if you slip after

clear proofs have come to you, then know that Allah is All-Mighty, All-Wise.

210. Are they waiting for Allah to reveal **Himself** to them in the shadows of the clouds and the Angels, and the matter is decreed? And to Allah return all matters.

211. Ask the Children of Israel, how many clear Signs **We** have given them. And whoever changes the Favor of Allah after it has come to him - then indeed, Allah is severe in chastising.

212. Beautified is the life of this world for those who disbelieve, and they ridicule those who believe. But those who fear Allah will be above them on the Day of Resurrection. And Allah provides whom **He** wills without measure.

213. Mankind was one single community, and Allah raised up Prophets as bearers of glad tidings and as warners, and sent down with them the Book in truth to decide between the people concerning that in which they differed. And only those who were given the Book differed in it - after clear proofs came to them - out of jealousy among themselves. And Allah, by **His** permission, guided those who believed to the truth concerning that over which

Surah 2: The cow (v. 210-213)   **Part - 2**

they had differed. And Allah guides whom **He** wills to a straight path.

214. Or do you think that you will enter Paradise while such (trial) has not (yet) come to you as came to those who passed away before you? They were afflicted with adversity and hardship and they were so shaken that even the Messenger and those who believed along with him said, "When will Allah's help come?" Unquestionably, Allah's help is near.

215. They ask you what they should spend. Say, "Whatever you spend of good is for parents, and the relatives, and the orphans, and the needy, and the wayfarer. And whatever good you do, indeed, Allah is All-Aware of it.

216. Fighting is prescribed upon you while it is disliked by you. But perhaps you dislike a thing and it is good for you; and perhaps you love a thing and it is bad for you. And Allah knows, while you do not know.

217. They ask you about fighting in the sacred months. Say, "Fighting therein is a great sin; but hindering (people) from the way of Allah and disbelief in **Him** and (preventing access to) Al-Masjid Al-Haraam

Surah 2: The cow (v. 214-217)   Part - 2

and driving out its people from it is greater sin in the sight of Allah. And oppression is worse than killing." They will not cease to fight with you until they turn you away from your religion if they can. And whoever amongst you turns away from his religion and dies while he is a disbeliever - for those, their deeds have become worthless in this world and the Hereafter. Those are the companions of the Fire; they will abide in it forever.

218. Indeed, those who believed and emigrated and strove in the way of Allah - they hope for the Mercy of Allah. And Allah is Oft-Forgiving, Most Merciful.

219. They ask you about intoxicants and the games of chance. Say, "In both of them there is great sin and (some) benefits for people. But their sin is greater than their benefits." And they ask you about what they should spend. Say, "Whatever you can spare." Thus Allah makes clear the Verses to you, so that you may ponder,

220. Concerning this world and the Hereafter. They ask you concerning the orphans. Say, "Setting right their affairs for them is best. And if you associate with them, then they are your brothers.

Surah 2: The cow (v. 218-220)

البقرة-٢ / سيقول-٢

شَآءَ اللّٰهُ	وَلَوْ	الْمُصْلِحِ	مِنَ	الْمُفْسِدَ	يَعْلَمُ	وَاللّٰهُ	
Allah (had) willed	And if	the amender.	from	the corrupter	knows	And Allah	
حَكِيمٌ	عَزِيزٌ	اللّٰهَ	إِنَّ	لَأَعْنَتَكُمْ			
All-Wise."	(is) All-Mighty,	Allah	Indeed,	surely He (could have) put you in difficulties.			
يُؤْمِنَّ	حَتّٰى	الْمُشْرِكٰتِ	وَلَا	تَنْكِحُوا		٢٢٠	
they believe.	until	[the] polytheistic women	And (do) not	[you] marry		220	
وَلَوْ	مُشْرِكَةٍ	مِّنْ	خَيْرٌ	مُّؤْمِنَةٌ	وَلَأَمَةٌ		
[and] even if	a polytheistic woman	than	(is) better	And a believing bondwoman			
الْمُشْرِكِينَ		تُنْكِحُوا	وَلَا	أَعْجَبَتْكُمْ			
(to) [the] polytheistic men	give in marriage (your women)	And (do) not	she pleases you.				
مُشْرِكٍ	مِّنْ	خَيْرٌ	وَلَعَبْدٌ مُّؤْمِنٌ	يُؤْمِنُوا	حَتّٰى		
a polytheistic man	than	(is) better	and a believing bondman	they believe,	until		
يَدْعُوا	وَاللّٰهُ	النَّارِ	إِلَى	يَدْعُونَ	أُولٰئِكَ	أَعْجَبَكُمْ	وَلَوْ
invites	and Allah	the Fire,	to	they invite	[Those]	he pleases you.	[and] even if
اٰيٰتِهِ	وَيُبَيِّنُ	بِإِذْنِهِ	وَالْمَغْفِرَةِ	الْجَنَّةِ	إِلَى		
His Verses	And He makes clear	by His permission.	and [the] forgiveness	Paradise	to		
عَنِ	وَيَسْأَلُونَكَ	٢٢١	يَتَذَكَّرُونَ	لَعَلَّهُمْ	لِلنَّاسِ		
about	And they ask you	221	take heed.	so that they may	for the people		
النِّسَآءَ	فَاعْتَزِلُوا	أَذًى	هُوَ	قُلْ	الْمَحِيضِ		
[the] women	so keep away (from)	(is) a hurt,	"It	Say,	[the] menstruation.		
حَتّٰى	تَقْرَبُوهُنَّ	وَلَا	الْمَحِيضِ	فِي			
until	approach them	And (do) not	(their) [the] menstruation.	during			
مِنْ	فَأْتُوهُنَّ	تَطَهَّرْنَ	فَإِذَا	يَطْهُرْنَ			
from	then come to them	they are purified,	Then when	they are cleansed			
التَّوَّابِينَ	يُحِبُّ	اللّٰهَ	إِنَّ	أَمَرَكُمُ اللّٰهُ	حَيْثُ		
those who turn in repentance	loves	Allah	Indeed,	Allah has ordered you."	where		
وَيُحِبُّ		نِسَآؤُكُمْ	حَرْثٌ	لَّكُمْ	٢٢٢	الْمُتَطَهِّرِينَ	
and loves	those who purify themselves.	222	Your wives	(are) a tilth	for you,		
لِأَنْفُسِكُمْ	وَقَدِّمُوا	حَرْثَكُمْ	أَنّٰى شِئْتُمْ	فَأْتُوا			
for yourselves.	and send forth (good deeds)	you wish,	when	(to) your tilth	so come		

And Allah knows the corrupter from the amender. And if Allah had willed He could have put you in difficulties. Indeed, Allah is All-Mighty, All-Wise."

221. And do not marry women who associate others with Allah until they believe. And a believing bondwoman is better than a woman who associates others with Allah, even if she pleases you. And do not give your women in marriage to men who associate others with Allah until they believe and a believing bondman is better than a man who associates others with Allah, even if he pleases you. They invite to the Fire, and Allah invites to Paradise and forgiveness by His permission. And He makes clear His Verses for people so that they may take heed.

222. And they ask you about menstruation. Say, "It is a hurt, so keep away from women during their menstruation. And do not approach them until they are cleansed. Then when they have purified themselves, approach them from where Allah has ordered you." Indeed, Allah loves those who turn in repentance and those who purify themselves.

223. Your wives are a tilth for you so come to your tilth when you wish, and sent forth (good deeds) for yourselves.

Surah 2: The cow (v. 221-223)   Part - 2

And be conscious of Allah and know that you will meet **Him**. And give glad tidings to the believers.

224. And do not make Allah's name an excuse in your oaths against doing good and being righteous and making peace between people. And Allah is All-Hearing, All-Knowing.

225. Allah will not take you to task for what is unintentional in your oaths but **He** takes you to task for what your hearts have earned. And Allah is Oft-Forgiving, Most Forbearing.

226. For those who swear not to approach their wives is a waiting period of four months, but if they go back, then indeed, Allah is Oft-Forgiving, Most Merciful.

227. And if they resolve on divorce - then indeed, Allah is All-Hearing, All-Knowing.

228. And the divorced women shall wait concerning themselves for three (monthly) periods. And it is not lawful for them to conceal what Allah has created in their wombs, if they believe in Allah and the Last Day. And their husbands are more entitled to take them back in that period, if they wish for reconciliation. And they (wives) have rights similar to those (of husbands) over them

Surah 2: The cow (v. 224-228)

229. Divorce is twice. Then retain (her) in a reasonable manner or release (her) with kindness. And it is not lawful for you to take back (from your wives) whatever you have given them, except if both fear that they will not be able to keep the limits of Allah. But if you fear that they both will not keep the limits of Allah, then there is no sin on them if she ransoms herself concerning it. These are the limits of Allah, so do not transgress them. And whoever transgresses the limits of Allah - then those are the wrongdoers.

230. Then if he divorces her (the third time) then she is not lawful for him until she marries a spouse other than him. Then if he divorces her, then there is no sin on them if they return to each other (for marriage), if they believe that they will be able to keep the limits of Allah. And these are the limits of Allah, which He makes clear to a people who know.

231. And when you divorce women and they reach their term, then either retain them in a fair manner or release them in a fair manner. And do not

retain them to hurt them so that you transgress. And whoever does that, then indeed, he wrongs himself. And do not take the Verses of Allah in jest, and remember the Favors of Allah upon you and that **He** revealed to you of the Book and the wisdom by which **He** instructs you. And fear Allah and know that Allah is All-Knower of everything.

232. And when you divorce women and they reach their waiting term, then do not hinder them from (re)marrying their husbands if they agree between themselves in a fair manner. This is an admonition for whoever among you believes in Allah and the Last Day; this is more virtuous and purer for you. And Allah knows and you do not know.

233. And the mothers shall suckle their children for two complete years, for those who wish to complete the suckling. And upon the father is their (mother's and child's) provision and their clothing in a fair manner. No person is burdened with more than his capacity. Neither shall a mother be made to suffer because of her child nor the father. And on the (father's) heirs is (a duty) like that. Then if they both desire weaning through

Surah 2: The cow (v. 232-233) **Part - 2**

عَلَيْهِمَا	جُنَاحَ	فَلَا	وَتَشَاوُرٍ	مِّنْهُمَا	تَرَاضٍ
on both of them.	blame	then no	and consultation,	of both of them	mutual consent
جُنَاحَ	فَلَا	أَوْلَادَكُمْ	أَن تَسْتَرْضِعُوا	أَرَدتُّمْ	وَإِنْ
blame	then (there is) no	your child	to ask another women to suckle	you want	And if
عَلَيْكُمْ	إِذَا	سَلَّمْتُم	مَّا	ءَاتَيْتُم	بِالْمَعْرُوفِ	وَاتَّقُوا اللَّهَ
And fear Allah	in a fair manner.	you give	what	you pay	when	on you,
وَالَّذِينَ	۝	بَصِيرٌ	تَعْمَلُونَ	بِمَا	اللَّهَ	أَنَّ	وَاعْلَمُوا
And those who	233	(is) All-Seer.	you do	of what	Allah	that	and know
بِأَنفُسِهِنَّ	يَتَرَبَّصْنَ	أَزْوَاجًا	وَيَذَرُونَ	مِنكُمْ	يُتَوَفَّوْنَ
(the widows) should wait for themselves	wives,	and leave behind	among you	pass away
أَجَلَهُنَّ	بَلَغْنَ	فَإِذَا	وَعَشْرًا	أَشْهُرٍ	أَرْبَعَةَ
their (specified) term,	they reach	Then when	and ten (days).	months	(for) four
فِي أَنفُسِهِنَّ	فَعَلْنَ	فِيمَا	عَلَيْكُمْ	جُنَاحَ	فَلَا
concerning themselves	they do	for what	upon you	blame	then (there is) no
وَلَا	۝	خَبِيرٌ	تَعْمَلُونَ	بِمَا	وَاللَّهُ	بِالْمَعْرُوفِ
And (there is) no	234	(is) All-Aware.	you do	of what	And Allah	in a fair manner.
النِّسَاءِ	خِطْبَةِ	مِنْ	بِهِ	عَرَّضْتُم	فِيمَا	عَلَيْكُمْ	جُنَاحَ
[to] the women	marriage proposal	[with it] of	you hint	in what	upon you	blame
سَتَذْكُرُونَهُنَّ	أَنَّكُمْ	اللَّهُ	عَلِمَ	أَنفُسِكُمْ	فِي	أَكْنَنتُمْ	أَوْ
will mention them,	that you	Allah knows	yourselves.	in	you conceal it	or
قَوْلًا	تَقُولُوا	أَن	إِلَّا	سِرًّا	تُوَاعِدُوهُنَّ	لَّا	وَلَٰكِن
a saying	you say	that	except	secretly	promise them (widows)	(do) not	[and] but
يَبْلُغَ	حَتَّىٰ	النِّكَاحِ	عُقْدَةَ	تَعْزِمُوا	وَلَا	مَّعْرُوفًا
reaches	until	the marriage knot	resolve (on)	And (do) not	honorable.
فِي	مَا	يَعْلَمُ	اللَّهَ	أَنَّ	وَاعْلَمُوا	أَجَلَهُ	الْكِتَابُ
(is) within	what	knows	Allah	that	And know	its end.	the prescribed term
غَفُورٌ	اللَّهَ	أَنَّ	وَاعْلَمُوا	فَاحْذَرُوهُ	أَنفُسِكُمْ
(is) Oft-Forgiving,	Allah	that	And know	so beware of Him.	yourselves
طَلَّقْتُمُ	إِن	عَلَيْكُمْ	جُنَاحَ	لَّا	۝	حَلِيمٌ
you divorce	if	upon you	blame	(There is) no	235	Most Forbearing.

mutual consent and consultation, then there is no blame on both of them. And if you desire a wet-nurse for your child then there is no sin on you, when you pay what is due from you in a fair manner. And fear Allah and know that Allah is All-Seer of what you do.

234. And those of you who die and leave wives behind them, the widows should wait (as regards their remarriage) for four months and ten days. And when they complete their specified term, then there is no blame on you for what the widows do concerning themselves in a fair manner. And Allah is All-Aware of what you do.

235. And there is no blame on you if you hint concerning a marriage proposal to the women or conceal it in your hearts. Allah knows that you will mention them, but do not make a secret promise with them (widows) except that you speak an honorable saying. And do not resolve on the marriage knot until the prescribed term reaches its end. And know that Allah knows what is within your hearts, so beware of Him. And know that Allah is Oft-Forgiving, Most Forbearing.

236. There is no blame upon you if you divorce women

whom you have not touched nor specified for them an obligation (*Mahr*). And make provision for them - the wealthy according to his means and the poor according to his means - in a fair manner, a duty upon the good-doers.

237. And if you divorce them before you have touched them while already you have specified for them an obligation (dower), then give half of what you have specified, unless they (the women) forgo it or the one in whose hand is the marriage knot forgoes it. And if you forgo, it is nearer to righteousness. And do not forget the graciousness among you. Indeed, Allah is All-Seer of what you do.

238. Guard strictly the prayers, and (especially) the middle prayer, and stand up before Allah devoutly obedient.

239. And if you fear, then pray on foot or while riding. But when you are secure, then remember Allah, as **He** has taught that which you did not know.

240. And those who die among you and leave their wives behind, should make a will for their wives - provision for a year without

Surah 2: The cow (v. 237-240) Part - 2

Surah 2: The cow (v. 241-246)

Word-by-word (verses continue):

...driving (them) out. But if they leave then no blame upon you in what they do concerning themselves [of] honorably. And Allah (is) All-Mighty, All-Wise. 240

And for the divorced women, (is) a provision in a fair manner - a duty upon the righteous. Thus Allah makes clear for you 241 His Verses so that you may use your intellect. 242

Did you not see [to] those who went out from their homes and they (were in) thousands (in) fear (of) [the] death? Then said to them Allah, "Die;" then He restored them to life. Indeed, Allah (is) surely Possessor of bounty for [the] mankind [and] but most (of) the people (are) not grateful. 243

And fight in (the) way (of) Allah, and know that Allah (is) All-Hearing, All-Knowing. 244

Who (is) the one who will lend (to) Allah - a loan, good, so (that) He multiplies it for him - manifolds And Allah withholds and grants abundance, and to Him you will be returned. 245

Did you not see [towards] the chiefs of (the) Children (of) Israel after Musa, when they said to a Prophet of theirs, "Appoint for us a king so that we may fight in (the) way (of) Allah?" He said, "Would

---

241. And for divorced women is a provision - a duty upon the righteous.

242. Thus Allah makes clear **His** Verses for you, so that you may use your intellect.

243. Are you not aware of those who left their homes in thousands fearing death? Then Allah said to them, "Die;" then **He** restored them to life. Indeed, Allah is full of bounty to mankind, but most of them are ungrateful.

244. And fight in the way of Allah, and know that Allah is All-Hearing, All-Knowing.

245. Who is the one who will lend to Allah a goodly loan (of noble deeds), so that **He** multiplies it for him manifolds? And Allah withholds and grants abundance, and to **Him** you will be returned.

246. Are you not aware of the chiefs of the Children of Israel after Musa when they said to their Prophet, "Appoint for us a king so that we may fight in the way of Allah?" He (the Prophet) said, "Would you perhaps refrain from fighting if it was prescribed upon you?" They said, "Why should we not fight in the way of Allah, verily we have been driven out from our homes and our children?" So when fighting was prescribed upon them they turned away except a few among them. And Allah is All-Knowing of the wrongdoers.

تُقَاتِلُوا	اَلَّا	الْقِتَالُ	عَلَيْكُمُ	كُتِبَ	اِنْ	عَسَيْتُمْ
you fight?"	that not	[the] fighting,	upon you	prescribed	if	you perhaps -

وَقَدْ	اللهِ	سَبِيْلِ	فِيْ	نُقَاتِلَ	اَلَّا	لَنَا	وَمَا	قَالُوْا
while surely	(of) Allah	(the) way	in	we fight	that not	for us	"And what	They said,

فَلَمَّا	وَاَبْنَآئِنَا	دِيَارِنَا	مِنْ	اُخْرِجْنَا
Yet, when	and our children?"	our homes	from	we have been driven out

اِلَّا	تَوَلَّوْا	الْقِتَالُ	عَلَيْهِمُ	كُتِبَ
except	they turned away,	the fighting	upon them	was prescribed

بِالظّٰلِمِيْنَ	عَلِيْمٌ	وَاللهُ	مِّنْهُمْ	قَلِيْلًا
of the wrongdoers.	(is) All-Knowing	And Allah	among them.	a few

اِنَّ	نَبِيُّهُمْ	لَهُمْ	وَقَالَ	۲۴۶
"Indeed,	their Prophet,	to them	And said	246

247. And their Prophet said to them, "Indeed Allah has appointed for you Talut as king." They said, "How can he have kingship over us while we are more entitled to kingship than him, and he has not been given abundant wealth?" He (the Prophet) said, "Allah has chosen him over you and has increased him abundantly in knowledge and physique. And Allah gives **His** kingdom to whom **He** wills. And Allah is All-Encompassing, All-Knowing."

طَالُوْتَ	لَكُمْ	بَعَثَ	قَدْ	اللهَ
Talut	for you	raised	(has) surely	Allah

الْمُلْكُ	لَهُ	اَنّٰى يَكُوْنُ	قَالُوْٓا	مَلِكًا
the kingship	for him	How can be	They said,	(as) a king."

مِنْهُ	بِالْمُلْكِ	اَحَقُّ	وَنَحْنُ	عَلَيْنَا
than him,	to kingship	(are) more entitled	while we	over us,

الْمَالِ	مِّنَ	سَعَةً	وَلَمْ يُؤْتَ
[the] wealth?"	of	abundance	and he has not been given

عَلَيْكُمْ	اصْطَفٰىهُ	اللهَ	اِنَّ	قَالَ
over you	has chosen him	Allah	"Indeed,	He said,

الْعِلْمِ	فِى	بَسْطَةً	وَزَادَهُ
[the] knowledge	in	abundantly	and increased him

مُلْكَهُ	يُؤْتِىْ	وَاللهُ	وَالْجِسْمِ
His kingdom	gives	And Allah	and [the] physique.

وَاسِعٌ	وَاللهُ	يَشَآءُ	مَنْ
(is) All-Encompassing,	And Allah	**He** wills.	(to) whom

248. And their Prophet said to them,

نَبِيُّهُمْ	لَهُمْ	وَقَالَ	۲۴۷	عَلِيْمٌ
their Prophet,	to them	And said	247	All-Knowing."

Surah 2: The cow (v. 247-248)   **Part - 2**

"Indeed, a sign of his kingship is that the ark will come to you in which is tranquility from your Lord and a remnant left by the family of Musa and the family of Harun carried by the Angels. Indeed, in that is a sign for you if you are believers."

إِنَّ	آيَةَ	مُلْكِهِ	أَن
"Indeed,	a sign	(of) his kingship	(is) that

يَأْتِيَكُمُ	التَّابُوتُ	فِيهِ	سَكِينَةٌ
will come to you	the ark,	in it	(is) tranquility

مِّن	رَّبِّكُمْ	وَبَقِيَّةٌ	مِّمَّا	تَرَكَ
from	your Lord,	and a remnant	of what	(was) left

آلُ	مُوسَىٰ	وَآلُ	هَارُونَ	تَحْمِلُهُ
(by the) family	(of) Musa	and family	(of) Harun	will carry it

الْمَلَائِكَةُ	إِنَّ	فِي	ذَٰلِكَ	لَآيَةً
the Angels.	Indeed,	in	that	(is) surely a sign

لَّكُمْ	إِن	كُنتُم	مُّؤْمِنِينَ
for you	if	you are	believers."

248

فَلَمَّا	فَصَلَ	طَالُوتُ	بِالْجُنُودِ
Then when	set out	Talut	with the forces

قَالَ	إِنَّ	اللَّهَ	مُبْتَلِيكُم
he said,	"Indeed,	Allah	will test you

بِنَهَرٍ	فَمَن	شَرِبَ	مِنْهُ	فَلَيْسَ
with a river.	So whoever	drinks	from it	then he is not

مِنِّي	وَمَن	لَّمْ	يَطْعَمْهُ	فَإِنَّهُ
from me,	and whoever	(does) not	taste it	then indeed, he

مِنِّي	إِلَّا	مَنِ	اغْتَرَفَ	غُرْفَةً
(is) from me	except	whoever	takes	(in the) hollow

بِيَدِهِ	فَشَرِبُوا	مِنْهُ	إِلَّا
(of) his hand."	Then they drank	from it	except

قَلِيلًا	مِّنْهُمْ	فَلَمَّا	جَاوَزَهُ	هُوَ
a few	of them.	Then when	he crossed it	

وَالَّذِينَ	آمَنُوا	مَعَهُ	قَالُوا
and those who	believed	with him,	they said,

لَا	طَاقَةَ	لَنَا	الْيَوْمَ	بِجَالُوتَ
"No	strength	for us	today	against Jalut

249. Then when Talut set out with the forces, he said, "Indeed, Allah will test you with a river. So whoever drinks from it is not of me. And whoever does not taste it is indeed of me, except the one who takes in the hollow of his hand." Then they drank from it except a few of them. Then when Talut crossed it (the river) with those who believed with him, they said, "We have no strength today against Jalut and his troops." But those who were certain that they would meet Allah said, "How often by Allah's permission has a small company overcome a large company. And Allah is with those who are patient."

وَجُنُودِهِ	قَالَ	الَّذِيْنَ	يَظُنُّوْنَ
and his troops."	Said	those who	were certain

أَنَّهُمْ	مُّلٰقُوا	اللّٰهِ	كَمْ	مِّنْ
that they	(would) meet	Allah,	"How many	of

فِئَةٍ قَلِيْلَةٍ	غَلَبَتْ	فِئَةً كَثِيْرَةً	بِإِذْنِ
a small company	overcame	a large company	by (the) permission

اللّٰهِ ۭ	وَاللّٰهُ	مَعَ	الصّٰبِرِيْنَ
(of) Allah.	And Allah	(is) with	the patient ones."

249	وَلَمَّا	بَرَزُوْا	لِجَالُوْتَ	وَجُنُوْدِهٖ
249	And when	they went forth	to (face) Jalut	and his troops

250. And when they went forth to (face) Jalut and his troops, they said, "Our Lord! Pour patience on us and make firm our feet and help us against the disbelieving people."

قَالُوْا	رَبَّنَاۤ	أَفْرِغْ	عَلَيْنَا	صَبْرًا
they said,	"Our Lord!	Pour	on us	patience

وَثَبِّتْ	أَقْدَامَنَا	وَانْصُرْنَا	عَلَى
and make firm	our feet,	and help us	against

الْقَوْمِ الْكٰفِرِيْنَ	250	فَهَزَمُوْهُمْ	بِإِذْنِ
the disbelieving people."	250	So they defeated them	by (the) permission

251. So they defeated them by the permission of Allah and Dawood killed Jalut, and Allah gave him the kingdom and the wisdom and taught him that which He willed. And if Allah had not repelled some of the people by some others, the earth would have been corrupted, but Allah is Full of bounty to the worlds.

اللّٰهِ ۣ	وَقَتَلَ	دَاوٗدُ	جَالُوْتَ	وَاٰتٰىهُ اللّٰهُ
(of) Allah,	and killed	Dawood	Jalut,	and Allah gave him

الْمُلْكَ	وَالْحِكْمَةَ	وَعَلَّمَهٗ	مِمَّا
the kingdom	and the wisdom	and taught him	that which

يَشَآءُ ۭ	وَلَوْلَا	دَفْعُ اللّٰهِ	النَّاسَ	بَعْضَهُمْ
He willed.	And if not	(for) Allah's repelling	[the] people -	some of them

بِبَعْضٍ	لَّفَسَدَتِ الْأَرْضُ	وَلٰكِنَّ	اللّٰهَ
with others,	certainly the earth (would have been) corrupted,	[and] but	Allah

ذُوْ فَضْلٍ	عَلَى	الْعٰلَمِيْنَ	251	تِلْكَ
(is) Possessor of bounty	to	the worlds.	251	These

252. These are the Verses of Allah We recite to you in truth. And indeed, you are surely of the Messengers.

اٰيٰتُ	اللّٰهِ	نَتْلُوْهَا	عَلَيْكَ	بِالْحَقِّ ۭ
(are the) Verses	(of) Allah,	We recite them	to you	in [the] truth.

وَإِنَّكَ	لَمِنَ	الْمُرْسَلِيْنَ	252
And indeed, you	(are) surely of	the Messengers.	252

253.
These Messengers! **We** preferred some over others. Among them were those with whom Allah spoke, and **He** raised some of them in degrees. And **We** gave Isa, son of Maryam, clear proofs and supported him with the Holy Spirit. And if Allah had willed, those succeeding them would not have fought each other after clear proofs had come to them. But they differed, some of them believed and some denied. And if Allah had willed, they would not have fought each other, but Allah does what **He** intends.

254.
O you who believe! Spend out of what **We** have provided you, before a Day comes when there will be no bargaining, no friendship, and no intercession. And the deniers - they are the wrongdoers.

255.
Allah - there is no God except **Him**, the Ever-Living, the Sustainer of all that exists. Neither slumber overtakes **Him** nor sleep. To **Him** belongs whatever is in the heavens and the earth. Who is the one who can intercede with **Him** except by **His** permission? **He** knows what lies before them and what

Surah 2: The cow (v. 253-255) — Part - 3

lies behind them. And they do not encompass anything of **His** knowledge except what **He** wills. **His** Throne extends over the heavens and the earth and the guarding of both of them does not tire **Him**. And **He** is the Most High, the Most Great.

256. There is no compulsion in religion. Surely, the right path has become distinct from the wrong. Then whoever disbelieves in false deities and believes in Allah, he has grasped a firm handhold, which will never break. And Allah is All-Hearing, All-Knowing.

257. Allah is the Protecting Guardian of those who believe. **He** brings them out of darkness into light. And those who disbelieve, their guardians are the evil ones, they bring them out of light into darkness. Those are the companions of the Fire and they will abide in it forever.

258. Are you not aware about the one who argued with Ibrahim about his Lord because Allah gave him the kingdom? When Ibrahim said, "My Lord is the **One Who** - grants life and causes death." He said, "I too give life and cause death." Ibrahim said, "Indeed, Allah brings up the sun

Surah 2: The cow (v. 256-258) Part - 3

from the east, so you bring it up from the west." So the disbeliever became dumbfounded, and Allah does not guide the wrongdoing people.

259. Or like the one, who passed by a township, which had been overturned on its roofs. He said, "How will Allah bring this (town) to life after its death?" Then Allah caused him to die for one hundred years and then revived him. He asked, "How long have you remained?" He said, "I remained for a day or part of a day." He said, "Nay, you have remained for one hundred years. Look at your food and your drink, they have not rotted. And look at your donkey; and **We** will make you a sign for the people. And look at the bones, how **We** raise them and then **We** cover them with flesh." Then when it became clear to him, he said, "I know that Allah has power over everything."

260. And when Ibrahim said, "My Lord, show me how **You** give life to the dead." **He** said, "Have you not believed?" He replied, "Yes, but (let me see it) so that my heart may be satisfied." He said, "Then take four birds and incline them towards you (i.e., tame them), then (after slaughtering them)

Surah 2: The cow (v. 259-260)   Part - 3

put on each hill a portion of them, then call them, they will come (flying) to you in haste. And know that Allah is All-Mighty, All-Wise.

261. The example of those who spend their wealth in the way of Allah is like a grain (which) grows seven ears, in each ear are a hundred grains. And Allah gives manifold to whom He wills. And Allah is All-Encompassing, All-Knowing.

262. Those who spend their wealth in the way of Allah and do not follow up what they have spent with reminders of generosity or hurt - they will have their reward from their Lord and they will have no fear nor will they grieve.

263. A kind word and (seeking) forgiveness are better than a charity followed by hurting (the feelings of the needy). And Allah is All-Sufficient, All-Forbearing.

264. O you who believe! Do not make your charities worthless by reminders of your generosity and by hurting (the feelings of the needy), like the one who spends his wealth to be seen by people and does not believe in Allah and the Last Day. Then his example is like that of a smooth rock on which is dust, then heavy rain fell on it and left it

Surah 2: The cow (v. 261-264)   **Part - 3**

265. And the example of those who spend their wealth seeking the pleasure of Allah and with certainty of their inner souls, is like a garden on a height, falls on it heavy rain, so it yields double harvest. And (even) if it does not receive a heavy rain, then a drizzle (is sufficient). And Allah is All-Seer of what you do.

266. Would any of you like to have a garden of date-palms and grapevines, underneath which rivers flow, and therein he has all kinds of fruits, while he is stricken with old age and has weak children, then it is struck with whirlwind containing fire and hence it is burnt? Thus Allah makes (His) Signs clear to you so that you may ponder.

267. O you who believe! Spend from the good things, which you have earned and whatever We bought forth for you from the earth. And do not aim at that which is bad to spend from it, while you would not take it except with closed eyes. And know that Allah is Self-Sufficient, Praiseworthy.

Surah 2: The cow (v. 265-267) — Part - 3

268. Shaitaan threatens you with poverty and orders you to immorality, while Allah promises you forgiveness from Him and bounty. And Allah is All-Encompassing, All-Knowing.

269. He grants wisdom to whom He wills, and whoever is granted wisdom, then certainly he has been granted abundant good. And none remembers it except those of understanding.

270. And whatever you spend of your expenditures or whatever vows you make (to spend), then indeed Allah knows it. And for the wrongdoers there will be no helpers.

271. If you disclose your charity, it is good. But if you keep it secret and give it to the poor, then it is better for you. And He will remove your evil deeds. And Allah is All-Aware of what you do.

272. Not on you is their guidance, but Allah guides whom He wills. And whatever good you spend (on others) is for your own good, and do not spend except seeking the pleasure of Allah. And whatever good you spend - it will be repaid to you in full and you will not be wronged.

273. (Charity is) for the poor who are wrapped up in the way of Allah,

Surah 2: The cow (v. 268-273)   Part - 3

they are unable to move about in the earth. An ignorant (person) would think that they are self-sufficient because of their restraint, but you can recognize them by their mark. They do not ask people with importunity. And whatever you spend of good, indeed Allah knows it.

274. Those who spend their wealth by night and by day, secretly and openly, they will have their reward with their Lord. And they will have no fear nor will they grieve.

275. Those who consume usury cannot stand (on the Day of Resurrection) except like the standing of a person whom Shaitaan has confounded by his touch. That is because they say, "Trade is only like usury." While Allah has permitted trade but has forbidden usury. Then whoever after receiving the admonition from **His** Lord refrains from it, then whatever has passed, his case is with Allah. And those who repeat - they are the companions of the Fire; they will abide in it forever.

276. Allah destroys usury and gives increase for charities. And Allah does not love any ungrateful sinner.

Surah 2: The cow (v. 274-276) — Part - 3

277. Indeed, those who believe and do good deeds and establish the prayer and give the *zakah*, they will have their reward from their Lord, and they will have no fear nor will they grieve.

278. O you who believe! Fear Allah and give up (what) remains (due to you) of usury, if you are believers.

279. And if you do not, then be informed of a war from Allah and **His** Messenger. And if you repent, then for you is your capital (amount) - do no wrong and you will not be wronged.

280. If the (debtor) is in difficulty, then grant him time until ease. And if you remit it as charity, it is better for you, if you only knew.

281. And fear the Day when you will be brought back to Allah. Then every soul will be repaid in full what it earned, and they will not be wronged.

282. O you who believe! When you contract a debt with one another for a fixed term, then write it. And let a scribe write it down with justice between you. And the scribe should not refuse to write as Allah has taught him. So let him write and let the one who has the obligation (i.e., debtor) dictate. And let him fear

Surah 2: The cow (v. 278-282)

Part - 3

Allah, his Lord; and do not diminish anything from it. And if the one on whom is the obligation is of limited understanding or weak or unable to dictate, then let his guardian dictate in justice. And call for evidence two witnesses from among your men. And if two men are not (available), then a man and two women from those whom you agree as witnesses - (so) if one of them errs then the other can remind her. And the witnesses should not refuse when they are called upon. And do not be weary of writing it - small or large - for its term. That is more just in the sight of Allah, and more upright for evidence and nearest in preventing doubt among you. However, if it is an immediate transaction which you conduct among yourselves, then there is no sin upon you if you do not write it. And take witness when you make a commercial transaction. And let neither scribe nor witness suffer harm, and if you do, then indeed it is sinful conduct on your part. And fear Allah. And Allah teaches you (herewith). And Allah is All-Knower of everything.

283. And if you are on a journey and you do not find a scribe, then take pledge in hand. And if one of you entrusts another, then let the one who is entrusted discharge his trust, and let him fear Allah, his Lord. And do not conceal the evidence. And whoever conceals it - then indeed his heart is sinful. And Allah is All-Knower of what you do.

284. To Allah belongs whatever is in the heavens and whatever is in the earth. Whether you disclose what is in your minds or conceal it, Allah will call you to account for it. Then He will forgive whom He wills and punish whom He wills. And Allah on everything is All-Powerful.

285. The Messenger has believed in what was revealed to him from his Lord, and (so have) the believers. All of them have believed in Allah and His Angels and His Books and His Messengers, (saying) "We do not make distinction between any of His Messengers." And they said, "We hear and we obey. Grant us Your forgiveness, our Lord, and to You is the return."

286. Allah does not burden a soul beyond its capacity. For him what he earned (of good deeds) and against him what he earned (of evil deeds). "Our Lord! Do not take us to task if we forget or if we err. Our Lord! Do not lay upon us a burden like that which You laid on those who

Surah 2: The cow (v. 284-286)   **Part - 3**

were before us. Our Lord! And burden us not with that which we have no strength to bear. And pardon us, and forgive us, and have mercy on us. **You** are our protector, so help us against the disbelieving people.

Surah Al-e-Imran

In the name of Allah, the Most Gracious, the Most Merciful.

1. *Alif Laam Meem.*

2. Allah - there is no God except **Him**, the Ever-Living, the Sustainer of all that exists.

3. **He** revealed to you the Book in truth which confirms that which was before it and **He** revealed the Taurat and the Injeel,

4. Before this, as guidance for mankind. And **He** revealed the Criterion. Verily, those who disbelieved in the Verses of Allah, for them is a severe punishment. And Allah is All-Mighty, All-Able of retribution.

5. Indeed, nothing is hidden from Allah in the earth and in the heaven.

6. **He** is the **One Who** shapes you in the wombs as **He** wills. There is no god except **Him,** the All-Mighty, the All-Wise.

Surah 2: The cow (v. 286) ; Surah 3: The family of Imran (v. 1-6) Part - 3

7. He is the One Who revealed to you the Book, in it are Verses which are absolutely clear - they are the foundation of the Book and others are allegorical. Then as for those in whose hearts is perversity - they follow what is allegorical from the Book, seeking discord and seeking its interpretation. And none except Allah knows its (true) interpretation. And those who are firm in knowledge say, "We believe in it. All (of it) is from our Lord." And not will take heed except men of understanding.

8. "Our Lord! Do not deviate our hearts after You have guided us and grant us mercy from Yourself. Indeed, You Alone are the Bestower.

9. Our Lord! Indeed, You will gather mankind on a Day about which there is no doubt. Indeed, Allah does not break His Promise."

10. Indeed, those who disbelieve - never will their wealth or their children avail them against Allah at all. And those will be the fuel for the Fire.

11. Like the behavior of the people of Firaun and those who were before them. They denied Our Signs, so Allah seized them for their sins. And Allah is severe in punishment.

12. Say to those who disbelieve, "You will be overcome

Surah 3: The family of Imran (v. 7-12)   Part - 3

and gathered towards Hell, an evil resting place.

13. Surely there has been for you a sign in the two hosts which met (in combat) - one fighting in the way of Allah and another of disbelievers. They saw them twice their number with their eyes. And Allah supports with His help whom He wills. Indeed, in that there is a lesson for those having vision.

14. Beautified for mankind is the love of the things they desire - of women and sons, and heaped up treasures of gold and silver, branded horses, and cattle and tilled land. Such are the possessions of the worldly life, but with Allah is an excellent abode to return to.

15. Say, "Shall I inform you of something better than that. For those who fear Allah, with their Lord, will be Gardens beneath which rivers flow, wherein they will abide forever, and they will have pure spouses and approval from Allah. And Allah is All-Seer of (His) slaves."

16. Those who say, "Our Lord! Indeed, we have believed, so forgive our sins, and save us from the punishment of the Fire."

17. The patient,

Surah 3: The family of Imran (v. 12-17)   Part - 3

the truthful, the obedient, those who spend (in Allah's way), and those who seek forgiveness before dawn.

18. Allah bears witness that there is no god except **Him**, and (so do) the Angels and those of knowledge - standing in justice. There is no god except **Him**, the All-Mighty, the All-Wise.

19. Indeed, the religion in the sight of Allah is Islam. And those who were given the Book did not differ except after knowledge had come to them - out of envy among them. And whoever disbelieves in the Verses of Allah, then indeed, Allah is swift in (taking) account.

20. Then if they argue with you, say, "I have submitted myself to Allah and (so have) those who follow me." And say to those who were given the Book and the unlettered people, "Have you submitted yourselves?" Then if they submit, then surely they are guided. But if they turn back then on you is only to convey (the Message). And Allah is All-Seer of (His) slaves.

21. Indeed, those who disbelieve in the Signs of Allah and kill the Prophets without right, and kill those who order justice among

Surah 3: The family of Imran (v. 18-21)

people - give them tidings of a painful punishment.

22. Those are the ones whose deeds have become worthless in this world and in the Hereafter. And for them there will be no helpers.

23. Have you not seen those who were given a portion of the Scripture? They are invited to the Book of Allah that it should arbitrate between them; then a party of them turns away and they are averse.

24. That is because they say, "Never will the Fire touch us except for (a few) numbered days." And they were deceived in their religion by what they were inventing.

25. Then how will it be when **We** will gather them on a Day about which there is no doubt. Every soul will be paid in full what it earned and they will not be wronged.

26. Say, "O Allah! Owner of the Dominion, **You** give the dominion to whom **You** will and **You** take away the dominion from whom **You** will, and **You** honor whom **You** will, and **You** humiliate whom **You** will. In **Your** hand is all the good. Indeed, **You** have power over everything.

27. **You** cause the night to enter the day and **You** cause the day to enter

Surah 3: The family of Imran (v. 22-27)   Part - 3

the night, and **You** bring forth the living from the dead, and **You** bring forth the dead from the living. And **You** give provision to whom **You** will without measure.

28. Let not the believers take the disbelievers as allies instead of the believers. And whoever does that, then he has no (connection) with Allah in anything except that you fear from them a threat. And Allah warns you of **Himself** and to Allah is the final return.

29. Say, "Whether you conceal what is in your breasts or disclose it, Allah knows it. And **He** knows what is in the heavens and what is in the earth. And Allah is on everything All-Powerful.

30. On the Day when every soul will find what it did of good presented (before him) and the evil it did, it will wish that there were a great distance between itself and the (evil it committed). And Allah warns you against **Himself**, and Allah is Most Kind to (**His**) slaves."

31. Say, "If you love Allah, then follow me, Allah will love you and forgive for you your sins. And Allah is Oft-Forgiving, Most Merciful.

32. Say, "Obey Allah and **His** Messenger." Then if they turn away then indeed, Allah does not love the disbelievers.

Surah 3: The family of Imran (v. 28-32)   **Part - 3**

33. Indeed, Allah chose Adam and Nuh, and the family of Ibrahim and the family of Imran over the worlds.

34. Descendents, some of them from others. And Allah is All-Hearing, All-Knowing.

35. When the wife of Imran said, "My Lord! Indeed, I have vowed to **You** what is in my womb, dedicated (to **Your** service), so accept from me. Indeed, **You** are All-Hearing, All-Knowing.

36. Then when she delivered her, she said, "My Lord, indeed, I have delivered a female." And Allah knows better what she delivered, and the male is not like the female. "And I have named her Maryam, and I seek **Your** protection for her and her offspring from Shaitaan, the rejected."

37. So her Lord accepted her with a goodly acceptance and made her grow in a good manner and put her in the care of Zakariya. Whenever Zakariya visited her prayer chamber, he found with her provision. He asked, "O Maryam! From where has this come to you." She said, "This is from Allah. Indeed, Allah gives provision to whom **He** wills without measure."

38. There itself,

Surah 3: The family of Imran (v. 33-38)   Part - 3

Zakariya invoked his Lord, he said, "My Lord grant me from **Yourself** a pure offspring. Indeed, **You** are All-Hearer of the prayer."

39. Then the Angels called him while he was standing in prayer in the prayer chamber. "Indeed, Allah gives you glad tidings of Yahya, confirming the word from Allah and (he will be) noble, chaste, and a Prophet from among the righteous.

40. He said, "My Lord, how will I have a son when I have reached old age and my wife is barren?" He (the Angel) said, "Thus; Allah does what **He** wills."

41. He said, "O my Lord give me a sign." **He** said, "Your sign is that you will not speak with people for three days except with gestures. And remember your Lord much, and glorify (**Him**) in the evening and in the morning."

42. And when the Angels said, "O Maryam! Indeed, Allah has chosen you and purified you and preferred you over the women of the worlds."

43. "O Maryam! Be obedient to your Lord and prostrate and bow down with those who bow down."

44. That is from the news of the unseen which **We** reveal to you.

Surah 3: The family of Imran (v. 39-44)   **Part - 3**

45. When the Angels said, "O Maryam! Indeed, Allah gives you glad tidings of a word from **Him**, his name is Messiah, Isa, son of Maryam, held in honor in this world and in the Hereafter and among those brought near (to Allah).

46. And he will speak to the people in the cradle and in maturity; and he will be of the righteous."

47. She said' "My Lord how will I have a child when no man has touched me?" He said, "Thus Allah creates what **He** wills. When **He** decrees a matter, then **He** only says to it, 'Be,' and it becomes.

48. And **He** will teach him the Book, and wisdom, and the Taurat, and the Injeel.

49. And (make him) a Messenger to the Children of Israel, (saying), 'Indeed, I have come to you with a sign from your Lord - that I design for you from clay (that which is) like the form of a bird, then I breath into it and it becomes a bird by the permission of Allah. And I cure the blind

Surah 3: The family of Imran (v. 45-49)

and the leper and give life to the dead by the permission of Allah. And I inform you of what you eat and what you store in your houses. Indeed, in that is surely a sign for you, if you are believers.

50. And (I have come) to confirm that which was before me of the Taurat, and to make lawful for you some of that which was forbidden to you. And I have come to you with a sign from your Lord. So fear Allah and obey me.

51. Indeed, Allah is my Lord and your Lord, so worship **Him Alone**. This is the straight path.'"

52. But when Isa perceived disbelief from them, he said, "Who will be my helpers (in the cause) of Allah." The disciples said, "We will be the helpers (in the cause) of Allah, we believe in Allah and bear witness that we are Muslims.

53. Our Lord, we believe in what **You** revealed and we follow the Messenger, then write us among the witnesses."

54. And they (disbelievers) schemed, and Allah planned. And Allah is the best of planners.

55. When Allah said, "O Isa! Indeed, **I** will take you and raise you towards **Myself**, and purify you from those who disbelieve and **I** will make those who follow you superior

Surah 3: The family of Imran (v. 50-55) Part - 3

to those who disbelieve on the Day of Resurrection. Then to **Me** is your return and **I** will judge between you concerning that about which you used to differ.

56. Then as for those who disbelieve, **I** will punish them with a severe punishment in this world and in the Hereafter. And they will have no helpers.

57. And as for those who believe and do righteous deeds, **He** will grant them in full their reward. And Allah does not love the wrongdoers.

58. That is what **We** recite to you of the Verses and the Wise Reminder.

59. Indeed, the likeness of Isa with Allah is like that of Adam. **He** created him from dust; then **He** said to him, "Be," and he was.

60. The truth is from your Lord, so do not be among the doubters.

61. Then whoever argues with you concerning it after knowledge has come to you - then say, "Come, let us call our sons and your sons, our women and your women, ourselves and yourselves, then let us humbly pray and invoke the curse of Allah on the liars.

62. Indeed, this is the true narration.

Surah 3: The family of Imran (v. 56-62)

And there is no god except Allah. And indeed, Allah is the All-Mighty, the All-Wise.

63. And if they turn back, then indeed, Allah is All-Knowing of the corrupters.

64. Say, "O People of the Book! Come to a word that is equitable between us and you that we worship none but Allah nor associate any partners with **Him** and that we will not take others as lords besides Allah." Then if they turn away, then say, "Bear witness that we are Muslims."

65. O People of the Book! Why do you argue about Ibrahim while the Taurat and Injeel were not revealed until after him? Then why don't you use your intellect?

66. Here you are - those who argue about that of which you have (some) knowledge, but why do you argue about that of which you have no knowledge? And Allah knows, while you do not know.

67. Ibrahim was neither a Jew nor a Christian, but he was a true Muslim and he was not of those who associated partners with Allah.

68. Indeed, the most worthy people to claim relationship to Ibrahim are those who follow him and this Prophet (Muhammad SAWS) and those who believe. And Allah is the Guardian

Surah 3: The family of Imran (v. 63-68)

لَوْ	الْكِتَابِ	مِّنْ	طَّآئِفَةٌ	وَدَّت	﴿٦٨﴾	الْمُؤْمِنِينَ
if	(of) the Book	from	a group	Wished	68	(of) the believers.

وَمَا	أَنفُسَهُمْ	إِلَّا	يُضِلُّونَ	وَمَا	يُضِلُّونَكُمْ
and not	themselves	except	they lead astray	and not	they could lead you astray,

بِآيَاتِ	تَكْفُرُونَ	لِمَ	الْكِتَابِ	يَاأَهْلَ	﴿٦٩﴾	يَشْعُرُونَ
[in] the Signs	you deny	Why do	(of) the Book!	O People	69	they perceive.

لِمَ	الْكِتَابِ	يَاأَهْلَ	﴿٧٠﴾	تَشْهَدُونَ	وَأَنتُمْ	اللَّهِ
Why	(of) the Book!	O People	70	bear witness?	while you	(of) Allah

تَعْلَمُونَ	وَأَنتُمْ	الْحَقَّ	وَتَكْتُمُونَ	بِالْبَاطِلِ	الْحَقَّ	تَلْبِسُونَ
know?	while you	the truth	and conceal	with the falsehood	the truth	do you mix

بِالَّذِي	آمِنُوا	الْكِتَابِ	أَهْلِ	مِّنْ	طَّآئِفَةٌ	وَقَالَت
in what	"Believe	(of) the Book,	(the) People	of	a group	And said

وَاكْفُرُوا	النَّهَارِ	وَجْهَ	آمَنُوا	الَّذِينَ	عَلَى	أُنزِلَ
and reject	(of) the day,	(at the) beginning	believe[d]	those who	on	was revealed

إِلَّا	تُؤْمِنُوا	وَلَا	﴿٧١﴾	يَرْجِعُونَ	لَعَلَّهُمْ	آخِرَهُ
except	believe	And (do) not	71	return.	perhaps they may	(at) its end,

الْهُدَى	إِنَّ	قُلْ	دِينَكُمْ	تَبِعَ	لِمَن
the (true) guidance	"Indeed,	Say,	your religion."	follows	(the one) who

أُوتِيتُمْ	مَّا	مِثْلَ	أَحَدٌ	يُؤْتَى	أَن	هُدَى اللَّهِ
was given to you	(of) what	(the) like	(to) one -	is given	lest	(is the) Guidance of Allah -

الْفَضْلَ	إِنَّ	قُلْ	رَبِّكُمْ	عِندَ	يُحَاجُّوكُمْ	أَوْ
the Bounty	"Indeed,	Say,	your Lord."	near	they may argue with you	or

وَاسِعٌ	وَاللَّهُ	يَشَاءُ	مَن	يُؤْتِيهِ	بِيَدِ اللَّهِ
(is) All-Encompassing,	and Allah	He wills,	(to) whom	He gives it	(is) in the Hand of Allah.

عَلِيمٌ	﴿٧٣﴾	يَشَاءُ	مَن	بِرَحْمَتِهِ	يَخْتَصُّ	وَاللَّهُ
All-Knowing."	73	He wills.	whom	for His Mercy	He chooses	And Allah

الْكِتَابِ	أَهْلِ	وَمِنْ	﴿٧٤﴾	الْعَظِيمِ	ذُو الْفَضْلِ
(of) the Book	(the) People	And from	74	[the] great.	(is) the Possessor of Bounty -

إِلَيْكَ	يُؤَدِّهِ	بِقِنطَارٍ	تَأْمَنْهُ	إِن	مَّن
to you.	he will return it	with a great amount of wealth	you entrust him	if	(is he) who,

Surah 3: The family of Imran (v. 69-75)

of the believers.

69. A group of the People of the Book wish to lead you astray, and not they lead astray except themselves and they do not perceive.

70. O People of the Book! Why do you deny the Signs of Allah to which you yourselves bear witness?

71. O People of the Book! Why do you mix the truth with falsehood and conceal the truth knowingly?

72. And a group of the People of the Book said, "Believe in that which was revealed to the believers at the beginning of the day and reject it at its end, perhaps they may return.

73. And do not believe except those who follow your religion." Say, "Indeed the true guidance is the Guidance of Allah - lest someone be given the like of that which was given to you or that they may argue with you before your Lord." Say, "Indeed, the Bounty is in the Hand of Allah - He gives it to whom He wills, and Allah is All-Encompassing, All-Knowing.

74. He chooses for His Mercy whom He wills. And Allah is the Possessor of Great Bounty.

75. And among the People of the Book is he who, if you entrust him with a great amount of wealth, he will return it to you.

And among them is he who, if you entrust him with a single coin, he will not return it to you unless you constantly stand demanding (it). That is because they say, "There is no blame upon us concerning the unlettered people." And they speak a lie about Allah while they know.

76. Nay, whoever fulfills his covenant and fears Allah, then indeed Allah loves those who fear **Him**.

77. Indeed, those who exchange the Covenant of Allah and their oaths for a little price will have no share in the Hereafter, and Allah will not speak to them nor look at them on the Day of Resurrection, nor will He purify them; and for them is a painful punishment.

78. And indeed, among them is a group who distort the Book with their tongues so that you may think it is from the Book, but it is not from the Book. And they say, "This is from Allah," but it is not from Allah. And they tell a lie about Allah while they know.

79. It is not for any human to whom Allah has given the Book, and wisdom and Prophethood to say to the people, "Be my worshippers

Surah 3: The family of Imran (v. 76-79)

كُوْنُوْا	وَلٰكِنْ	مِنْ دُوْنِ اللّٰهِ	لِّيْ	
"Be	but (would say)	besides Allah,	of me	
الْكِتٰبَ	تُعَلِّمُوْنَ	كُنْتُمْ	بِمَا	رَبّٰنِيّٖنَ
the Book	teaching	you have been	because	worshippers of the Lord
وَلَا	٧٩	تَدْرُسُوْنَ	كُنْتُمْ	وَبِمَا
And not	79	studying (it)."	you have been	and because
وَالنَّبِيّٖنَ	الْمَلٰٓئِكَةَ	تَتَّخِذُوْا	اَنْ	يَاْمُرَكُمْ
and the Prophets	the Angels,	you take	that	he will order you
اِذْ	بَعْدَ	بِالْكُفْرِ	اَيَاْمُرُكُمْ	اَرْبَابًا
[when]	after	to [the] disbelief	Would he order you	(as) lords.
اَخَذَ اللّٰهُ	وَاِذْ	۸۰	مُسْلِمُوْنَ	اَنْتُمْ
Allah took	And when	80	Muslims?	you (have become)
مِنْ	اٰتَيْتُكُمْ	لَمَآ	النَّبِيّٖنَ	مِيْثَاقَ
of	I (have) given you	"Certainly, whatever	(of) the Prophets,	covenant
رَسُوْلٌ	جَآءَكُمْ	ثُمَّ	وَحِكْمَةٍ	كِتٰبٍ
a Messenger	comes to you	then	and wisdom	(the) Book
بِهٖ	لَتُؤْمِنُنَّ	مَعَكُمْ	لِّمَا	مُّصَدِّقٌ
in him	you must believe	(is) with you,	that which	confirming
وَاَخَذْتُمْ	ءَاَقْرَرْتُمْ	قَالَ	وَلَتَنْصُرُنَّهٗ	
and take	"Do you affirm	He said,	and you must help him."	
اَقْرَرْنَا	قَالُوْٓا	اِصْرِيْ	ذٰلِكُمْ	عَلٰى
"We affirm."	They said,	My Covenant?"	that (condition)	on
مِّنَ	مَعَكُمْ	وَاَنَا	فَاشْهَدُوْا	قَالَ
among	with you	and I (am)	"Then bear witness,	He said,
بَعْدَ	تَوَلّٰى	فَمَنْ	۸۱	الشّٰهِدِيْنَ
after	turns away	Then whoever	81	the witnesses."
۸۲	الْفٰسِقُوْنَ	هُمُ	فَاُولٰٓئِكَ	ذٰلِكَ
82	(are) the defiantly disobedient.	they	then those	that,
يَبْغُوْنَ	اللّٰهِ	دِيْنِ	اَفَغَيْرَ	
they seek?	(of) Allah	(the) religion	So is (it) other than	

besides Allah," but (on the contrary) he would say, "Be worshippers of the Lord because you have been teaching the book and you have been studying it."

80. Nor would he order you to take the Angels and the Prophets as lords. Would he order you to disbelief after you have become Muslims?

81. And when Allah took the covenant of the Prophets (saying)," Certainly, whatever I have given you of the Book and the wisdom, then there comes to you a Messenger confirming that which is with you, you must believe in him and support him." He said, "Do you affirm and take on that (condition) My Covenant?" They said, "We affirm." He said, "Then bear witness, and I am with you among the witnesses."

82. Then whoever turns away after that - then those are the defiantly disobedient.

83. Do they seek other than the religion of Allah?

While to **Him** have submitted whatever is in the heavens and the earth willingly or unwillingly, and to **Him** they will be returned.

84. Say, "We believe in Allah and what is revealed to us and what was revealed to Ibrahim and Ismail, and Ishaq, and Yaqub, and the descendents and what was given to Musa, and Isa, and the Prophets from their Lord. We do not make any distinction between them and to **Him** we are submissive.

85. And whoever seeks a religion other than Islam - it will never be accepted from him, and he, in the Hereafter, will be among the losers.

86. How shall Allah guide a people who disbelieved after they had believed and had witnessed that the Messenger is true, and clear proofs had come to them? And Allah does not guide

Surah 3: The family of Imran (v. 84-86)   **Part - 3**

جَزَآؤُهُمْ	أُو۟لَٰٓئِكَ	۝ ٨٦	ٱلظَّٰلِمِينَ
their recompense,	Those -	86	[the] wrongdoers.
وَٱلْمَلَٰٓئِكَةِ	ٱللَّهِ	لَعْنَةَ	عَلَيْهِمْ	أَنَّ
and the Angels	(of) Allah	(is the) curse	on them	that
فِيهَا	خَٰلِدِينَ	۝ ٨٧	أَجْمَعِينَ	وَٱلنَّاسِ
in it.	(They will) abide forever	87	all together.	and the people
وَلَا	ٱلْعَذَابُ	عَنْهُمُ	يُخَفَّفُ	لَا
and not	the punishment	for them	will be lightened	Not
ٱلَّذِينَ	إِلَّا	۝ ٨٨	يُنظَرُونَ	هُمْ
those who	Except	88	will be reprieved.	they
وَأَصْلَحُوا۟	ذَٰلِكَ	مِنۢ بَعْدِ	تَابُوا۟
and reform[ed] themselves.	that,	after	repent
رَّحِيمٌ	غَفُورٌ	ٱللَّهَ	فَإِنَّ
۝ ٨٩	Most Merciful.	(is) Oft-Forgiving,	Allah	Then indeed,
89				
إِيمَٰنِهِمْ	بَعْدَ	كَفَرُوا۟	ٱلَّذِينَ	إِنَّ
their belief	after	disbelieved	those who	Indeed,
تُقْبَلَ	لَّن	كُفْرًا	ٱزْدَادُوا۟	ثُمَّ
will be accepted	never	(in) disbelief,	they increased	then
ٱلضَّآلُّونَ	هُمْ	وَأُو۟لَٰٓئِكَ	تَوْبَتُهُمْ
(are) those who have gone astray.	they	and those -	their repentance,
وَمَاتُوا۟	كَفَرُوا۟	ٱلَّذِينَ	إِنَّ	۝ ٩٠
and died	disbelieve[d]	those who	Indeed,	90
مِّنْ	يُقْبَلَ	فَلَن	كُفَّارٌ	وَهُمْ
from	will be accepted	then never	(are) disbelievers,	while they
وَلَوِ	ذَهَبًا	مِلْءُ ٱلْأَرْضِ	أَحَدِهِم
[and] (even) if	(of) gold	earth full	any one of them
أَلِيمٌ	عَذَابٌ	لَهُمْ	أُو۟لَٰٓئِكَ	ٱفْتَدَىٰ بِهِۦ
painful	(is) a punishment	for them	Those -	he offered it as ransom.
۝ ٩١	نَّٰصِرِينَ	مِّن	لَهُم	وَمَا
91	helpers.	any	(will be) for them	and not

87. Those - their recompense is that on them is the curse of Allah and the Angels and the people, all together.

88. They will abide therein forever. The punishment will not be lightened for them, nor will they be reprieved.

89. Except those who repent after that and reform themselves. Then indeed, Allah is Oft-Forgiving, Most Merciful.

90. Indeed, those who disbelieved after their belief and then they increased in disbelief, their repentance will never be accepted and they are the ones who have gone astray.

91. Indeed, those who disbelieve and die while they are disbelievers even if any one of them offered all the gold on the earth as ransom it will not be accepted from him. For them is a painful punishment and they will have no helpers.

Surah 3: The family of Imran (v. 87-91)

92. Never will you attain righteousness until you spend from that which you love. And whatever you spend - indeed, Allah is All-Knowing of it.

93. All food was lawful for the Children of Israel except what Israel made unlawful to himself before the Taurat was revealed. Say, "So bring the Taurat and recite it, if you are truthful."

94. Then whoever fabricates a lie about Allah after that - then those are the wrongdoers.

95. Say, "Allah has spoken the truth, so follow the religion of Ibrahim - the upright; and he was not of those who associated others with Allah.

96. Indeed, the First House set up for mankind is at Bakkah (i.e., Makkah) - blessed and a guidance for the worlds.

97. In it are clear signs, standing place of Ibrahim, and whoever enters it is safe. And pilgrimage to the House is a duty that mankind owes to Allah for those who are able to find the means. And whoever disbelieves, then indeed, Allah is free from the need of the universe.

98. Say, "O People of the Book! Why do you disbelieve in the Verses of Allah

Surah 3: The family of Imran (v. 92-98)   **Part - 4**

while Allah is a Witness over what you do?"

99. Say, "O People of the Book! Why do you hinder those who believe from the way of Allah, seeking to make it (seem) crooked, while you are witnesses (to the truth)? And Allah is not unaware of what you do.

100. O you who believe! If you obey a group from those who were given the Book they will turn you back, after your belief, to disbelievers.

101. And how could you disbelieve while it is you to whom the Verses of Allah are being recited and among you is His Messenger? And whoever holds firmly to Allah then surely, he is guided to a straight path.

102. O you who believe! Fear Allah as He has the right to be feared and do not die except as Muslims.

103. And hold firmly to the rope of Allah all together, and do not be divided. And remember the Favor of Allah on you when you were enemies, then He made friendship between your hearts and by His Favor you became brothers. And when you were on the brink of the pit of the Fire,

Surah 3: The family of Imran (v. 99-103)   Part - 4

then **He** saved you from it. Thus Allah makes clear for you **His** Verses so that you may be guided.

104. And let there be among you a (group) of people inviting to the good, enjoining what is right and forbidding what is wrong, and those are the successful.

105. And do not be like those who became divided and differed after the clear proofs came to them. And they will have a great punishment.

106. On the Day (some) faces will turn white and some faces will turn black. As for those whose faces will turn black (it will be said to them), "Did you disbelieve after your belief? Then taste the punishment for what you used to disbelieve."

107. But as for those whose faces will turn white, they will be in the Mercy of Allah and they will abide in it forever.

108. These are the Verses of Allah. **We** recite them to you in truth. And Allah does not want any injustice to the worlds.

109. And to Allah belongs whatever is in the heavens and whatever is on the earth. And to Allah all matters will be returned.

110. You are the best of people

Surah 3: The family of Imran (v. 104-110) — Part - 4

وَتَنْهَوْنَ عَنِ	بِالْمَعْرُوفِ	تَأْمُرُونَ	لِلنَّاسِ	أُخْرِجَتْ
and forbidding [from]	the right	enjoining	for the mankind -	raised

أَهْلُ	ءَامَنَ	وَلَوْ	بِاللَّهِ	وَتُؤْمِنُونَ	الْمُنكَرِ
(the) People	believed	And if	in Allah.	and believing	the wrong

مِّنْهُمُ	لَّهُمْ	خَيْرًا	لَكَانَ	الْكِتَابِ
Among them	for them.	good	surely would have been	(of) the Book

۞	الْفَاسِقُونَ	وَأَكْثَرُهُمُ	الْمُؤْمِنُونَ
110	(are) defiantly disobedient.	but most of them	(are) [the] believers,

وَإِن	أَذًى	إِلَّا	يَضُرُّوكُمْ	لَن
And if	a hurt.	except	will they harm you	Never

يُنصَرُونَ	لَا	ثُمَّ	الْأَدْبَارَ	يُوَلُّوكُمُ	يُقَاتِلُوكُمْ
they will be helped.	not	then	the backs,	they will turn (towards) you	they fight you,

ثُقِفُوا	مَا	أَيْنَ	الذِّلَّةُ	عَلَيْهِمُ	ضُرِبَتْ	۞
they are found	wherever		the humiliation	on them	Struck	111

النَّاسِ	مِّنَ	وَحَبْلٍ	اللَّهِ	مِّنَ	بِحَبْلٍ	إِلَّا
the people.	from	and a rope	Allah	from	with a rope	except

عَلَيْهِمُ	وَضُرِبَتْ	اللَّهِ	مِّنَ	بِغَضَبٍ	وَبَاءُو
on them	and struck	Allah	from	wrath	And they incurred

بِآيَاتِ	يَكْفُرُونَ	كَانُوا	بِأَنَّهُمْ	ذَٰلِكَ	الْمَسْكَنَةُ
in (the) Verses	disbelieve	they used to	(is) because	That	the poverty.

بِمَا	ذَٰلِكَ	حَقٍّ	بِغَيْرِ	الْأَنبِيَاءَ	وَيَقْتُلُونَ	اللَّهِ
(is) because	That	right.	without	the Prophets	and they killed	(of) Allah

سَوَاءً	لَيْسُوا	۞	يَعْتَدُونَ	وَكَانُوا	عَصَوا
(the) same;	They are not	112	transgress.	and they used to	they disobeyed

مِّنْ	أَهْلِ	الْكِتَابِ	أُمَّةٌ	قَائِمَةٌ	يَتْلُونَ
(and) reciting	standing	(is) a community	(of) the Book	(the) People	among

يَسْجُدُونَ	وَهُمْ	اللَّيْلِ	ءَانَاءَ	اللَّهِ	ءَايَاتِ
prostrate.	and they	(of) the night	(in the) hours	(the) Verses of Allah

الْآخِرِ	وَالْيَوْمِ	بِاللَّهِ	يُؤْمِنُونَ	۞
the Last	and the Day	in Allah	They believe	113

raised for mankind - enjoining what is right and forbidding what is wrong and believing in Allah. And if the People of the Book had believed, it would have been better for them. Among them are believers but most of them are defiantly disobedient.

111. They will never be able to harm you except a (trifling) hurt. And if they fight you, they will turn their backs (i.e., retreat), then they will not be helped.

112. They have been struck by humiliation wherever they are found except for a rope (covenant) from Allah and a rope (treaty) from the people. And they incurred the wrath of Allah and struck on them poverty. That is because they used to disbelieve in the Verses of Allah and they killed the Prophets without right. That is because they disobeyed and transgressed.

113. They are not the same; among the People of the Book is a community standing and reciting the Verses of Allah in the hours of night and they prostrate.

114. They believe in Allah and the Last Day

Surah 3: The family of Imran (v. 111-114)   **Part - 4**

and they enjoin what is right and forbid what is wrong and they hasten in doing good deeds. And those are among the righteous.

115. And whatever good they do, they will never be denied its (reward). And Allah is All-Knowing of the God-fearing.

116. Indeed, those who disbelieve - never will their wealth and their children avail them against Allah at all, and those are the companions of the Fire; they will abide therein forever.

117. The example of what they spend in the life of this world is like that of a wind containing frost, which strikes the harvest of people who have wronged themselves and destroys it. And Allah has not wronged them, but they wronged themselves.

118. O you who believe! Do not take as intimates other than yourselves (i.e., believers), for they will not spare you any ruin. They wish to distress you. Indeed, hatred has become apparent from their mouths, and what their breasts conceal is greater. We have certainly made clear to you the Verses, if

Surah 3: The family of Imran (v. 115-118)

وَلَا	تُحِبُّونَهُمْ	أُولَاءِ	هَاأَنْتُمْ	(١١٨)	تَعْقِلُونَ	كُنْتُمْ
but not	you love them	those,	Lo! You are	118	(to use) reason.	you were

لَقُوكُمْ	وَإِذَا	كُلِّهٖ ۚ	بِالْكِتٰبِ	وَتُؤْمِنُونَ	يُحِبُّونَكُمْ
they meet you	And when	all of it.	in the Book -	and you believe	they love you

الْأَنَامِلَ	عَلَيْكُمُ	عَضُّوا	خَلَوْا	وَإِذَا	اٰمَنَّا ۚ	قَالُوا
the finger tips	at you	they bite	they are alone	And when	"We believe."	they say,

اللّٰهَ	إِنَّ	بِغَيْظِكُمْ ؕ	مُوتُوا	قُلْ	الْغَيْظِ ؕ	مِنَ
Allah	Indeed.	in your rage.	Die	Say,	[the] rage.	(out) of

تَمْسَسْكُمْ	إِنْ	(١١٩)	الصُّدُورِ	بِذَاتِ	عَلِيمٌۢ
touches you	If	119	(is in) the breasts."	of what	(is) All-Knowing

بِهَا ؕ	يَفْرَحُوا	سَيِّئَةٌ	تُصِبْكُمْ	وَإِنْ	تَسُؤْهُمْ	حَسَنَةٌ
at it.	they rejoice	misfortune,	strikes you	and if	it grieves them	a good,

كَيْدُهُمْ	يَضُرُّكُمْ	لَا	وَتَتَّقُوا	تَصْبِرُوا	وَإِنْ
their plot	will harm you	not	and fear (Allah),	you are patient	And if

مُحِيطٌ	يَعْمَلُونَ	بِمَا	اللّٰهَ	إِنَّ	شَيْئًا ؕ
(is) All-Encompassing.	they do	of what	Allah,	Indeed,	(in) anything.

تُبَوِّئُ	أَهْلِكَ	مِنْ	غَدَوْتَ	وَإِذْ	ع (١٢٠)
to post	your household	from	you left early morning	And when	120

عَلِيمٌ	سَمِيعٌ	وَاللّٰهُ	لِلْقِتَالِ ؕ	مَقَاعِدَ	الْمُؤْمِنِينَ
All-Knowing.	(is) All-Hearing,	And Allah	for the battle.	(to take) positions	the believers

تَفْشَلَا ۙ	أَنْ	مِنْكُمْ	طَّائِفَتَانِ	هَمَّتْ	إِذْ	ۙ (١٢١)
they lost heart,	that	among you	two parties	inclined	When	121

الْمُؤْمِنُونَ	فَلْيَتَوَكَّلِ	اللّٰهِ	وَعَلَى	وَلِيُّهُمَا ؕ	وَاللّٰهُ
the believers.	let put (their) trust	Allah	And on	(was) their protector.	but Allah

أَذِلَّةٌ ۚ	وَأَنْتُمْ	بِبَدْرٍ	اللّٰهُ	نَصَرَكُمُ	وَلَقَدْ	(١٢٢)
weak.	while you (were)	in Badr	Allah	helped you	And certainly	122

تَقُولُ	إِذْ	(١٢٣)	تَشْكُرُونَ	لَعَلَّكُمْ	اللّٰهَ	فَاتَّقُوا
you said	When	123	(be) grateful.	so that you may	Allah	So fear

رَبُّكُمْ	يُمِدَّكُمْ	أَنْ	يَكْفِيَكُمْ	أَلَنْ	لِلْمُؤْمِنِينَ
your Lord	reinforces you	that	enough for you	"Is it not	to the believers,

you use reason.

119. Lo! You are those who love them, but they do not love you and you believe in the Book - all of it. And when they meet you, they say, "We believe." And when they are alone they bite their fingers tips at you in rage. Say, "Die in your rage. Indeed, Allah is All-Knowing of what is in the breasts."

120. If any good touches you, it grieves them; and if any misfortune strikes you, they rejoice at it. And if you are patient and fear Allah, their plot will not harm you at all. Indeed, Allah of what they do is All-Encompassing.

ع ١٢ ١١ ٣

121. And when you left your household early morning to post the believers to take positions for the battle - and Allah is All-Hearing, All-Knowing.

122. When two parties among you were about to lose courage, but Allah was their protector. And in Allah the believers should put their trust.

123. And Allah had already helped you in Badr when you were weak. So fear Allah, so that you may be grateful.

124. When you said to the believers, "Is it not enough for you that your Lord helped you

with three thousand Angels sent down?

125. Yes, if you are patient and fear Allah and they (enemy) come upon you suddenly, your Lord will reinforce you with five thousand Angels having marks.

126. And Allah made it not except as good news for you and to reassure your hearts. And there is no victory except from Allah, the All-Mighty, the All-Wise.

127. That **He** may cut off a part from those who disbelieved or suppress them so that they turn back disappointed.

128. Not for you is the decision whether **He** turns to them or punishes them, for indeed, they are wrongdoers.

129. And to Allah belongs whatever is in the heavens and whatever is in the earth, **He** forgives whom **He** wills and punishes whom **He** wills. And Allah is Oft-Forgiving, Most Merciful.

130. O you who believe! Do not consume usury doubled and multiplied. And fear Allah so that you may be successful.

131. And fear the Fire which is prepared for the disbelievers.

132. And obey Allah and the Messenger so that you may

Surah 3: The family of Imran (v. 125-132)   **Part - 4**

133. And hasten towards forgiveness from your Lord and a Garden as wide as the heavens and the earth, prepared for the pious.

134. Those who spend in ease and hardship and those who restrain their anger and pardon people - and Allah loves the good-doers.

135. And those when they do immorality or wrong themselves, they remember Allah and seek forgiveness for their sins - and who can forgive sins except Allah? And they do not persist knowingly in what they have done.

136. Those - their reward is forgiveness from their Lord and Gardens beneath which rivers flow, wherein they will abide forever. An excellent reward for the (righteous) workers.

137. Similar situations have passed before you, so travel in the earth and see how was the end of those who denied.

138. This is a declaration for the people and guidance and admonition for the God-fearing.

139. And do not weaken and do not grieve

Surah 3: The family of Imran (v. 133-139) — Part - 4

139. and you will be superior, if you are believers.

140. If a wound has touched you, then certainly a similar wound has touched the people. And these days (of varying fortunes), We alternate among the people so that Allah makes evident those who believe and take from among you martyrs. And Allah does not love the wrongdoers.

141. And so that Allah may purify those who believe and destroy the disbelievers.

142. Or do you think that you will enter Paradise while Allah has not yet made evident among you who strove hard (in His way) and made evident those who are steadfast.

143. And certainly you used to wish for death before you met it, then indeed you had seen it while you were looking on.

144. Muhammad (SAWS) is not but a Messenger, certainly many Messengers have passed away before him. So if he died or is slain, will you turn back on your heels? And whoever turns back on his heels not the least harm will he do to Allah, and Allah will reward those who are grateful.

145. And it is not

Surah 3: The family of Imran (v. 140-145)

بِاِذْنِ اللّٰهِ	اِلَّا	اَنْ	تَمُوْتَ	لِنَفْسٍ	كَانَ
by (the) permission of Allah,	except	that	he dies	for a soul	is

الدُّنْيَا	ثَوَابَ	يُرِدْ	وَمَنْ	مُّؤَجَّلًا	كِتٰبًا
(of) the world -	reward	desires	And whoever	determined.	(at a) decree

الْاٰخِرَةِ	ثَوَابَ	يُرِدْ	وَمَنْ	مِنْهَا	نُؤْتِهٖ
(of) the Hereafter	reward	desires	and whoever	thereof;	We will give him

الشّٰكِرِيْنَ	وَسَنَجْزِى	مِنْهَا	نُؤْتِهٖ		۱٤٥
the grateful ones.	And We will reward	thereof.	We will give him		145

رِّبِّيُّوْنَ كَثِيْرٌ	مَّعَهٗ	قٰتَلَ	نَّبِىٍّ	مِّنْ	وَكَاَيِّنْ
(were) many religious scholars.	with him	fought;	a Prophet	from	And how many

اللّٰهِ	سَبِيْلِ	فِىْ	اَصَابَهُمْ	لِمَاۤ	وَهَنُوْا	فَمَا
(of) Allah	(the) way	in	befell them	for what	they lost heart	But not

يُحِبُّ	وَاللّٰهُ	اسْتَكَانُوْا	وَمَا	ضَعُفُوْا	وَمَا
loves	And Allah	they gave in.	and not	they weakened	and not

اَنْ	اِلَّاۤ	قَوْلَهُمْ	كَانَ	وَمَا	۱٤٦	الصّٰبِرِيْنَ
that	except	their words	were	And not	146	the patient ones.

فِىْ	وَاِسْرَافَنَا	ذُنُوْبَنَا	لَنَا	اغْفِرْ	رَبَّنَا	قَالُوْا
in	and our excesses	our sins	for us	forgive	"Our Lord	they said,

الْقَوْمِ	عَلَى	وَانْصُرْنَا	اَقْدَامَنَا	وَثَبِّتْ	اَمْرِنَا
[the people]	over	and give us victory	our feet	and make firm	our affairs

وَحُسْنَ	الدُّنْيَا	ثَوَابَ	فَاٰتٰىهُمُ اللّٰهُ	۱٤٧	الْكٰفِرِيْنَ
and good	(in) the world	reward	So Allah gave them	147	the disbelievers."

يٰۤاَيُّهَا	۱٤٨	الْمُحْسِنِيْنَ	يُحِبُّ	وَاللّٰهُ	الْاٰخِرَةِ	ثَوَابِ
O you	148	the good-doers.	loves	And Allah	(in) the Hereafter.	reward

كَفَرُوْا	الَّذِيْنَ	تُطِيْعُوا	اِنْ	اٰمَنُوْۤا	الَّذِيْنَ
disbelieve,	those who	you obey	If	believe!	who

خٰسِرِيْنَ	فَتَنْقَلِبُوْا	اَعْقَابِكُمْ	عَلٰۤى	يَرُدُّوْكُمْ
(as) losers.	then you will turn back	your heels,	on	they will turn you back

خَيْرُ	وَهُوَ	مَوْلٰىكُمْ	اللّٰهُ	بَلِ	۱٤٩
(is the) best	and He	(is) your Protector	Allah	Nay,	149

Surah 3: The family of Imran (v. 146-150)

---

for a soul to die except by the permission of Allah at a decree determined. And whoever desires the reward of this world, **We** will give him thereof; and whoever desires the reward of the Hereafter, **We** will give him thereof. And **We** will reward those who are grateful.

146. And how many a Prophet fought; with him fought many religious scholars. But they never lost heart for what befell them in the way of Allah, nor did they weaken or give in. And Allah loves those who are patient.

147. And their words were not except that they said, "Our Lord, forgive our sins and our excesses in our affairs and make our feet firm and give us victory over the disbelieving people."

148. So Allah gave them the reward in this world and good reward in the Hereafter. And Allah loves the good-doers.

149. O you who believe! If you obey those who disbelieve, they will turn you back on your heels, then you will turn back as losers.

150. Nay, Allah is your Protector and **He** is best

Part - 4

151. We will cast terror in the hearts of those who disbelieve because they associated partners with Allah for which He had not sent down any authority. And their refuge will be the Fire and wretched is the abode of the wrongdoers.

152. And certainly Allah had fulfilled His promise to you when you were killing them by His permission until you lost courage and fell into dispute concerning the order and disobeyed after He had shown you that which you love. Among you are some who desire this world and among you are some who desire the Hereafter. Then He diverted you from them so that He may test you. And surely He has forgiven you. And Allah is the Possessor of Bounty for the believers.

153. (Remember) when you were running uphill without casting a glance at anyone while the Messenger was calling you from behind. So He repaid you with distress upon distress so that you would not grieve for that which had escaped you or that which had befallen you.

Surah 3: The family of Imran (v. 151-153)   **Part - 4**

And Allah is All-Aware of what you do.

154. Then He sent down on you, after the distress, security - slumber overcoming a group of you, while another group worried about themselves, thinking about Allah other than the truth - the thought of ignorance, saying, "Is there anything for us in this matter." Say, "Indeed all the matter belongs to Allah." They hide in themselves what they do not reveal to you. They say, "If there was anything for us in this matter we would not have been killed here." Say, "Even if you had been in your houses, those on whom death was decreed would have surely gone forth to their places of death. And that Allah might test what is in your breasts and purge what is in your hearts. And Allah is All-Aware of what is in the breasts."

155. Indeed, those who turned back among you on the day when the two hosts met - Shaitaan made them slip for what they had earned.

Surah 3: The family of Imran (v. 154-155)

And surely Allah forgave them and indeed, Allah is Oft-Forgiving, All-Forbearing.

156. O you who believe! Do not be like those who disbelieved and said about their brothers when they traveled in the earth or they went out fighting, "If they had been with us, they would not have died nor been killed." So Allah makes that a regret in their hearts. And it is Allah who gives life and causes death and Allah is All-Seer of what you do.

157. And if you are killed in the way of Allah or die - certainly forgiveness and Mercy from Allah are better than what they accumulate.

158. And if you die or are killed, to Allah you will be gathered.

159. Because of Mercy from Allah you dealt gently with them. And if you had been rude and harsh at heart, surely they would have dispersed from around you. Then pardon them and ask forgiveness for them, and consult them in the matters. Then when you have decided, then put your trust in Allah. Indeed, Allah

Surah 3: The family of Imran (v. 156-159)

loves those who put their trust in **Him**.

160. If Allah helps you, then none can overcome you; and if **He** forsakes you, who is there who can help you after **Him**? And on Allah let the believers put their trust.

161. And not is for any Prophet that he defrauds. And whoever defrauds will bring whatever he had defrauded on the Day of Resurrection. Then every soul will be repaid in full what it earned and they will not be wronged.

162. So is the one who pursues the pleasure of Allah like the one who draws upon himself the wrath of Allah, and his abode is hell, a wretched destination?

163. They are in varying degrees in the sight of Allah, and Allah is All-Seer of what they do.

164. Certainly Allah bestowed **His** Favor upon the believers when **He** raised among them a Messenger from themselves, reciting to them **His** Verses and purifying them and teaching them the Book and wisdom, although they had been in clear error before.

Surah 3: The family of Imran (v. 160-164) Part - 4

165. Or when disaster struck you, surely you had struck them with twice of it, you said, "From where is this?" Say, "It is from yourselves." Indeed, Allah is on everything All-Powerful.

166. And what struck you on the day the two hosts met was by the permission of Allah that He might make evident the believers.

167. And that He might make evident those who are hypocrites. And it was said to them, "Come, fight in the way of Allah or defend." They said, "If we knew fighting, certainly we would have followed you." That day they were nearer to disbelief than to faith, saying with their mouths what was not in their hearts. And Allah is Most Knowing of what they conceal.

168. Those who said about their brothers while sitting (at home), "If they had obeyed us they would not have been killed." Say, "Then avert death from yourselves if you are truthful."

169. And do not think of those who are killed in the way of Allah as dead. Nay! They are alive;

Surah 3: The family of Imran (v. 165-169) — Part - 4

they are receiving provision from their Lord.

170. Rejoicing in what Allah bestowed on them of **His** Bounty and they receive good tidings about those who have not yet joined them but are left behind - they will have no fear, nor will they grieve.

171. They receive good tidings of Favor from Allah and Bounty and that Allah does not let go waste the reward of the believers.

172. Those who responded to Allah and the Messenger after injury befell them - for those who did good among them and feared Allah is a great reward.

173. Those to whom the people said, "Indeed, the people have gathered against you, so fear them." But it only increased their faith and they said, "Sufficient for us is Allah and **He** is the best Disposer of affairs."

174. So they returned with Favor from Allah and Bounty, no harm having touched them. And they pursued the pleasure of Allah, and Allah is the Possessor of great Bounty.

175. It is only Shaitaan who frightens you of his allies. So do not fear them, but fear **Me**, if you are believers.

176. And do not be grieved by those who

Surah 3: The family of Imran (v. 170-176)   **Part - 4**

177. Indeed, those who hasten in disbelief. Indeed, they will never harm Allah in anything. Allah intends that **He** will not give them any portion in the Hereafter, and for them is a great punishment.

177. Indeed, those who purchase disbelief (in exchange) for faith - never will they harm Allah in anything, and for them is a painful punishment.

178. And let not think those who disbelieve that **Our** respite to them is good for them. **We** only give respite to them so that they may increase in sins, and for them is a humiliating punishment.

179. Allah does not leave the believers in the state you are until **He** separates the evil from the good. Nor does Allah inform you about the unseen, but Allah chooses from **His** Messengers whom **He** wills. So believe in Allah and **His** Messengers, and if you believe and fear **Him**, then for you is a great reward.

180. And do not think about those who (greedily) withhold what Allah has given them of **His** Bounty that it is good for them. Nay, it is bad for them. Their necks will be encircled by what they withheld

Surah 3: The family of Imran (v. 177-180)

on the Day of Resurrection. And to Allah belongs the heritage of the heavens and the earth. And Allah is All-Aware of what you do.

181. Certainly, Allah has heard the saying of those who said, "Indeed, Allah is poor and we are rich." **We** will record what they said and their killing the Prophets without right, and **We** will say, "Taste the punishment of the Burning Fire."

182. That is because of what your hands have sent forth and Allah is not unjust to **His** slaves.

183. Those who said, "Indeed, Allah has taken a promise that we should not believe in a Messenger until he brings to us a sacrifice that is consumed by fire." Say, "Surely came to you Messengers before me with clear Signs and with what you speak. So why did you kill them, if you are truthful?"

184. Then if they reject you, then certainly many Messengers were rejected before you, who came with clear Signs and Scriptures and the Enlightening Book.

185. Every soul will taste death, and you will be paid your reward in full only

Surah 3: The family of Imran (v. 181-185)   Part - 4

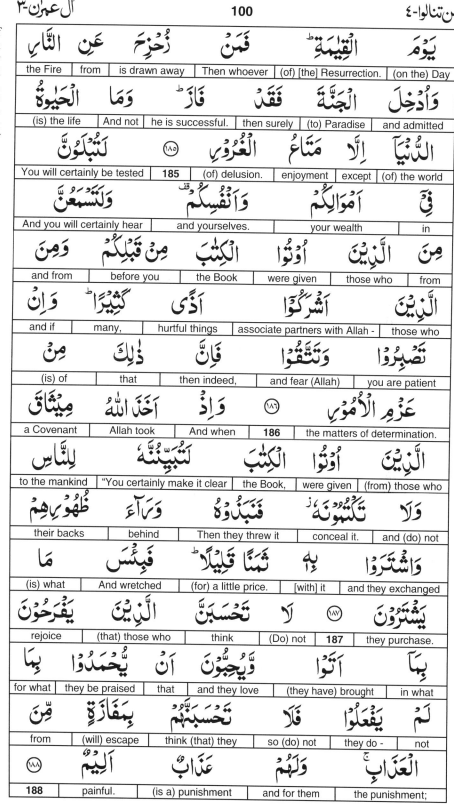

186. You will certainly be tested in your wealth and yourselves. And you will certainly hear hurtful things from those who were given the Book before you and from those who associate partners with Allah. But if you are patient and fear Allah - indeed, that is of the matters of determination.

187. And when Allah took a Covenant from those who were given the Book (saying), "You certainly make it clear to mankind and do not conceal it." Then they threw it behind their backs and exchanged it for a little price. And wretched is what they purchased.

188. Do not think that those who rejoice in what they have brought and they love to be praised for what they have not done - so do not think that they will escape from the punishment; and for them is a painful punishment.

189. And to Allah belongs the dominion of the heavens and the earth, and Allah has power over everything.

190. Indeed, in the creation of the heavens and earth and the alternation of the night and day are surely Signs for men of understanding.

191. Those who remember Allah standing and sitting and on their sides and they reflect on the creation of the heavens and the earth (saying), "Our Lord, You have not created this in vain. Glory be to You; so save us from the punishment of the Fire.

192. Our Lord, indeed whom You admit to the Fire, then surely You have disgraced him, and for the wrongdoers there are no helpers.

193. Our Lord, indeed we heard a caller calling to faith (saying), 'Believe in your Lord,' so we have believed. Our Lord, so forgive for us our sins and remove from us our evil deeds, and cause us to die with the righteous.

194. Our Lord grant us what You promised us through Your Messengers and do not disgrace us on the Day of Resurrection. Indeed, You never

Surah 3: The family of Imran (v. 189-194)　　Part - 4

195. Then their Lord responded to them, "Indeed, I will not let go waste the deeds of the doer among you, whether male or female; you are of one another. So those who emigrated and were driven out from their homes and were harmed in **My** way and fought and were killed - surely I will remove from them their evil deeds, and surely I will admit them to Gardens beneath which rivers flow as a reward from Allah. And with Allah is the best reward."

196. Be not deceived by the movement of those who disbelieved in the land.

197. A little enjoyment, then their abode is hell - a wretched resting place.

198. But those who fear their Lord, for them will be Gardens beneath which rivers flow, they will abide in it forever - a hospitality from Allah. And that which is with Allah is best for the righteous.

199. And indeed, among the People of the Book are those who believe in Allah and what has been revealed to you and what was revealed to them, humbly submissive to Allah. They do not exchange

Surah 3: The family of Imran (v. 195-199)

the Verses of Allah for a little price They will have their reward with their Lord. Indeed, Allah is swift in (taking) the account.

200. O you who believe! Be steadfast and patient and constant and fear Allah so that you may be successful.

Surah An-Nisa

In the name of Allah, the Most Gracious, the Most Merciful.

1. O mankind! Fear your Lord the **One Who** created you from a single soul and created from it its mate and dispersed from them many men and women. And fear Allah through **Whom** you claim (your mutual rights) and (revere) the wombs (that bore you). Indeed, Allah is Ever-Watchful over you.

2. And give the orphans their wealth and do not exchange the bad for the good, and do not consume their wealth with your wealth. Indeed, it is a great sin.

3. And if you fear that not you will be able to do justice with the orphans, then marry what seems suitable to you from the women - two, three, or four. But if you fear that you will not be just, then marry one or what your right hands possess.

Surah 3: The family of Imran (v. 200); Surah 4: The women (v. 1-3)   Part - 4

That is more appropriate so that you may not oppress.

4. And give the women their dower graciously. But if they remit to you anything on their own accord then consume it in satisfaction and ease.

5. And do not give the foolish (weak-minded) your wealth, which Allah made a means of support for you, but provide for them with it and clothe them and speak to them words of kindness.

6. And test the orphans until they reach the age of marriage, then if you perceive sound judgement in them, then deliver to them their wealth. And do not consume it extravagantly and hastily (fearing) that they will grow up. And whoever is rich should refrain (from taking wages) and whoever is poor, then let him consume what is reasonable. Then when you deliver their wealth to them, then take witnesses. And Allah is sufficient as a Reckoner.

7. For the men is a portion of what is left by parents and the near relatives, and for the women is a portion of what is left by parents and near relatives whether little or much - an obligatory portion.

8. And when

Surah 4: The women (v. 4-8)

وَالْمَسَاكِينُ	وَالْيَتَامَىٰ	أُولُو الْقُرْبَىٰ	الْقِسْمَةَ		حَضَرَ	
and the poor,	and the orphans	the relatives	(at) the (time of) division		present	
٨	مَعْرُوفًا	قَوْلًا	لَهُمْ	وَقُولُوا	مِنْهُ	فَارْزُقُوهُمْ
8	(of) kindness.	words	to them	and speak	from it	then provide them
ضِعَافًا	ذُرِّيَّةً	مِنْ خَلْفِهِمْ	تَرَكُوا	لَوْ	الَّذِينَ	وَلْيَخْشَ
weak	offspring	behind	they left	if	those who,	And let fear -
وَلْيَقُولُوا	اللَّهَ	فَلْيَتَّقُوا	عَلَيْهِمْ		خَافُوا	
and let them speak	Allah	So let them fear	about them.		(and) they would have feared	
أَمْوَالَ	يَأْكُلُونَ	الَّذِينَ	إِنَّ	٩	سَدِيدًا	قَوْلًا
wealth	consume	those who	Indeed,	9	appropriate.	words
نَارًا	بُطُونِهِمْ	فِي	يَأْكُلُونَ	إِنَّمَا	ظُلْمًا	الْيَتَامَىٰ
fire,	their bellies	in	they consume	only	wrongfully,	(of) the orphans
فِي		يُوصِيكُمُ اللَّهُ	١٠	سَعِيرًا		وَسَيَصْلَوْنَ
concerning		Allah instructs you	10	(in) a Blazing Fire.		and they will be burned
فَإِنْ	الْأُنْثَيَيْنِ	حَظِّ	مِثْلُ	لِلذَّكَرِ		أَوْلَادِكُمْ
But if	(of) two females.	(the) portion	like	for the male		your children -
مَا	ثُلُثَا	فَلَهُنَّ	اثْنَتَيْنِ	فَوْقَ	نِسَاءً	كُنَّ
(of) what	two thirds	then for them	two,	more (than)	(only) women	there are
تَرَكَ	وَلِأَبَوَيْهِ	النِّصْفُ	فَلَهَا	وَاحِدَةً	كَانَتْ	وَإِنْ
And for his parents,	(is) half.	then for her	(only) one,	(there) is	And if	he left.
إِنْ	تَرَكَ	مِمَّا	السُّدُسُ	مِنْهُمَا	وَاحِدٍ	لِكُلِّ
if	(is) left,	of what	a sixth	of them	one	for each
وَلَدٌ	لَهُ	يَكُنْ	لَمْ	فَإِنْ	وَلَدٌ	كَانَ لَهُ
any child	for him is		not	But if	a child.	for him is
الثُّلُثُ	فَلِأُمِّهِ		أَبَوَاهُ		وَوَرِثَهُ	
(is) one third.	then for his mother		his parents,		and inherit[ed] him	
فَلِأُمِّهِ		إِخْوَةٌ		كَانَ لَهُ		فَإِنْ
then for his mother		brothers and sisters,		for him are		And if
أَوْ	بِهَا	يُوصِي	وَصِيَّةٍ	مِنْ بَعْدِ		السُّدُسُ
or	[of which]	he has made	any will	after		(is) the sixth

9. And let those have the same fear as they would have for their own, if they had left behind weak offspring. So let them fear Allah and speak appropriate words.

10. Indeed, those who consume the wealth of orphans wrongfully, they are only consuming fire in their bellies. And they will be burned in a Blazing Fire.

11. Allah instructs you concerning your children - for the male a portion equal to that of two females. But if there are (only) daughters, two or more, then for them two thirds of what he left. And if there is only one, then for her is half. And for the parents, to each one of them is a sixth of what is left, if he has a child. But if he does not have a child and his parents (alone) inherit from him, then for his mother is one third. And if he has brothers and sisters, then for his mother is a sixth after (fulfilling) any will he has made or (payment of)

any debt. Your parents or your children - you do not know which of them are nearer to you in benefit. An obligation from Allah. Indeed, Allah is All-Knowing, All-Wise.

اَقْرَبُ	اَيُّهُمْ	لَا تَدْرُوْنَ	وَاَبْنَآؤُكُمْ	اٰبَآؤُكُمْ	دَيْنٍ
(is) nearer	which of them	you know not	and your children -	Your parents	any debt.

اللّٰهَ	اِنَّ	اللّٰهِ	مِّنَ	فَرِيْضَةً	نَفْعًا	لَكُمْ
Allah	Indeed,	Allah.	from	An obligation	(in) benefit.	to you

وَلَكُمْ	۞	حَكِيْمًا	عَلِيْمًا	كَانَ
And for you	11	All-Wise.	All-Knowing,	is

لَّمْ	اِنْ	اَزْوَاجُكُمْ	تَرَكَ	مَا	نِصْفُ
not	if	by your wives	(is) left	(of) what	(is) half

وَلَدٌ	يَكُنْ لَّهُنَّ	فَاِنْ	وَلَدٌ	لَّهُنَّ	يَكُنْ
a child,	for them is	But if	a child.		for them is

مِنْۢ بَعْدِ	تَرَكْنَ	مِمَّا	الرُّبُعُ	فَلَكُمُ
after	they left,	of what	(is) the fourth	then for you

وَلَهُنَّ	دَيْنٍ	اَوْ	بِهَآ	يُوْصِيْنَ	وَصِيَّةٍ
And for them	any debt.	or	[for which]	they have made	any will

12. And for you is half of what your wives leave if they have no child. But if they have a child, then for you is a fourth of what they leave, after (fulfilling) any will they have made and (payment) of any debt. And for them (women) is a fourth of what you leave, if you have no child. But if you leave a child, then for them is an eighth of what you leave after (fulfilling) any will you have made and (payment) of any debt. And if a man or woman whose wealth is to be inherited has no parent or child but has a brother or sister, then for each one of them is a sixth. But if they are more than two, then they share a third after (fulfilling) any will that may have been made

يَكُنْ لَّكُمْ	لَّمْ	اِنْ	تَرَكْتُمْ	مِمَّا	الرُّبُعُ
for you is	not	if	you left,	of what	(is) the fourth

فَلَهُنَّ	وَلَدٌ	لَكُمْ	كَانَ	فَاِنْ	وَلَدٌ
then for them	a child,	for you is		But if	a child.

تُوْصُوْنَ	وَصِيَّةٍ	مِنْۢ بَعْدِ	تَرَكْتُمْ	مِمَّا	الثُّمُنُ
you have made	any will	after	you left	of what	(is) the eighth

يُّوْرَثُ	رَجُلٌ	كَانَ	وَاِنْ	دَيْنٍ	اَوْ	بِهَآ
(whose wealth) is to be inherited	a man	[is]	And if	any debt.	or	[for which]

اَوْ	اَخٌ	وَّلَهٗٓ	اِمْرَاَةٌ	اَوِ	كَلٰلَةً
or	(is) a brother	and for him	a women	or	(has) no parent or child

فَاِنْ	السُّدُسُ	مِنْهُمَا	وَاحِدٍ	فَلِكُلِّ	اُخْتٌ
But if	(is) the sixth.	of (the) two	one	then for each	a sister,

شُرَكَآءُ	فَهُمْ	ذٰلِكَ	مِنْ	اَكْثَرَ	كَانُوْٓا
(are) partners	then they	that,	than	more	they are

بِهَآ	يُوْصٰى	مِنْۢ بَعْدِ	وَصِيَّةٍ	الثُّلُثِ	فِى
[for which]	was made	after	any will	the third,	in

and (payment) of any debt without being harmful. An ordinance from Allah. And Allah is All-Hearing, All-Forbearing.

13. These are the limits of Allah, and whoever obeys Allah and **His** Messenger, **He** will admit him into Gardens underneath which rivers flow, he will abide in it forever. And that is a great success.

14. And whoever disobeys Allah and **His** Messenger and transgresses the limits of Allah, **He** will admit him into the Fire, he will abide in it forever. And for him is a humiliating punishment.

15. And those who commit immorality from your women, then bring against them four witnesses from among you. And if they testify, then confine them in their houses until death takes them or Allah ordains for them (some other) way.

16. And the two among you who commit it (immorality), then punish both of them. But if they repent and correct themselves, then turn away from both of them. Indeed, Allah is Oft-Forgiving, Most Merciful.

17. The repentance accepted by Allah is only for those who do

Surah 4: The women (v. 13-17)   Part - 4

evil in ignorance and then repent soon after. It is those to whom Allah will turn in forgiveness and Allah is All-Knowing, All-Wise.

soon after.	they repent	then	in ignorance,	the evil
and Allah is	upon them,	(from) Allah	will have forgiveness	Then those
(is) the acceptance of repentance		And not	17 All-Wise.	All-Knowing,

18. The repentance is not accepted from those who (continue to) do evil deeds until when death approaches one of them, he says, "Indeed, I repent now;" nor for those who die while they are disbelievers. For them **We** have prepared a painful punishment.

approaches	when	until	the evil deeds	do	for those who
and not	now;'	repent	'Indeed I	he says,	[the] death,	one of them
Those -	(are) disbelievers.	while they	die	those who
O you	18	painful.	a punishment	for them	We have prepared

19. O you who believe! It is not lawful for you to inherit women by force. And do not constrain them so that you may take a part of what you have given them unless they commit an open immorality. And live with them in kindness. For if you dislike them - perhaps you dislike a thing and Allah has placed much good in it.

you inherit	that	for you	(is) lawful	Not	believe[d]!	who
so that you may take	you constraint them	And not	(by) force.	the women
they commit	that	except	you have given them	(of) what	a part
But if	in kindness.	And live with them	open.	immorality
a thing	you dislike	that	then perhaps	you dislike them,
you intend	And if	19	much good.	in it	and Allah placed

20. And if you intend replacing one wife with another and you have given one of them a heap of gold, then do not take away anything from it.

and you have given	(of) a wife	(in) place	a wife	replacing
anything.	from it	take away	then (do) not	heap (of gold)	one of them

Surah 4: The women (v. 18-20)

Surah 4: The women (v. 21-23)

Would you take it by slander and as a manifest sin?

21. And how could you take it while you have gone in unto each other, and they have taken a strong covenant from you?

22. And do not marry those women whom your fathers married, except what has already passed. Indeed, it was an immorality and a hateful (deed) and an evil way.

23. Forbidden to you are your mothers, your daughters, your sisters, your father's sisters, your mother's sisters, daughters of brothers, daughters of sisters, your foster mothers, your foster sisters, mothers of your wives and your step daughters who are under your guardianship (born) of your wives you have had relations with, but if you have not had relations with them, then there is no sin on you. And (also forbidden) are wives of your sons who are from your loins, and that you take (in marriage) two sisters simultaneously, except what has already passed. Indeed, Allah is Oft-Forgiving, Most Merciful.

24. And also (prohibited are) those women who are already married except whom you rightfully possess (through wedlock). (This is) the decree of Allah upon you. And lawful to you are (all) beyond these, (provided) that you seek them (in marriage) with your wealth desiring chastity and not lust. So for whatever you benefit from them, give them their bridal due as an obligation. And there is no sin on you concerning what you mutually agree to, beyond the obligation. Indeed, Allah is All-Knowing, All-Wise.

25. And whoever among you is not able to marry free chaste believing women, then (marry) from those whom your right hands possess of believing slave girls. And Allah knows all about your faith. You (believers) are of one another. So marry them with the permission of their family and give them their bridal due in a fair manner, they being chaste, not committing immorality or taking secret lovers. Then if after marriage they commit adultery, then their punishment is half of that which is prescribed for free chaste women. This is for him among you who fears committing sin, but to be patient

Surah 4: The women (v. 24-25)

is better for you. And Allah is Oft-Forgiving, Most Merciful.

26. Allah wishes to make clear to you and to guide you to the ways of those who were before you and to accept your repentance. And Allah is All-Knowing, All-Wise.

27. Allah wishes to accept your repentance, but those who follow their passions wish that you deviate (into) a great deviation.

28. Allah wishes to lighten for you (your difficulties); and mankind was created weak.

29. O you who believe! Do not consume one another's wealth unjustly; instead do business with mutual consent. And do not kill yourselves. Indeed, Allah is Most Merciful to you.

30. And whoever does that in aggression and injustice, then soon We will cast him into a Fire. And that is easy for Allah.

31. If you avoid major sins, which you are forbidden, We will remove from you your evil deeds and We will admit you to a noble entrance.

32. And do not covet for that by which Allah has made some of you exceed others. For men is a share of what they have earned

Surah 4: The women (v. 26-32) — Part - 5

and for women is a share of what they have earned. And ask Allah of His Bounty. Indeed, Allah is All-Knower of everything.

33. And for all, We have made heirs to what is left by their parents and relatives. And as to those whom your right hands pledged, give them their share. Indeed, Allah is a Witness over everything.

34. Men are protectors and maintainers of women because Allah has bestowed some of them over others and because they spend from their wealth. So the righteous women are obedient, guarding in the husbands absence what Allah orders them to guard. And those from whom who fear ill-conduct, then advise them, forsake them in bed, and set forth (the impending separation) to them. Then if they obey you, then seek no means against them. Indeed, Allah is Most High, Most Great.

35. And if you fear a breach between the two of them, then send an arbitrator from his family and an arbitrator from her family. If they both wish reconciliation, Allah will cause reconciliation between them. Indeed,

Surah 4: The women (v. 33-35) — Part - 5

Surah 4: The women (v. 36-40)

وَلَا	اللَّهَ	وَاعْبُدُوا	﴿٣٥﴾	خَبِيرًا	عَلِيمًا	كَانَ	اللَّهَ
And (do) not	Allah	And worship	35	All-Aware.	All-Knower,	is	Allah
وَبِذِي الْقُرْبَىٰ	إِحْسَانًا	وَبِالْوَالِدَيْنِ	شَيْئًا	بِهِ	تُشْرِكُوا
and with the relatives,	(do) good,	and to the parents	anything,	with Him	associate
وَالْجَارِ	ذِي الْقُرْبَىٰ	وَالْجَارِ	وَالْمَسَاكِينِ	وَالْيَتَامَىٰ
and the neighbor	(who is) near,	and the neighbor	and the needy	and the orphans,
وَمَا	وَابْنِ السَّبِيلِ	بِالْجَنْبِ	وَالصَّاحِبِ	الْجُنُبِ
and what	and the traveler	by your side	and the companion	(who is) farther away,
مَن	يُحِبُّ	لَا	اللَّهَ	إِنَّ	أَيْمَانُكُمْ	مَلَكَتْ
(the one) who	love	(does) not	Allah	Indeed,	your right hands.	possess[ed]
وَيَأْمُرُونَ	يَبْخَلُونَ	الَّذِينَ	﴿٣٦﴾	فَخُورًا	مُخْتَالًا	كَانَ
and order	are stingy	Those who	36	(and) [a] boastful.	[a] proud	is
اللَّهُ آتَاهُمْ	مَا	وَيَكْتُمُونَ	بِالْبُخْلِ	النَّاسَ
Allah (has) given them	what	and hide	[of] stinginess	the people
عَذَابًا	لِلْكَافِرِينَ	وَأَعْتَدْنَا	فَضْلِهِ	مِن
a punishment	for the disbelievers	and We (have) prepared	His Bounty -	of
رِئَاءَ	أَمْوَالَهُمْ	يُنفِقُونَ	وَالَّذِينَ	﴿٣٧﴾	مُهِينًا
to be seen	their wealth	spend	And those who	37	humiliating.
الْآخِرِ	بِالْيَوْمِ	وَلَا	بِاللَّهِ	يُؤْمِنُونَ	وَلَا	النَّاسِ
the Last,	in the Day	and not	in Allah	they believe	and not	(by) the people
فَسَاءَ	قَرِينًا	لَهُ	الشَّيْطَانُ	يَكُن	وَمَن
then evil	(as) companion -	for him	the Shaitaan	has	and whoever
آمَنُوا	لَوْ	عَلَيْهِمْ	وَمَاذَا	﴿٣٨﴾	قَرِينًا
they believed	if	(is) against them	And what	38	(is he as) a companion.
اللَّهُ رَزَقَهُمُ	مِمَّا	وَأَنفَقُوا	الْآخِرِ	وَالْيَوْمِ	بِاللَّهِ
Allah (has) provided them?	from what	and spent	the Last	and the Day	in Allah
لَا	اللَّهَ	إِنَّ	﴿٣٩﴾	عَلِيمًا	بِهِمْ	وَكَانَ اللَّهُ
(does) not	Allah	Indeed,	39	All-Knower.	about them	And Allah is
يُضَاعِفْهَا	حَسَنَةً	تَكُ	وَإِن	ذَرَّةٍ	مِثْقَالَ	يَظْلِمُ
He doubles it	a good	there is	And if	(of) an atom.	(as much as) weight	wrong

Allah is All-Knower, All-Aware.

36. And worship Allah and do not associate anything with **Him**, and do good to parents, relatives, orphans, needy, the neighbor who is near, the neighbor who is farther away, the companion by your side, the traveler and those whom your right hands possess. Indeed, Allah does not love those who are proud and boastful.

37. Those who are stingy and enjoin upon (other) people stinginess and hide what Allah has given them of **His** Bounty - and **We** have prepared for the disbelievers a humiliating punishment.

38. And those who spend their wealth to be seen by people and do not believe in Allah and the Last Day. And whoever has Shaitaan as a companion, then evil is he as a companion.

39. And what (harm would come) upon them if they believed in Allah and the Last Day and spend from what Allah has provided them? And Allah is All-Knower about them.

40. Indeed, Allah does not wrong (even as much as) an atom's weight. And if there is a good (deed) **He** doubles it

41. So how (will it be) when **We** bring from every nation a witness and **We** bring you as a witness against these people.

42. And on that Day those who disbelieved and disobeyed the Messenger will wish that the earth was leveled with them. But they will not (be able) to hide any statement from Allah.

43. O you who believe! Do not approach prayer while you are intoxicated until you know what you are saying or (when you are) impure, except (when) passing through a way, until you have bathed. And if you are ill or on a journey or one of you comes from the toilet or you have touched women and you do not find water, then do *tayammum* with clean earth and wipe over your faces and your hands. Indeed, Allah is Oft-Pardoning, Oft-Forgiving.

44. Did you not see those who were given a portion of the Book, purchasing error and wishing that you stray from the (straight) way?

45. And Allah knows better about your enemies and sufficient is Allah as a Protector, and sufficient is Allah as a Helper.

46. Among

Surah 4: The women (v. 41-46) — Part - 5

the Jews are those who distort the words from their places and they say, "We hear and we disobey" and "Hear as one who does not hear" and "*Raina*," twisting their tongues and defaming the religion. And if they had said, "We hear and we obey" and "Hear and look at us," surely it would have been better and more suitable for them. But Allah cursed them for their disbelief, so they do not believe, except a few.

47. O you who have been given the Book, believe in what **We** have revealed confirming what is with you, before **We** efface the faces and turn them on their backs or curse them as **We** cursed the Sabbath-breakers. And the command of Allah is (always) executed.

48. Indeed, Allah does not forgive that partners be associated with **Him**, but **He** forgives other than that for whom **He** wills. And whoever associates partners with Allah, then surely he has fabricated a tremendous sin.

49. Do you not see those who claim purity for themselves? Nay, Allah purifies whom **He** wills, and they will not be wronged (even as much as) a hair on a date-seed.

50. See how

they invent a lie about Allah, and sufficient is that as a manifest sin.

51. Do you not see those who were given a portion of the Book? They believe in superstition and false deities, and they say about the disbelievers "These are better guided to the way than the believers."

52. Those are the ones whom Allah has cursed, and whoever Allah curses - you will never find any helper for him.

53. Or have they a share in the Kingdom? Then they would not give the people (even as much as) the speck on a date seed.

54. Or are they jealous of the people for what Allah has given them from **His** Bounty? But surely **We** gave the family of Ibrahim the Book and wisdom and gave them a great kingdom.

55. Then of them are some who believed in him and of them are some who turned away from him. And sufficient is Hell as a Blazing Fire.

56. Indeed, those who disbelieve in **Our** Signs, soon **We** will burn them in a Fire. Every time their skins are roasted, **We** will replace their skins with another skin, so that they may taste the punishment. Indeed, Allah is

Surah 4: The women (v. 51-56)

57. And those who believe and do good deeds **We** will admit them in Gardens underneath which rivers flow, wherein they will abide forever. For them therein are purified spouses, and **We** will admit them in the thick shade.

58. Indeed, Allah orders you to render trusts to their owners, and when you judge between people to judge with justice. Excellent is what Allah advises you with. Indeed, Allah is All-Hearing, All-Seeing.

59. O you who believe! Obey Allah and obey the Messenger and those having authority among you. Then if you disagree in anything, refer it to Allah and the Messenger, if you believe in Allah and the Last Day. That is best and more suitable for (final) determination.

60. Do you not see those who claim that they believe in what is revealed to you and what was revealed before you? They wish to go for judgment to false deities, while they were ordered to reject it. And Shaitaan wishes to mislead them far astray.

61. And when it is said to them, "Come to

Surah 4: The women (v. 57-61) — Part - 5

to what Allah has revealed and to the Messenger," you see the hypocrites turning away from you in aversion.

62. So how would it be when disaster befalls them because of what their hands had sent forth? Then they come to you swearing by Allah saying, "We intended nothing but good and reconciliation."

63. Those are the ones about whom Allah knows what is in their hearts, so turn away from them and admonish them and speak to them penetrating words.

64. And We did not send any Messenger except to be obeyed by the permission of Allah. And if, when they wronged themselves, they had come to you and asked Allah's forgiveness and the Messenger had asked forgiveness for them, surely they would have found Allah Oft-Forgiving, Most-Merciful.

65. But no, by your Lord, they will not believe until they make you judge about whatever arises between them and then do not find within themselves any discomfort about what you have decided and submit in (full) submission.

66. And if We had decreed on them, "Kill yourselves" or "Leave your homes," they would have not done it except a few

Surah 4: The women (v. 62-66)

of them. But if they had done what they were advised, surely it would have been better for them and more strengthening (for their faith).

67. And then **We** would have given them from **Ourselves** a great reward.

68. And **We** would have guided them to the straight way.

69. And whoever obeys Allah and the Messenger, then they will be with those on whom Allah has bestowed **His** Favor - the Prophets, the truthful, the martyrs, and the righteous. And excellent are those as companions.

70. That is the Bounty of Allah, and Allah is sufficient as All-Knower.

71. O you who believe! Take your precautions and advance in groups or advance all together.

72. And indeed, there is among you he who lags behind, and if disaster befalls you, he says "Verily, Allah has favored me in that I was not present with them."

73. And if bounty comes to you from Allah, he would surely say, as if there had not been any affection between you and him, "Oh! I wish I had been with them then I would have attained a great success."

74. So let those fight in

the way of Allah who sell the life of this world for the Hereafter. And whoever fights in the way of Allah and is killed or achieves victory **We** will grant him a great reward.

75. And what is (the matter) with you that you do not fight in the way of Allah, and (for) the ones who are weak among men and women and children who say, "Our Lord, take us out of this town whose people are oppressors and appoint for us from **Yourself** a protector and a helper.

76. Those who believe, they fight in the way of Allah; and those who disbelieve, they fight in the way of the false deities. So fight against the friends of Shaitaan. Indeed, the strategy of Shaitaan is weak.

77. Have you not seen those who were told, "Restrain your hands and establish prayer and give *zakah*?" Then when fighting was ordained on them, then a group of them feared people as they fear Allah or with more intense fear. And they said, "Our Lord why have **You** ordained upon us fighting? If only **You** postponed (it for) us for

Surah 4: The women (v. 75-77)   Part - 5

a short period." Say, "The enjoyment of this world is little, and the Hereafter is better for those who fear Allah. And you will not be wronged (even as much as) a hair on a date-seed."

78. Wherever you may be, death will overtake you even if you are in lofty towers. And if any good comes to them, they say, "This is from Allah." And if any evil befalls them, they say, "This is from you." Say, "All is from Allah." So what is (wrong) with these people that they do not seem to understand any statement.

79. Whatever good comes to you is from Allah, and whatever evil befalls you is from yourself. And **We** have sent you for the people as a Messenger, and Allah is sufficient as a Witness.

80. He who obeys the Messenger then surely he has obeyed Allah, and whoever turns away, then **We** have not sent you as a guardian over them.

81. And they say, "We pledge obedience." Then when they leave you, a group of them plan by night other than what you say. But Allah records what they plan by night. So turn away from them

81. and put your trust in Allah. And Allah is sufficient as a Trustee.

82. Then do they not ponder on the Quran? If it had been from other than Allah, surely they would have found much contradiction in it.

83. And when there comes to them a matter of security or fear, they spread it. But if they had referred it to the Messenger and to those having authority among them, surely those who can draw correct conclusion from it would have known about it. And if not for the Bounty of Allah upon you and **His** Mercy, surely you would have followed Shaitaan except for a few.

84. So fight in the way of Allah; you are not responsible except for yourself. And encourage the believers that perhaps Allah will restrain the might of those who disbelieve. And Allah is Greater in Might and Stronger in punishment.

85. Whoever intercedes for a good cause will have for himself a share of it; and whoever intercedes for an evil cause will have a portion of it. And Allah is on everything a Keeper.

86. And when you are greeted with a greeting, greet

Surah 4: The women (v. 82-86)

with a better greeting or (at least) return it (in a like manner). Indeed, Allah is over everything, an Accountant.

87. Allah - there is no god except **Him**, surely **He** will gather you on the Day of Resurrection, about which there is no doubt. And who is more truthful than Allah in statement.

88. So what is (the matter) with you (that you have) become two parties concerning the hypocrites? And Allah cast them back for what they earned. Do you wish to guide those whom Allah has let go astray? And whoever Allah lets go astray - never will you find for him a way (of guidance).

89. They wish if you disbelieve as they disbelieved so that you would be alike. So do not take from among them allies until they emigrate in the way of Allah. But if they turn back, seize them and kill them wherever you find them. And do not take from among them any ally or helper,

90. Except those who join a group between whom and you there is a treaty or those who come to you with hearts restraining them from fighting you or fighting their people. And if Allah had willed, surely **He** would have given them power over you

and they would have fought you. So if they withdraw from you and do not fight against you and offer you peace, then Allah has not made for you a way against them.

91. You will find others who wish to obtain security from you and (to) obtain security from their people. Every time they are returned to the temptation, they plunge into it. So if they do not withdraw from you or offer you peace or restrain their hands, then seize them and kill them wherever you find them. And those - **We** have made for you against them a clear authority.

92. It is not for a believer to kill a believer except by mistake. And whoever kills a believer by mistake - then he should free a believing slave and blood money should be paid to his family except that they remit it as charity. But if he was from a people hostile to you and he was a believer, then freeing of a believing slave. And if he was from a people with whom you have a treaty - then the blood money should be paid to his family and a believing slave should be freed. And whoever does not find (one or cannot afford to buy one) - then he should fast

for two months consecutively, (seeking) repentance from Allah. And Allah is All-Knowing, All-Wise.

93. And whoever kills a believer intentionally, then his reward is Hell, abiding in it forever; and Allah's wrath will fall on him and He has cursed him and He has prepared for him a great punishment.

94. O you who believe! When you go forth in the way of Allah, investigate, and do not say to the one who offers you the (greetings of) peace, "You are not a believer," seeking the transitory gains of this worldly life; for with Allah are abundant booties. You were like them before; then Allah conferred favor upon you; so investigate. Indeed, Allah is All-Aware of what you do.

95. Not equal are those among the believers who sit (at home) - except those who are disabled - and those who strive in the way of Allah with their wealth and their lives. And Allah has preferred in rank those who strive with their wealth and their lives to those who sit (at home). And to all Allah has promised the best. And Allah has preferred those who strive over

Surah 4: The women (v. 93-95) Part - 5

those who sit (at home) with a great reward,

96. Ranks from **Him** and forgiveness and mercy. And Allah is Oft-Forgiving, Most Merciful.

97. Indeed, those whom the Angels take (in death) while they were wronging themselves - they (the Angels) will say, "In what (condition) were you?" They will say, "We were oppressed in the earth." They (the Angels) will say, "Was not the earth of Allah spacious (enough) for you to emigrate therein?" Then those will have their abode in Hell - and evil it is as a destination.

98. Except the oppressed among the men and women and children who cannot devise a plan nor are they directed to a way.

99. Then for those, may be, Allah will pardon them, and Allah is Oft-Pardoning, Oft-Forgiving.

100. And whoever emigrates in the way of Allah will find on the earth many places of refuge and abundance. And whoever leaves from his home as an emigrant to Allah and **His** Messenger and then death overtakes him then certainly his reward has become incumbent on Allah. And Allah is Oft-Forgiving, Most Merciful.

101. And when you travel in the earth,

Surah 4: The women (v. 96-101)

there is no blame upon you that you shorten the prayer, if you fear that those who disbelieve may harm you. Indeed, the disbelievers are your open enemies.

102. And when you are among them and you lead them in prayer, then let a group of them stand with you and let them take their arms. Then when they have prostrated, let them be behind you and let the other group come forward, which has not (yet) prayed and let them pray with you, taking their precautions and their arms. Those who disbelieve wish that you neglect your arms and your baggage, so that they can assault you in a single attack. But there is no blame upon you, if you are troubled by rain or are sick, for laying down your arms, but take your precautions. Indeed, Allah has prepared a humiliating punishment for the disbelievers.

103. Then when you have finished the prayer, then remember Allah standing, sitting, and (lying) on your sides. But when you are secure, then re-establish the (regular) prayer.

Surah 4: The women (v. 102-103)

Indeed, prayer is prescribed for the believers at fixed times.

104. And do not be weak in pursuing the people (enemy). If you are suffering, then indeed they are also suffering like you are suffering, and you hope from Allah what they do not hope. And Allah is All-Knowing, All-Wise.

105. Indeed, We have revealed to you the Book with the truth so that you may judge between the people with what Allah has shown you. And do not be a pleader for the deceitful.

106. And seek forgiveness of Allah. Indeed, Allah is Oft-Forgiving, Most Merciful.

107. And do not argue on behalf of those who deceive themselves. Indeed, Allah does not love the one who is treacherous and sinful.

108. They seek to hide from the people but they cannot hide from Allah and **He** is with them when they plot by night in words that **He** does not approve. And Allah encompasses what they do.

109. Here you are - those who argue on their behalf in the life of this world - but who will argue with Allah for them on the Day of Resurrection or who

Surah 4: The women (v. 104-109)   Part - 5

110. And whoever does evil or wrongs his soul and then seeks forgiveness of Allah he will find Allah Oft-Forgiving, Most Merciful.

111. And whoever earns sin only earns it against himself. And Allah is All-Knowing, All-Wise.

112. And whoever earns a fault or a sin and then blames it on an innocent (person), then surely he has burdened himself with a slander and a manifest sin.

113. And if it was not for the Grace of Allah upon you and **His** Mercy, a group of them had resolved to mislead you. But they do not mislead except themselves, and they will not harm you in anything. And Allah has revealed to you the Book and the Wisdom and taught you what you did not know. And Allah's Grace upon you is great.

114. There is no good in most of their secret talk except he who orders charity or kindness or conciliation between people. And whoever does that seeking the pleasure of Allah then soon **We** will give him a great reward.

115. And whoever opposes the Messenger after guidance has become clear

Surah 4: The women (v. 110-115)   Part - 5

to him and follows other than the way of the believers - **We** will turn him to what he has turned to and **We** will burn him in Hell; and it is an evil destination.

116. Indeed, Allah does not forgive that you associate partners with **Him,** but **He** forgives other than that for whom **He** wills. And whoever associates partners with Allah, then surely he has lost the way, straying far away.

117. They invoke besides **Him** none but female (deities), and they (actually) invoke none but the rebellious Shaitaan.

118. Allah cursed him and he (Shaitaan) said, "I will surely take from your slaves an appointed portion.

119. And I will surely mislead them and I will surely arouse (sinful) desires in them, and I will surely order them so they will surely cut off the ears of the cattle and I will surely order them so they will surely change the creation of Allah." And whoever takes Shaitaan as a friend besides Allah, then surely he has suffered a manifest loss.

120. He promises them and arouses (sinful) desires in them. And Shaitaan does not promise them except deception.

121. Those will have their abode

Surah 4: The women (v. 116-121) — **Part - 5**

121. ...in Hell and they will not find any escape from it.

122. And those who believe and do righteous deeds, We will admit them in Gardens underneath which rivers flow, wherein they will abide forever. A Promise of Allah in truth, and who is truer than Allah in statement?

123. Neither your desire nor the desire of the People of the Book (can prevail). Whoever does evil will be recompensed for it, and he will not find besides Allah any protector or any helper.

124. And whoever does righteous deeds, whether male or female and is a believer - those will enter Paradise and they will not be wronged, (even as much as) the speck on a date-seed.

125. And who is better in religion than he who submits his face to Allah and he is a good-doer and follows the religion of Ibrahim - the upright? And Allah took Ibrahim as a friend.

126. And to Allah belongs whatever is in the heavens and whatever is on the earth. And Allah encompasses everything.

127. And they seek your ruling concerning women. Say, "Allah gives you the ruling

Surah 4: The women (v. 122-127) — Part - 5

about them and what has been recited to you in the Book concerning the orphan girls to whom you do not give what is ordained for them and you desire to marry them, and (concerning) the weak among children and to deal justly with orphans. And whatever good you do, then indeed, Allah is All-Knowing of it.

128. And if a woman fears ill-conduct or desertion from her husband, then there is no sin upon them that they make terms of peace between themselves and reconciliation is best. And souls are swayed by greed. But if you do good and fear Allah, then indeed, Allah is All-Aware of what you do.

129. And you will never be able to deal justly between the women even if you desire, but do not incline completely (towards one) and leave another hanging. And if you reconcile and fear Allah - then indeed, Allah is Oft-Forgiving, Most Merciful.

130. And if they separate, Allah will enrich each of them from **His** abundance. And Allah is All-Encompassing,

Surah 4: The women (v. 128-130) — Part - 5

All-Wise.

131. To Allah belongs whatever is in the heavens and whatever is on the earth. And surely We have instructed those who were given the Book before you and yourselves to fear Allah. But if you disbelieve - then indeed, to Allah belongs whatever is in the heavens and whatever is on the earth. And Allah is Free of need and Praiseworthy.

132. To Allah belongs whatever is in the heavens and whatever is on the earth. And Allah is sufficient as a Disposer of affairs.

133. If He wills, He can eliminate you O people, and bring others (in your place). And Allah is over that All-Powerful.

134. Whoever desires the reward of this world - then with Allah is the reward of this world and the Hereafter. And Allah is All-Hearing, All-Seeing.

135. O you who believe! Be custodians of justice as witnesses to Allah, even if it is against yourselves or your parents or relatives whether rich or poor, for Allah is nearer to both of them. So do not follow the desires, lest you deviate (from doing justice). And if you distort (your testimony) or refrain (from giving it), then indeed, Allah is All-Aware of what you do.

Surah 4: The women (v. 131-135) — Part - 5

136. O you who believe! Believe in Allah and **His** Messenger, and the Book, which **He** revealed upon **His** Messenger and the Book which **He** revealed before. And whoever disbelieves in Allah, **His** Angels, **His** Books, **His** Messengers and the Last Day, then surely he has lost the way, straying far away.

137. Indeed, those who believed then disbelieved, then believed, then (again) disbelieved, and then increased in disbelief - Allah will not forgive them, nor will **He** guide them to the (right) way.

138. Give tidings to the hypocrites that for them is a painful punishment -

139. Those who take the disbelievers as allies instead of the believers. Do they seek honor with them? But indeed, all honor belongs to Allah.

140. And surely **He** has revealed to you in the Book that when you hear the Verses

Surah 4: The women (v. 136-140)

of Allah being rejected and ridiculed, then do not sit with them until they engage in some other conversation. Indeed, you would then be like them. Indeed, Allah will gather the hypocrites and disbelievers in Hell all together.

141. Those (hypocrites) are waiting for you; then if you gain a victory from Allah, they say, "Were we not with you?" But if the disbelievers have a success, they say, "Did we not gain the advantage over you and we protected you from the believers?" And Allah will judge between you on the Day of Resurrection, and never will Allah give the disbelievers over the believers a way.

142. Indeed, the hypocrites seek to deceive Allah and it is **He Who** deceives them. And when they stand for prayer, they stand lazily, showing off

except	Allah	they remember	and not	(to) the people

to people and they do not remember Allah except a little.

that,	between	Wavering	142	a little.

those.	to	and not	these	to	not

143. Wavering between them, neither to these (i.e., the believers) nor to those (i.e., the disbelievers). And whoever Allah lets go astray - then never will you find a way for him.

for him	you will find	then never	Allah lets go astray -	And whoever

(Do) not	believe[d]!	who	O you	143	a way.

the believers.	instead of	(as) allies	the disbelievers	take

144. O you who believe! Do not take the disbelievers as allies instead of the believers. Do you wish to give Allah clear evidence against yourselves?

against you	for Allah	you make	that	Do you wish

the hypocrites	Indeed,	144	clear?	an evidence

145. Indeed, the hypocrites will be in the lowest depths of the Fire, and never will you find any helper for them

and never	the Fire,	of	the lowest depths	(will be) in

those who	Except	145	any helper	for them	you will find

146. Except those who repent, correct themselves and hold fast to Allah, and are sincere in their religion for Allah, then those will be with the believers. And soon Allah will give the believers a great reward.

and are sincere	to Allah	and hold fast	and correct (themselves)	repent

the believers.	with	then those (will be)	for Allah,	(in) their religion

146	a great reward.	the believers	Allah will give	And soon

147. What would Allah do by punishing you if you are grateful and you believe? And Allah is All Appreciative, All-Knowing.

you are grateful	if	by punishing you	would Allah do	What

147	All-Knowing.	All-Appreciative,	And Allah is	and you believe?

Surah 4: The women (v. 143-147)

148. Allah does not love the public mention of evil words, except by the one who has been wronged. And Allah is All-Hearing, All-Knowing.

149. If you disclose a good or conceal it or pardon an evil, then indeed, Allah is Oft-Pardoning, All-Powerful.

150. Indeed, those who disbelieve in Allah and **His** Messengers and wish to differentiate between Allah and **His** Messengers and say, "We believe in some and disbelieve in others." And they wish to take a way in between that.

151. Truly, they are disbelievers. And **We** have prepared for the disbelievers a humiliating punishment.

152. And those who believe in Allah and **His** Messengers and they do not differentiate between any one of them - to those, **He** will give them their reward. And Allah is Oft-Forgiving, Most Merciful.

153. The People of the Book ask you to bring down to them a book from the heaven. Indeed, they had asked Musa even greater

Surah 4: The women (v. 148-153)   Part - 6

than that for they said, "Show us Allah manifestly," so the thunderbolt struck them for their wrongdoing. Then they took the calf (for worship) after clear proofs came to them, then **We** forgave them for that. And **We** gave Musa a clear authority.

154. And **We** raised the mount over them for their covenant, and **We** said to them, "Enter the gate bowing humbly." And **We** said to them, "Do not transgress in (the matter of) the Sabbath." And **We** took a solemn covenant from them.

155. Then because of their breaking of the covenant and their disbelief in the Signs of Allah and their killing of the Prophets without any right and their saying, "Our hearts are wrapped." Nay, Allah has set a seal on their hearts for their disbelief, so they do not believe except a few.

156. And for their disbelief and their saying against Maryam a great slander.

157. And for their saying, "Indeed, we have killed the Messiah, Isa, son of Maryam, the Messenger of Allah." And they did not kill him nor did they crucify him; but it was made to appear so

Surah 4: The women (v. 154-157)

158. Nay, Allah raised him towards **Him**. And Allah is All-Mighty, All-Wise.

159. And there is none from the People of the Book but must believe in him before his death. And on the Day of Resurrection he will be a witness against them.

160. Then for the wrongdoing of the Jews, **We** made unlawful for them good things which were lawful for them, and for their hindering many (people) from the way of Allah.

161. And for their taking of usury while they were forbidden from taking it and for their consuming wealth of people wrongfully. And **We** have prepared for the disbelievers among them a painful punishment.

162. But those who are firm in knowledge among them and the believers believe in what has been revealed to you and what was revealed before you. And those who establish prayer

Surah 4: The women (v. 158-162) — Part - 6

167. Indeed, those who disbelieved and did wrong, they have strayed, straying far away.

168. Indeed, those who disbelieve and do wrong, Allah will not forgive them nor will He guide them to a way,

169. Except the way to Hell, they will abide in it forever. And that is easy for Allah.

170. O mankind! Surely the Messenger has come to you with the truth from your Lord, so believe, it is better for you. But if you disbelieve, then indeed, to Allah belongs whatever is in the heavens and the earth. And Allah is All-Knowing, All-Wise.

171. O People of the Book! Do not commit excess in your religion nor say anything about Allah except the truth. The Messiah, Isa, son of Maryam, was only a Messenger of Allah and His word, which He conveyed to Maryam and a spirit from Him. So believe in Allah and His Messengers. And do not say, "Trinity," desist - it is better for you. Allah is the only One God. Glory be to Him! (Far Exalted is He) above having a son. To Him belongs whatever is in the heavens

Surah 4: The women (v. 168-171) Part - 6

172. Never would the Messiah disdain to be a slave of Allah nor the Angels near (Allah). And whoever disdains **His** worship and is arrogant, then **He** will gather them towards **Him** all together.

173. Then as for those who believe and do righteous deeds, **He** will give them their reward in full and give them more from **His** Bounty. And as for those who disdain and are arrogant, **He** will punish them with a painful punishment, and they will not find for themselves besides Allah any protector or helper.

174. O mankind! Surely a convincing proof has come to you from your Lord, and **We** have sent down to you a clear light.

175. So as for those who believe in Allah and hold fast to **Him** - **He** will admit them in **His** Mercy and Bounty and will guide them to **Himself** on a straight way.

176. They seek your ruling. Say, "Allah gives you a ruling concerning

Surah 4: The women (v. 172-176)   Part - 6

Kalala (one having no descendants or ascendants as heirs)." If a man dies, leaving no child but (only) a sister, she will have half of what he left. And he inherits from her if she (dies and) has no child. But if there are two sisters, they will have two thirds of what he left. But if there are (both) brothers and sisters, the male will have the share of two females. Allah makes clear to you lest you go astray. And Allah is All-Knower of everything.

176

Surah Al-Maidah

In the name of Allah, the Most Gracious, the Most Merciful.

1. O you who believe! Fulfil the contracts. Lawful for you are the quadrupeds of the grazing livestock except what is recited to you - hunting not being permitted while you are in the state of Ihram. Indeed, Allah decrees what **He** wills.

2. O you who believe! Do not violate the rites of Allah or the sacred month or the sacrificial animals or the garlanded or those coming to the Sacred House seeking

Bounty and pleasure of Allah. And when you come out of Ihram you may hunt. And do not let the hatred of a people who stopped you from Al-Masjid Al-Haraam lead you to transgression. And help one another in righteousness and piety, but do not help one another in sin and transgression. And fear Allah; indeed, Allah is severe in punishment.

3. Are made unlawful for you the dead animals, blood, the flesh of swine, and that which is dedicated to other than Allah, and that which is killed by strangling or by a violent blow or by a head-long fall or by the goring of horns, and that which is eaten up by the wild animal except what you slaughter (before its death), and that which is sacrificed on stone altars, and that you seek division by divining arrows - that is grave disobedience. This day those who disbelieve have despaired of (defeating) your religion; so do not fear them, but fear Me. This day I have perfected your religion for you and I have completed My Favor upon you, and I have approved for you Islam as a religion. But whoever is forced

Surah 5: The Table spread (v. 3)

by hunger with no inclination to sin, then indeed, Allah is Oft-Forgiving, Most Merciful.

4. They ask you what is made lawful for them. Say, "Lawful for you are the good things and what you have trained of hunting animals which you train as Allah has taught you. So eat of what they catch for you and mention the name of Allah on it, and fear Allah. Indeed, Allah is swift in taking account.

5. This day (all) good things have been made lawful; and the food of those who were given the Book is lawful for you and your food is lawful for them. And (lawful in marriage are) chaste women from the believers and chaste women from those who were given the Book before you, when you have given them their bridal due, desiring chastity, not lewdness nor taking them as secret lovers. And whoever denies the faith, then surely his deeds are wasted and in the Hereafter he will be among the losers.

6. O you who believe! When you stand up for prayer, wash your faces and your hands

Surah 5: The Table spread (v. 4-6)

Part - 6

till the elbows and wipe your heads and (wash) your feet till the ankles. But if you are in a state of ceremonial impurity, purify yourselves. But if you are ill or on a journey or one of you has come from the toilet or you have had contact with women and you do not find water, then do *tayammum* with clean earth by wiping your faces and your hands with it. Allah does not intend to make any difficulty for you but **He** intends to purify you and complete **His** Favor upon you, so that you may be grateful.

7. And remember the Favor of Allah upon you and **His** covenant with which **He** bound you when you said, "We hear and we obey;" and fear Allah. Indeed, Allah is All-Knower of what is in the breasts.

8. O you who believe! Be steadfast for Allah as witnesses in justice, and do not let the hatred of people prevent you from being just. Be just; it is nearer to piety. And fear Allah; indeed, Allah is All-Aware of what you do.

9. Allah has promised

Surah 5: The Table spread (v. 7-9)   Part - 6

147

مَغْفِرَةٌ	لَهُم	الصَّالِحَاتِ	وَعَمِلُوا	آمَنُوا	الَّذِينَ	
(is) forgiveness	for them	the righteous deeds -	and do	believe	those who	
وَكَذَّبُوا	كَفَرُوا	وَالَّذِينَ	۹	عَظِيمٌ	وَأَجْرٌ	
and deny	disbelieve	And those who	9	great.	and a reward	
يَا أَيُّهَا	۱۰	الْجَحِيمِ	أَصْحَابُ	أُولَٰئِكَ	بِآيَاتِنَا	
O you	10	(of) the Hellfire.	(are the) companions	those	Our Signs -	
عَلَيْكُمْ	اللَّهِ	نِعْمَتَ	اذْكُرُوا	آمَنُوا	الَّذِينَ	
upon you	(of) Allah	(the) Favor	Remember	believe!	who	
إِلَيْكُمْ	يَبْسُطُوا	أَن	قَوْمٌ	هَمَّ	إِذْ	
towards you	they stretch	that	a people	determined	when	
اللَّهَ	وَاتَّقُوا	عَنكُمْ	أَيْدِيَهُمْ	فَكَفَّ	أَيْدِيَهُمْ	
Allah.	And fear	from you.	their hands	but He restrained	their hands,	
وَلَقَدْ	۱۱	الْمُؤْمِنُونَ	فَلْيَتَوَكَّلِ	اللَّهِ	وَعَلَى	
And certainly	11	the believers.	so let put the trust	Allah	And upon	
وَبَعَثْنَا	إِسْرَائِيلَ	بَنِي	مِيثَاقَ	اللَّهُ	أَخَذَ	
and We appointed	(of) Israel	(from the) Children	a Covenant		Allah took	
مَعَكُمْ	إِنِّي	اللَّهُ	وَقَالَ	نَقِيبًا	اثْنَيْ عَشَرَ	مِنْهُمُ
with you,	"Indeed, I (am)		And Allah said,	leaders.	twelve	among them
وَآمَنتُم	الزَّكَاةَ	وَآتَيْتُمُ	الصَّلَاةَ	أَقَمْتُمُ	لَئِنْ	
and you believe	the zakah	and give	the prayer	you establish	if	
قَرْضًا حَسَنًا	اللَّهَ	وَأَقْرَضْتُمُ	وَعَزَّرْتُمُوهُمْ		بِرُسُلِي	
a goodly loan,	(to) Allah	and you loan	and you assist them		in My Messengers	
جَنَّاتٍ	وَلَأُدْخِلَنَّكُمْ	سَيِّئَاتِكُمْ	عَنكُمْ		لَأُكَفِّرَنَّ	
(to) gardens	and I will surely admit you	your evil deeds	from you		surely I will remove	
بَعْدَ	كَفَرَ	فَمَن	الْأَنْهَارُ	تَحْتِهَا	مِن	تَجْرِي
after	disbelieved	But whoever	the rivers.	underneath them	from	flow
۱۲	سَوَاءَ السَّبِيلِ	فَقَدْ	ضَلَّ	مِنكُمْ	ذَٰلِكَ	
12	(from) the right way.	then certainly	he strayed	among you,	that	
قُلُوبَهُمْ	وَجَعَلْنَا	لَعَنَّاهُمْ	مِيثَاقَهُمْ	نَقْضِهِم	فَبِمَا	
their hearts	and We made	We cursed them	(of) their covenant	their breaking	So for	

those who believe and do righteous deeds that for them is forgiveness and a great reward.

10. And those who disbelieve and deny **Our** Signs those are the companions of the Hellfire.

11. O you who believe! Remember the Favor of Allah upon you, when people determined to stretch their hands towards you, but **He** restrained their hands from you. And fear Allah; and upon Allah let the believers put their trust.

12. And certainly Allah took a Covenant from the Children of Israel and **We** appointed from among them twelve leaders. And Allah said, "Indeed, **I** am with you if you establish prayer and give *zakah* and you believe in **My** Messengers and assist them and loan Allah a goodly loan, surely **I** will remove from you your evil deeds and will admit you to gardens beneath which rivers flows. But whoever of you disbelieves after that, has certainly strayed from the right way.

13. So for their breaking of their covenant **We** cursed them and **We** made their hearts

Surah 5: The Table spread (v. 10-13)   **Part - 6**

hard. They distort words from their places and forgot a part of what they were reminded of. And you will not cease to discover treachery from them except a few of them. But forgive them and overlook (their misdeeds). Indeed, Allah loves the good-doers.

14. And from those who said, "We are Christians," **We** took their covenant; but they forgot a part of what they were reminded of. So **We** aroused enmity and hatred between them until the Day of Resurrection. And soon Allah will inform them about what they used to do.

15. O People of the Book! Surely there has come to you **Our** Messenger making clear to you much of what you used to conceal of the Scripture and overlooking much. Surely there has come to you from Allah a light and a clear Book

16. By which Allah guides those who seek **His** pleasure to the ways of peace and brings them out from darkness into light by **His** permission and guides them to

Surah 5: The Table spread (v. 14-16)

the straight way.

17. They have certainly disbelieved who say, "Indeed, Allah is the Messiah, the son of Maryam." Say, "Then who has the power against Allah if **He** intends to destroy Messiah, the son of Maryam and his mother and everyone on the earth?" And to Allah belongs the dominion of the heavens and the earth and whatever is between them. **He** creates what **He** wills, and Allah has power over everything.

18. The Jews and the Christian say, "We are the children of Allah and **His** beloved." Say, "Then why does **He** punish you for your sins." Nay, you are human beings from among those **He** created. **He** forgives whom **He** wills and punishes whom **He** wills. And to Allah belongs the dominion of the heavens and the earth and whatever is between them and to **Him** is the final return.

19. O People of the Book! Surely has come to you **Our** Messenger to make clear to you (the religion) after an interval of (cessation of) Messengers, lest you say, "There did not come to us any bearer of glad tidings or a warner."

Surah 5: The Table spread (v. 17-19)

But surely there has come to you a bearer of glad tidings and a warner. And Allah has power over everything.

20. And (remember) when Musa said, "O my people, remember the Favor of Allah upon you when He placed among you Prophets and made you kings and He gave you what He had not given anyone among the worlds.

21. "O my people! Enter the Holy land which Allah has ordained for you and do not turn your backs, for then you will turn back as losers."

22. They said, "O Musa! Indeed, within it are people of tyrannical strength and indeed, we will never enter it until they leave it; and if they leave it, then certainly we will enter it."

23. Said two men from those who feared (Allah) upon whom Allah had bestowed favor, "Enter upon them through the gate, for when you have entered it, then indeed you will be victorious. And put your trust in Allah if you are believers.

24. They said, O Musa! Indeed, we will never enter it, ever, as long as they are in it. So go, you and your Lord, and fight.

Surah 5: The Table spread (v. 20-24)

Indeed, we are sitting here.

25. He said, "O my Lord! Indeed, I do not have control except over myself and my brother, so separate us from the defiantly disobedient people."

26. Allah said, "Then indeed, it will be forbidden to them for forty years, they will wander in the earth. So do not grieve over the defiantly disobedient people."

27. And recite to them the story of the two sons of Adam in truth, when they both offered a sacrifice, and it was accepted from one of them but was not accepted from the other. Said (the latter), "Surely I will kill you." Said (the former), "Allah only accepts from the God fearing.

28. If you stretch your hand against me to kill me, I will not stretch my hand against you to kill you. Indeed, I fear Allah, the Lord of the worlds."

29. "Indeed, I wish that you be laden with my sin and your sin, so you will be among the companions of the Fire. And that is the recompense of the wrong-doers."

30. Then his soul prompted him

Surah 5: The Table spread (v. 25-30) Part - 6

to kill his brother, so he killed him and became of the losers.

| 30 | the losers. | of | and became | so he killed him | his brother, | (to) kill |

31. Then Allah sent a crow who scratched the ground to show him how to hide the dead body of his brother. He said, "Woe to me! Am I unable to be like this crow and hide the dead body of my brother?" Then he became of the regretful.

how	to show him	the earth	in	it (was) scratching	a crow,	Then Allah sent
Am I unable	"Woe to me!	He said,	(of) his brother.	(the) dead body	to hide
(the) dead body	and hide	[the] crow	this	like	I can be	that
From time	31	the regretful.	of	Then he became	(of) my brother?"

32. From that time, **We** ordained on the Children of Israel that whoever kills a soul other than for a life or for spreading corruption in the earth, then it is as if he has killed the whole mankind, and whoever saves it then it is as if he has saved the whole mankind. And surely **Our** Messengers came to them with clear Signs, yet even after that many of them committed excesses in the earth.

kills	who	that he	(of) Israel	(the) Children	on	We ordained	that,
the earth	in	(for) spreading corruption	or	(for) a soul	other than	a soul
saves it	and whoever	all [the] mankind,	he has killed	then (it) is as if
came to them	And surely	all [the] mankind.	he has saved	then (it) is as if
after	of them	many	indeed,	yet,	with clear Signs	**Our** Messengers
Only	32	(are) surely those who commit excesses.	the earth	in	that

33. Verily the punishment for those who wage a war against Allah and **His** Messenger and spread corruption in the earth is that they be killed or crucified or their hands and their feet of opposite sides be cut off or they be exiled from the land. That is their disgrace in

and **His** Messenger	(against) Allah	wage war	(for) those who	(the) recompense
or	they be killed	(is) that	spreading corruption	the earth	in	and strive
opposite sides	of	and their feet	their hands	be cut off	or	they be crucified
in	disgrace	(is) for them	That	the land.	from	they be exiled	or

Surah 5: The Table spread (v. 31-33)

this world, and in the Hereafter they will have a great punishment.

34. Except those who repent before you overpower them. And know that Allah is Oft-Forgiving, Most Merciful.

35. O you who believe! Fear Allah and seek the means (of nearness) to **Him** and strive hard in **His** way so that you may succeed.

36. Indeed, those who disbelieve, if they had all that is in the earth and the like of it with it by which to ransom themselves from the punishment of the Day of Resurrection, it will not be accepted from them, and for them is a painful punishment.

37. They will wish to come out of the Fire, but they will not come out of it. And for them is a lasting punishment.

38. And for the male and the female thief cut off their hands in recompense for what they have earned as an exemplary (punishment) from Allah. And Allah is All-Mighty, All-Wise.

39. But whoever repents after his wrongdoing and reforms (his ways), then indeed, Allah will turn towards him in forgiveness. Indeed, Allah is Oft-Forgiving, Most Merciful.

Surah 5: The Table spread (v. 34-39) Part - 6

40. Do you not know that to Allah belongs the dominion of the heavens and the earth? **He** punishes whom **He** wills and **He** forgives whom **He** wills. And Allah has power over everything.

41. O Messenger! Let not grieve you those who hasten into disbelief of those who say, "We believe" with their mouths, but their hearts believe not, and from among the Jews. They are listeners of falsehood and listeners for other people who have not come to you. They distort the words from their context, saying, "If you are given this, take it; but if you are not given it, then beware." And for whom Allah intends a trial never will you have power to do anything for him against Allah. Those are the ones for whom Allah did not intend to purify their hearts. For them in this world is disgrace and for them in the Hereafter is a great punishment.

42. (They are) listeners of falsehood and devourers of the forbidden. So if they come to you, then either judge between them or turn away from them. And if you turn away

Surah 5: The Table spread (v. 40-42)

from them, then they will never harm you in anything. And if you judge between them, then judge with justice. Indeed, Allah loves those who are just.

43. But how can they appoint you a judge while they have with them the Taurat, wherein is the Command of Allah? Then they turn away after that, and they are not believers.

44. Indeed, **We** revealed the Taurat wherein was Guidance and light. The Prophets who submitted (to Allah) judged by it for the Jews, as did the Rabbis and the scholars as they were entrusted with the Book of Allah and they were witnesses to it. So do not fear the people but fear **Me**, and do not sell **My** Verses for a little price. And whoever does not judge by what Allah has revealed, then those are the disbelievers.

45. And **We** ordained for them therein a life for a life, an eye for an eye, a nose for a nose, an ear for an ear, a tooth for a tooth, and for the wounds is a retribution. But whoever gives it (up as) charity, then it is an expiation for him. And whoever does

Surah 5: The Table spread (v. 43-45)   Part - 6

not judge by what Allah has revealed, then those are the wrongdoers.

46. And on their footsteps We sent Isa, son of Maryam, confirming what was before him of the Taurat, and We gave him the Injeel, in it was Guidance and light and confirming what was before him of the Taurat and a Guidance and an admonition for those who are God conscious.

47. And let the People of the Injeel judge by what Allah has revealed therein. And whoever does not judge by what Allah has revealed, then those are the defiantly disobedient.

48. And We have revealed to you the Book in truth, confirming the Book that came before it and as a guardian over it. So judge between them by what Allah has revealed and do not follow their vain desires when the truth has come to you. For each of you We have prescribed a law and a clear way. And if Allah had willed, He would have made you one community but (His plan) is to test you in what He has given you; so race to (all that is) good. Towards Allah you will all return, then He will inform you concerning that over which you used to differ.

49. And that you judge between them

by what Allah has revealed and do not follow their vain desires and beware of them lest they tempt you away from some of what Allah has revealed to you. And if they turn away, then know that Allah only intends to afflict them for some of their sins. And indeed, many among the people are defiantly disobedient.

50. Is it then the judgment of ignorance they seek? And who is better than Allah in judgment for a people who firmly believe.

51. O you who believe! Do not take the Jews and the Christians as allies. They are allies of one other. And whoever among you takes them as allies, then indeed he is of them. Indeed, Allah does not guide the wrongdoing people.

52. And you see those in whose hearts is a disease (i.e., hypocrisy), they hasten to them saying, "We fear that a misfortune may strike us." But perhaps Allah will bring victory or a decision from **Him**. Then they will become regretful over what they had been concealing within themselves.

53. And those who believe will say, "Are these the ones who swore by Allah their strongest oaths that indeed they were with you?" Their deeds have become worthless, and they have become losers.

Surah 5: The Table spread (v. 50-53)   **Part - 6**

54. O you who believe! Whoever among you turns back from his religion, then soon Allah will bring a people whom **He** loves and who will love **Him**, humble towards the believers and stern towards the disbelievers; striving in the way of Allah and not fearing the blame of a critic. That is the Grace of Allah; **He** grants to whom **He** wills. And Allah is All-Encompassing, All-Knowing.

55. Your ally is none but Allah and **His** Messenger and those who believe, and those who establish prayer and give *zakah* and those who bow down.

56. And whoever takes as an ally Allah and **His** Messenger and those who believe, then indeed the party of Allah - they are the victorious.

57. O you who believe! Do not take allies those who take your religion in ridicule and fun among those who were given the Book and the disbelievers. And fear Allah, if you are believers.

58. And when you make a call for prayer, they take it in ridicule and fun. That is because they are a people who do not understand.

59. Say,

Surah 5: The Table spread (v. 54-59)   Part - 6

اٰمَنَّا	اَنْ	اِلَّاۤ	مِنَّاۤ	تَنْقِمُوْنَ	هَلْ	الْكِتٰبِ	يٰۤاَهْلَ
we believe	that	except	[of] us	you resent	Do	(of) the Book!	"O People
مِنْ قَبْلُ	اُنْزِلَ	وَمَاۤ	اِلَيْنَا	اُنْزِلَ	وَمَاۤ	بِاللّٰهِ	
before,	was revealed	and what	to us	has been revealed	and what	in Allah	
اُنَبِّئُكُمْ	هَلْ	قُلْ	۵۹	فٰسِقُوْنَ	اَكْثَرَكُمْ	وَاَنَّ	
I inform you	"Shall	Say,	59	(are) defiantly disobedient."	most of you	and that	
بِشَرٍّ	مِنْ ذٰلِكَ	مَثُوْبَةً	عِنْدَ اللّٰهِ	مَنْ	لَّعَنَهُ اللّٰهُ		
(of) worse	than	that	(as) recompense	from	Allah?	Whom	Allah has cursed
وَالْخَنَازِيْرَ	الْقِرَدَةَ	مِنْهُمُ	وَجَعَلَ	عَلَيْهِ	وَغَضِبَ		
and [the] swines,	[the] apes	of them	and made	with him	and He became angry		
مَكَانًا	شَرٌّ	اُولٰٓئِكَ	الطَّاغُوْتَ	وَعَبَدَ			
(in) position	(are) worse	Those	the false deities.	and (who) worshipped			
وَاَضَلُّ	عَنْ	سَوَآءِ	السَّبِيْلِ	۶۰	وَاِذَا	جَآءُوْكُمْ	
and farthest astray	from	(the) even	way."	60	And when	they come to you	
قَالُوْۤا	اٰمَنَّا	وَقَدْ	دَّخَلُوْا	بِالْكُفْرِ	وَهُمْ	قَدْ	
they say,	"We believe."	But certainly	they entered	with disbelief	and they	certainly	
خَرَجُوْا	بِهٖ	وَاللّٰهُ	اَعْلَمُ	بِمَا	كَانُوْا	يَكْتُمُوْنَ	۶۱
went out	with it.	And Allah	knows best	[of] what	they were	hiding.	61
وَتَرٰى	كَثِيْرًا	مِّنْهُمْ	يُسَارِعُوْنَ	فِي الْاِثْمِ	وَالْعُدْوَانِ		
And you see	many	of them	hastening	into [the] sin	and [the] transgression		
وَاَكْلِهِمُ	السُّحْتَ	لَبِئْسَ	مَا	كَانُوْا	يَعْمَلُوْنَ	۶۲	
and eating	the forbidden.	Surely evil	(is) what	they were	doing.	62	
لَوْلَا	يَنْهٰىهُمُ	الرَّبّٰنِيُّوْنَ	وَالْاَحْبَارُ	عَنْ			
Why (do) not	forbid them,	the Rabbis	and the religious scholars	from			
قَوْلِهِمُ	الْاِثْمَ	وَاَكْلِهِمُ	السُّحْتَ	لَبِئْسَ	مَا		
their saying	the sinful	and their eating	(of) the forbidden?	Surely, evil	(is) what		
كَانُوْا	يَصْنَعُوْنَ	۶۳	وَقَالَتِ الْيَهُوْدُ	يَدُ اللّٰهِ	مَغْلُوْلَةٌ		
they used to	do.	63	And the Jews said,	"Allah's Hand	(is) chained."		
غُلَّتْ	اَيْدِيْهِمْ	وَلُعِنُوْا	بِمَا	قَالُوْا	بَلْ		
Are chained	their hands,	and they have been cursed	for what	they said.	Nay,		

"O People of the Book! Do you resent us except (for the fact) that we believe in Allah and what has been revealed to us and what was revealed before us and that most of you are defiantly disobedient."

60. Say, "Shall I inform you of something worse than that as recompense from Allah? Those whom Allah has cursed and He became angry with them, and He made some of them apes and swines and those who worshipped the false deities. Those are worse in position and farthest astray from the even (i.e., right) way."

61. And when they come to you, they say, "We believe." But certainly they entered with disbelief and they certainly went out with it. And Allah knows best what they were hiding.

62. And you see many of them hastening into sin and transgression and devouring (what is) forbidden. Surely, evil is what they were doing.

63. Why do the rabbis and the religious scholars not forbid them from saying what is sinful and devouring what is forbidden? Surely, evil is what they used to do.

64. And the Jews said, "The Hand of Allah is chained." Their hands are chained and they have been cursed for what they say. Nay,

Surah 5: The Table spread (v. 60-64)   **Part - 6**

His Hands are stretched out, **He** bestows as **He** wills. And that which has been revealed to you from your Lord will surely increase many of them in rebellion and disbelief. And **We** have cast among them enmity and hatred till the Day of Resurrection. Every time they kindled the fire of war, Allah extinguished it. And they strive in the earth spreading corruption. And Allah does not love the corrupters.

65. And if only the People of the Book had believed and feared Allah, surely **We** would have removed from them their evils deeds and would have admitted them to Gardens of Bliss.

66. And if only they had stood firmly by the Taurat and the Injeel and what was revealed to them from their Lord, surely they would have consumed (provision) from above them and from beneath their feet. Among them is a moderate community, but many of them do evil deeds.

67. O Messenger! Convey what has been revealed to you from your Lord, and if you do not, then you have not conveyed **His** Message. And Allah will protect you from the people. Indeed, Allah does not

Surah 5: The Table spread (v. 68-71)

68. O People of the Book! You are not on anything until you stand firmly by the Taurat and the Injeel, and what has been revealed to you from your Lord. And that which has been revealed to you from your Lord will surely increase many of them in rebellion and disbelief. So do not grieve over the disbelieving people.

69. Indeed, those who believed and those who are Jews and the Sabians and the Christians, whoever believed in Allah and the Last Day and did good deeds, then they will have no fear, nor will they grieve.

70. Surely We took a Covenant from the Children of Israel and sent to them Messengers. Whenever any Messenger came to them with what their souls did not desire, some (of the Messengers) they denied and some of them they killed.

71. And they thought there would be no trial for them, so they became blind and deaf. Then Allah turned to them (in forgiveness), then (again) many of them became blind and deaf. And Allah

72. They surely disbelieve who say, "Indeed, Allah is Messiah, the son of Maryam" while the Messiah said, "O Children of Israel! Worship Allah, my Lord and your Lord." Indeed, he who associates partners with Allah then surely Allah has forbidden Paradise for him, and his abode will be the Fire. And there will be no helpers for the wrongdoers.

73. Certainly they have disbelieved, those who say, "Indeed, Allah is the third of the three." And there is no god except the **One** God. And if they do not desist from what they are saying, a painful punishment will surely afflict those who disbelieve among them.

74. So will they not turn to Allah and seek **His** forgiveness? And Allah is Oft-Forgiving, Most Merciful.

75. The Messiah, son of Maryam, was not

Surah 5: The Table spread (v. 72-75)

مِن قَبۡلِهِ	خَلَتۡ	قَدۡ	رُسُلٌ	إِلَّا
before him	had passed	certainly	a Messenger,	but
يَأۡكُلَانِ	كَانَا	صِدِّيقَةٌ	وَأُمُّهُۥ	ٱلرُّسُلُ
eat	They both used to	(was) truthful.	And his mother	the Messengers.
لَهُمُ	نُبَيِّنُ	كَيۡفَ	ٱنظُرۡ	ٱلطَّعَامَۗ
to them	We make clear	how	See	[the] food.
يُؤۡفَكُونَ	أَنَّىٰ	ٱنظُرۡ	ثُمَّ	ٱلۡأٓيَٰتِ
they are deluded.	how	see	then	the Signs,
ٱللَّهِ	مِن دُونِ	أَتَعۡبُدُونَ	قُلۡ	٧٥
Allah	besides	"Do you worship	Say,	75
وَلَا	ضَرًّا	لَكُمۡ	يَمۡلِكُ	لَا	مَا
and not	any harm	to (cause) you	has power	not	what
ٱلۡعَلِيمُ	ٱلسَّمِيعُ	هُوَ	وَٱللَّهُ	نَفۡعًاۚ
the All-Knowing?	(is) the All-Hearing,	He	while Allah,	any benefit,
لَا	ٱلۡكِتَٰبِ	يَٰٓأَهۡلَ	قُلۡ	٧٦
(Do) not	(of) the Book!	"O People	Say,	76
وَلَا	ٱلۡحَقِّ	غَيۡرَ	دِينِكُمۡ	فِي	تَغۡلُواْ
and (do) not	the truth,	other than	your religion	in	exceed
ضَلُّواْ	قَدۡ	قَوۡمٍ	أَهۡوَآءَ	تَتَّبِعُوٓاْ
who went astray	certainly	(of) a people	(vain) desires	follow
عَن	وَضَلُّواْ	كَثِيرًا	وَأَضَلُّواْ	مِن قَبۡلُ
from	and they have strayed	many,	and they misled	before,
ٱلَّذِينَ	لُعِنَ	٧٧	ٱلسَّبِيلِ	سَوَآءِ
those who	Were cursed	77	[the] way.	(the) right
لِسَانِ	عَلَىٰ	إِسۡرَٰٓءِيلَ	بَنِيٓ	مِنۢ	كَفَرُواْ
(the) tongue	by	(of) Israel	(the) Children	from	disbelieved
ذَٰلِكَ	مَرۡيَمَۚ	ٱبۡنِ	وَعِيسَى	دَاوُۥدَ
that (was)	(of) Maryam,	son	and Isa	(of) Dawood
٧٨	يَعۡتَدُونَ	وَكَانُواْ	عَصَواْ	بِمَا
78	transgressing.	and they were	they disobeyed	because

but a Messenger, certainly Messengers had passed away before him. And his mother was truthful. They both used to eat food. See how **We** make clear to them the Signs; then see how they are deluded.

76. Say, "Do you worship besides Allah that which has no power either to harm you or benefit you while it is Allah **Who** is the All-Hearing, the All-Knowing?

77. Say, "O People of the Book! Do not exceed in your religion beyond the truth and do not follow the vain desires of a people who went astray before and misled many, and they have strayed from the right way.

78. Those who disbelieved from the Children of Israel were cursed by the tongue of Dawood and Isa, son of Maryam, because they disobeyed and they used to transgress.

Surah 5: The Table spread (v. 76-79) Part - 6

79. They did not forbid each other from any wrongdoing they did. Surely, evil was what they were doing.

80. You see many of them taking as allies those who disbelieved. Surely, evil is what they have sent forth for themselves (with the result) that Allah became angry with them, and in the punishment they will abide forever.

81. And if they had believed in Allah and the Prophet and what has been revealed to him, they would not have taken them as allies; but many of them are defiantly disobedient.

82. Surely, you will find the strongest among people in enmity towards the believers - the Jews and those who associate partners with Allah; and surely you will find nearest of them in affection to believers those who say, "We are Christians." That is because among them are priests and monks and because they are not arrogant.

Surah 5: The Table spread (v. 80-82)

83. And when they listen to what has been revealed to the Messenger, you see their eyes overflowing with tears because they have recognized the truth. They say, "Our Lord, we have believed, so write us among the witnesses.

84. And why should we not believe in Allah and what came to us of the truth? And we hope that our Lord will admit us (in Paradise) with the righteous people."

85. So Allah rewarded them for what they said with Gardens underneath which rivers flow, wherein they will abide forever. And that is the reward of the good-doers.

86. And those who disbelieve and deny **Our** Signs, those are the companions of the Hellfire.

87. O you who believe! Do not make unlawful good things, which Allah has made lawful for you and do not transgress. Indeed, Allah does not love the transgressors.

88. And eat what Allah has provided for you lawful and good things. And fear Allah, the **One** in **Whom** you believe.

89. Allah will not call you to account for your thoughtless utterances in your oaths but **He** will call you to account for your deliberate oaths.

Surah 5: The Table spread (v. 83-89)   Part - 7

So its expiation is the feeding of ten needy persons from the average of what you feed your families or clothing them or freeing a slave. But whoever does not find (or afford it) then a fasting of three days. That is the expiation of your oaths when you have sworn. Therefore guard your oaths. Thus Allah makes clear to you **His** Verses so that you may be grateful.

90. O you who believe! Verily, intoxicants and games of chance and (sacrifices at) altars and divining arrows are an abomination from the work of Shaitaan, so avoid it so that you may be successful.

91. Shaitaan only intends to cause enmity and hatred between you through intoxicants and gambling, and to hinder you from the remembrance of Allah and from the prayer. So will you abstain?

92. And obey Allah and obey the Messenger and beware. And if you turn away, then know that upon **Our** Messenger is only to clearly convey (the Message).

93. There is no sin on those who believe and do good deeds for what they ate (in the past) if they (now) fear Allah and believe and do good deeds, then

Surah 5: The Table spread (v. 90-93)   Part - 7

وَاللّٰهُ	وَأَحْسِنُوا	اتَّقَوْا	ثُمَّ	وَآمَنُوا	اتَّقَوْا		
and Allah	and do good,	they fear (Allah)	then	and believe,	they fear (Allah)		
	يُحِبُّ	الْمُحْسِنِينَ	۝٩٣	يَا أَيُّهَا	الَّذِينَ آمَنُوا	لَيَبْلُوَنَّكُمُ اللّٰهُ	
	loves	the good-doers.	93	O you	who believe!	Surely Allah will test you	
بِشَيْءٍ	مِّنَ	الصَّيْدِ	تَنَالُهُ	أَيْدِيكُمْ	وَرِمَاحُكُمْ		
through something	of	the game -	can reach it	your hands	and your spears		
لِيَعْلَمَ اللّٰهُ	مَن	يَخَافُهُ	بِالْغَيْبِ	فَمَنِ	اعْتَدَىٰ		
that Allah may make evident	who	fears Him	in the unseen.	And whoever	transgressed		
بَعْدَ	ذٰلِكَ	فَلَهُ	عَذَابٌ	أَلِيمٌ	۝٩٤	يَا أَيُّهَا	
after	that,	then for him	(is) a punishment	painful.	94	O you	
الَّذِينَ آمَنُوا	لَا	تَقْتُلُوا	الصَّيْدَ	وَأَنتُمْ	حُرُمٌ		
who	believe!	(Do) not	kill	the game	while you	(are in) Ihram.	
وَمَن	قَتَلَهُ	مِنكُم	مُّتَعَمِّدًا	فَجَزَاءٌ	مِّثْلُ	مَا	
And whoever	killed it	among you	intentionally,	then penalty	(is) similar	(to) what	
قَتَلَ	مِنَ	النَّعَمِ	يَحْكُمُ	بِهِ	ذَوَا عَدْلٍ	مِّنكُمْ	هَدْيًا
he killed	of	the cattle,	judging	it	two just men	among you	(as) an offering
بَالِغَ	الْكَعْبَةِ	أَوْ	كَفَّارَةٌ	طَعَامُ	مَسَاكِينَ	أَوْ	عَدْلُ
reaching	the Kabah	or	an expiation -	feeding	needy people	or	equivalent
ذٰلِكَ	صِيَامًا	لِّيَذُوقَ	وَبَالَ	أَمْرِهِ	عَفَا اللّٰهُ		
(of) that	(in) fasting,	that he may taste	(the) consequence	(of) his deed.	Allah pardoned		
عَمَّا	سَلَفَ	وَمَنْ	عَادَ	فَيَنتَقِمُ اللّٰهُ	مِنْهُ		
what	(has) passed,	but whoever	returned,	then Allah will take retribution	from him.		
وَاللّٰهُ	عَزِيزٌ	ذُو	انتِقَامٍ	۝٩٥	أُحِلَّ		
And Allah	(is) All-Mighty,	Owner	(of) Retribution.	95	Is made lawful		
لَكُمْ	صَيْدُ	الْبَحْرِ	وَطَعَامُهُ	مَتَاعًا	لَّكُمْ	وَلِلسَّيَّارَةِ	
for you	game	(of) the sea	and its food	(as) provision	for you	and for the travelers,	
وَحُرِّمَ	عَلَيْكُمْ	صَيْدُ	الْبَرِّ	مَا دُمْتُمْ	حُرُمًا		
and is made unlawful	on you	game	(of) the land	as long as you	(are) in Ihram.		
وَاتَّقُوا اللّٰهَ	الَّذِي	إِلَيْهِ	تُحْشَرُونَ	۝٩٦			
And be conscious of Allah	the One	to Him	you will be gathered.	96			

94. O you who believe! Surely Allah will test you through something of the game that your hands and your spears can reach, that Allah may make evident those who fear **Him** unseen. And whoever transgresses after that, then for him is a painful punishment.

95. O you who believe! Do not kill the game when you are in *Ihram*. And whoever of you killed it intentionally, then the penalty is an equivalent to what he killed of the cattle, as judged by two men among you as an offering reaching the Kabah or an expiation - feeding needy people or the equivalent of that in fasting, that he may taste the consequences of his deed. Allah pardoned what is past; but whoever returns, then Allah will take retribution from him. And Allah is All-Mighty, Owner of Retribution.

96. Is made lawful for you game of the sea and its food as provision for you and for travelers, but is made unlawful to you hunting on the land as long as you are in *Ihram*. And be conscious of Allah to **Whom** you will be gathered.

Surah 5: The Table spread (v. 94-96)   **Part - 7**

97. Allah has made Kabah, the Sacred House, an establishment for mankind and the sacred months and the animals for offering and the garlands (that mark them). That is so that you may know that Allah knows what is in the heavens and what is in the earth and that Allah is All-Knower of everything.

98. Know that Allah is severe in punishment and that Allah is Oft-Forgiving, Most Merciful.

99. The Messenger's duty is only to convey the Message. And Allah knows what you reveal and what you conceal.

100. Say, "The evil and the good are not equal even if the abundance of evil impresses you. So fear Allah, O men of understanding, so that you may be successful."

101. O you who believe! Do not ask about things, if they are made clear to you, will distress you. But if you ask about them while the Quran is being revealed, they will be made clear to you. Allah has pardoned it and Allah is Oft-Forgiving, All-Forbearing.

102. Indeed, people before you asked (such questions); then they became thereby disbelievers.

103. Allah has not made (superstitions like) *Bahirah*,

Surah 5: The Table spread (v. 97-103)

الَّذِينَ	وَلَٰكِنَّ	حَامٍ	وَلَا	وَصِيلَةٍ	وَلَا	سَائِبَةٍ	وَلَا
those who	[And] but	a Hami.	and not	a Wasilah	and not	a Saibah	and not
لَا	وَأَكْثَرُهُمْ	الْكَذِبَ	اللَّهِ	عَلَى	يَفْتَرُونَ	كَفَرُوا	
(do) not	and most of them	the lie,	Allah	against	they invent	disbelieved	
مَا	إِلَىٰ	تَعَالَوْا	لَهُمْ	قِيلَ	وَإِذَا	103	يَعْقِلُونَ
what	to	"Come	to them,	it is said	And when	103	use reason.
مَا	حَسْبُنَا	قَالُوا	الرَّسُولِ	وَإِلَى	اللَّهُ	أَنزَلَ	
(is) what	"Sufficient for us	they said,	the Messenger,"	and to	Allah has revealed		
لَا	آبَاؤُهُمْ	كَانَ	وَلَوْ	آبَاءَنَا	عَلَيْهِ	وَجَدْنَا	
not	their forefathers were	Eventhough	our forefathers."	upon it	we found		
الَّذِينَ	يَا أَيُّهَا	104	يَهْتَدُونَ	وَلَا	شَيْئًا	يَعْلَمُونَ	
who	O you	104	they (were) guided?	and not	anything	knowing	
مَن	يَضُرُّكُم	لَا	أَنفُسَكُمْ	عَلَيْكُمْ	آمَنُوا		
(those) who	Will not harm you		(is to guard) yourselves.	Upon you	believe!		
مَرْجِعُكُمْ	اللَّهِ	إِلَى	اهْتَدَيْتُمْ	إِذَا	ضَلَّ		
(is) your return -	Allah	To	you have been guided.	when	(have gone) astray		
يَا أَيُّهَا	105	تَعْمَلُونَ	كُنتُمْ	بِمَا	فَيُنَبِّئُكُم	جَمِيعًا	
O you	105	do.	you used to	of what	then He will inform you	all;	
أَحَدَكُمُ	حَضَرَ	إِذَا	بَيْنِكُمْ	شَهَادَةُ	آمَنُوا	الَّذِينَ	
one of you	approaches	when	among you	(Take) testimony	believe!	who	
مِنكُمْ	عَدْلٍ	ذَوَا	اثْنَانِ	الْوَصِيَّةِ	حِينَ	الْمَوْتُ	
among you,	just men		two	[the] a will	(at the) time (of making)	[the] death,	
فِي	ضَرَبْتُمْ	أَنتُمْ	إِنْ	غَيْرِكُمْ	مِنْ	آخَرَانِ	أَوْ
in	(are) travel(ing)	you	if	other than you	from	two others	or
تَحْبِسُونَهُمَا	الْمَوْتِ	مُصِيبَةُ	فَأَصَابَتْكُم	الْأَرْضِ			
Detain both of them	(of) [the] death.	calamity	then befalls you	the earth			
إِنِ ارْتَبْتُمْ	بِاللَّهِ	فَيُقْسِمَانِ	الصَّلَاةِ	بَعْدِ	مِن		
you doubt,	if	by Allah	and let them both swear	the prayer	after		
وَلَا	ذَا قُرْبَىٰ	كَانَ	وَلَوْ	ثَمَنًا	بِهِ	نَشْتَرِي	لَا
and not	a near relative,	he is	even if	a price	it for		"We will not exchange

Surah 5: The Table spread (v. 104-106)

Saibah, Wasilah, and *Hami* (all these animals were liberated in honor of idols as practiced by pagan Arabs in the pre-Islamic period). But those who disbelieve, invent a lie against Allah and most of them do not use reason.

104. And when it is said to them, "Come to what Allah has revealed and to the Messenger," they say, "Sufficient for us is that upon which we found our forefathers." Eventhough their forefathers knew nothing, nor were they guided.

105. O you who believe! Upon you is (to guard) yourselves. Those who have gone astray will not harm you when you have been guided. To Allah you will all return and He will inform you about what you used to do.

106. O you who believe! When death approaches one of you, take testimony among you at the time of making a will - two just men from among you or two others not of you, if you are traveling in the earth and the calamity of death befalls you. Detain both of them after prayer and let them both swear by Allah if you doubt (saying), "We will not exchange it for a price, even if he is a near relative and we will not

107. Then if it is found that those two were guilty of sin, then let two others stand in their place from those who have a lawful right over them (as against the former two). And let them swear by Allah that "Our testimony is truer than their testimony, and we have not transgressed. Indeed, we will then be of the wrongdoers."

108. That is more likely that they will give testimony in its true form, or they would fear that their oaths may be refuted by others' oaths. And fear Allah and listen; and Allah does not guide the defiantly disobedient people.

109. The Day Allah will gather the Messengers and say, "What was the response you received?" They will say, "We have no knowledge. Indeed, You are the Knower of the unseen."

110. When Allah said, "O Isa, son of Maryam! Remember **My Favor** upon you and upon your mother when I strengthened you with the Holy Spirit and you spoke to the people in the cradle and in maturity. And when

Surah 5: The Table spread (v. 107-110) Part - 7

I taught you the Book and the wisdom and the Taurat and the Injeel; and when you made from clay like the shape of a bird by **My** permission, then you breathed into it, and it became a bird by **My** permission; and you healed those born blind and the leper by **My** permission; and when you brought forth the dead by **My** permission. And when **I** restrained the Children of Israel from you when you came to them with the clear proofs, then those who disbelieved among them said, "This is nothing but clear magic."'

111. And when **I** inspired to the disciples to believe in **Me** and **My** Messenger they said, "We believe and bear witness that indeed we are Muslims."

112. When the disciples said, "O Isa, son of Maryam! Can your Lord send down to us a table spread from the heaven?" He said, "Fear Allah, if you are believers."

113. They said, "We wish to eat from it and satisfy our hearts and to know that certainly you have spoken the truth to us and be among the witnesses."

114. Said Isa, son of Maryam, "O Allah, our Lord, send down to us

Surah 5: The Table spread (v. 111-114)   Part - 7

a table spread from the heaven that it may be a festival for us - for the first and the last of us and a sign from **You**. And provide us and **You** are best of the providers.

115. Allah said, "Indeed, **I** will send it down to you, then whoever from among you disbelieves after that, then indeed, **I** will punish him with a punishment with which I have not punished anyone among the worlds."

116. And when Allah said, "O Isa, son of Maryam! Did you say to the people, "Take me and my mother as two gods besides Allah?"" He will say, "Glory be to **You**! It was not for me to say what I had no right to (say). If I had said it, then surely **You** would have known it. **You** know what is in myself and I do not know what is in **Yourself**. Indeed, **You**, **You Alone** are the All-Knower of the unseen.

117. I did not say to them except what **You** commanded me - that, 'You worship Allah my Lord and your Lord.' And I was over them a witness as long as I was among them, then when **You** raised me up, **You** were the Watcher over them, and **You** are Witness over all things.

118. If **You** punish them, then indeed they

Surah 5: The Table spread (v. 115-118)

are **Your** slaves, and if **You** forgive them, then indeed **You, You Alone** are the All-Mighty, the All-Wise."

118 the All-Wise." (are) the All-Mighty,

119. Allah will say, "This is the Day when the truthful will profit from their truthfulness. For them are Gardens underneath which rivers flow, wherein they will abide forever." Allah is pleased with them and they are pleased with **Him**. That is a great success.

120. To Allah belongs the dominion of the heavens and the earth and whatever is within them. And **He** has power over everything.

Surah Al-Anaam

In the name of Allah, the Most Gracious, the Most Merciful.

1. All praises and thanks be to Allah, the **One Who** created the heavens and the earth and made the darkness and the light. Yet those who disbelieve equate (others) with their Lord.

2. **He is the One Who** created you from clay and then decreed a term - a specified term (known to) **Him**, yet you are in doubt!

3. And **He** is Allah in the heavens and in the earth. **He** knows your secret and what you make public, and **He** knows

Surah 5: The Table spread (v. 119-120); Surah 6: The cattle (v. 1-3)   Part - 7

4. And no sign comes to them from the Signs of their Lord except that they turn away from it.

5. Then indeed, they denied the truth when it came to them, but soon news will come to them about what they used to mock.

6. Have they not seen how many generations We destroyed before them which We had established upon the earth as We have not established you? And We sent (rain) from the sky upon them in abundant showers and We made the rivers flow beneath them. Then We destroyed them for their sins and We raised after them other generations.

7. And even if We had sent down to you a written Scripture on parchment and they touched it with their hands, those who disbelieved would have said, "This is nothing but obvious magic."

8. And they said, "Why has not an Angel been sent down to him?" And if We had sent down an Angel, the matter would have been decided; then no respite would have been granted to them.

9. And if We had made him (i.e., the Messenger) an Angel, certainly We would have made him (appear as) a man and We would have obscured

Surah 6: The cattle (v. 4-9) — Part - 7

them with that in which they are obscuring themselves (i.e., confusion and doubt).

10. And indeed, the Messengers were mocked before you, but those who scoffed at them were surrounded by that which they used to mock.

11. Say, "Travel in the earth and see how was the end of the rejecters."

12. Say, "To whom belongs whatever is in the heavens and the earth?" Say, "To Allah." **He** has decreed upon **Himself** Mercy. Surely, **He** will assemble you on the Day of Resurrection, about which there is no doubt. Those who have lost themselves do not believe.

13. And to **Him** belongs whatever dwells in the night and the day, and **He** is All-Hearing, All-Knowing.

14. Say "Is it other than Allah I should take as a protector, Creator of the heavens and the earth, while it is **He Who** feeds and is not fed?" Say, "Indeed, I have been commanded to be the first to submit (to Allah) and not to be of those who associate partners with Allah."

15. Say, "Indeed, I fear, if I should disobey my Lord, the punishment of a Mighty Day."

16. Whoever is averted from such a punishment that Day, then surely **He** had Mercy on him. And that is the clear success.

17. And if Allah touches you with affliction, then there is no remover of it except **Him**. And if **He** touches you with good, then **He** has power over everything.

18. And **He** is the Subjugator over **His** slaves. And **He** is the All-Wise, the All-Aware.

19. Say, "What thing is greatest as a testimony?" Say, "Allah is Witness between me and you. And this Quran has been revealed to me so that I may warn you with it and whoever it reaches. Do you truly testify that there are other gods with Allah?" Say, "I do not testify." Say, "**He** is but One God, and indeed, I am free of what you associate (with **Him**)."

20. Those to whom **We** have given the Book recognize him as they recognize their sons. Those who have lost themselves do not believe.

21. And who is more unjust than he who invents a lie against Allah or rejects **His** Signs? Indeed, the wrongdoers will not be successful.

22. And the Day **We** will gather them all together, then **We** will say to those who associated others with Allah, "Where are your partners, those whom you used to claim.

23. Then they will have no plea

Surah 6: The cattle (v. 17-23)

24. Look how they lied against themselves. And what they used to invent will be lost from them.

25. And among them are those who listen to you, but **We** have placed over their hearts coverings lest they understand it, and in their ears deafness. And if they see every sign, they will not believe in it. Even when they come to you and argue with you those who disbelieve say, "This is nothing but the tales of the former people."

26. And they forbid (others) from it and they (themselves) keep away from it. And they do not destroy except themselves, and they do not perceive.

27. And if you could see when they are made to stand before the Fire, they will say, "Oh! Would that we were sent back, then we would not deny the Signs of our Lord and would be among the believers."

28. Nay, what they used to conceal before has become manifest to them. And even if they were sent back, certainly they would return to that which they were forbidden; and certainly, they are liars.

29. And they say, "There is nothing

Surah 6: The cattle (v. 24-29)   Part - 7

except our worldly life, and we will not be resurrected."

30. And if you could see when they will be made to stand before their Lord. **He** will say, "Is this not the truth?" They will say, "Yes, by our Lord." **He** will say, "So taste the punishment because you used to disbelieve."

31. Indeed, they have incurred loss who deny the meeting with Allah until, when the Hour comes on them suddenly, they will say, "Oh! Our regret over what we neglected concerning it," while they will bear their burdens on their backs. Unquestionably! Evil is what they bear.

32. And the worldly life is nothing but play and amusement; but the home of the Hereafter is best for those who are God conscious. Then, will you not reason?

33. Indeed, **We** know that it grieves you what they say. And indeed, they do not deny you, but the wrongdoers reject the Verses of Allah.

34. And surely Messengers were rejected before you, but they were patient on being rejected and they were harmed until **Our** help came to them. And none

Surah 6: The cattle (v. 30-34)

35. And if their aversion is difficult for you, then if you are able to seek a tunnel into the earth or a ladder into the sky to bring to them a Sign (then do so). And if Allah had willed, surely He would have gathered them to guidance. So do not be of the ignorant.

36. Only those who listen respond. But the dead - Allah will resurrect them, then to Him they will be returned.

37. And they say, "Why is not a Sign sent down to him from his Lord?" Say, "Indeed, Allah is Able to send down a Sign, but most of them do not know."

38. And there is no animal on the earth or a bird that flies with its wings, but they are communities like you. We have not neglected in the Book anything. Then to their Lord they will be gathered.

39. And those who reject Our Verses are deaf and dumb in the darkness. Whoever Allah wills - He lets him go astray; and whoever He wills - He places on

40. Say, "Have you considered - if there comes upon you the punishment of Allah or comes upon you the Hour - is it other than Allah you call, if you are truthful?"

41. "Nay, it is Him Alone you call, and He would remove that for which you called upon Him if He wills, and you will forget what you associate (with Him)."

42. And certainly We sent (Messengers) to the nations before you, then We seized them with adversity and hardship, so that they may humble themselves.

43. Then why, when Our punishment came to them, they did not humble themselves? But their hearts became hardened and Shaitaan made fair-seeming to them what they used to do.

44. So when they forgot what they were reminded of, We opened on them the gates of everything until, when they rejoiced in what they were given, We seized them suddenly, and then they were dumbfounded.

45. So the people who committed wrong were eliminated. And all praises and thanks be to Allah, the Lord of the worlds.

46. Say, "Have you considered: if Allah took away your hearing and your sight and sealed

Surah 6: The cattle (v. 40-46)   Part - 7

your hearts, which god other than Allah could restore them to you? See how **We** explain the Signs; yet they turn away."

47. Say, "Have you considered: if the punishment of Allah comes to you suddenly or openly, will any be destroyed except the wrongdoing people?

48. And **We** did not send the Messengers except as bearer of glad tidings and as warners. So whoever believes and reforms - then they will have no fear nor will they grieve.

49. And those who deny **Our** Verses, the punishment will touch them for what they used to defiantly disobey.

50. Say, (O Muhammad SAWS!) "I do not say to you that I have with me the treasures of Allah, nor do I know the unseen, nor do I say to you that I am an Angel. I only follow what is revealed to me." Say, "Can the blind and the seeing one be equal?" Then will you not give thought?

51. And warn with it those who fear that they will be gathered before their Lord, for them there will be no protector and no intercessor besides **Him**, so that they may become righteous.

52. And do not send away those who call

Surah 6: The cattle (v. 47-52)   Part - 7

their Lord in the morning and the evening, seeking **His** Countenance. Not upon you is anything of their account and not upon them is anything of your account. So were you to send them away, you would then be of the wrongdoers.

53. And thus **We** try some of them through others that they say, "Are these whom Allah has favored among us?" Is not Allah most knowing of those who are grateful?

54. And when those who believe in **Our** Verses come to you, say, "Peace be upon you. Your Lord has prescribed Mercy upon **Himself**, so that whoever of you does evil in ignorance and then reforms himself after that, then indeed, **He** is Oft-Forgiving, Most Merciful."

55. And thus **We** explain the Verses, so that the way of the criminals become manifest.

56. Say, "Indeed, I am forbidden to worship those whom you call besides Allah." Say, "I will not follow your vain desires, for I would then go astray, and I would not be of the guided-ones."

57. Say, "Indeed, I am on clear proof from my Lord, while you deny it. I do not have

Surah 6: The cattle (v. 53-57)

what you seek to hasten (i.e., the punishment). The decision is only for Allah. **He** relates the truth, and **He** is the best of the Deciders."

58. Say, "If I had what you seek to hasten, surely the matter would have been decided between me and you. And Allah is most knowing of the wrongdoers."

59. And with **Him** are the keys of the unseen, none knows them except **Him**. And **He** knows what is on the land and in the sea. And not a leaf falls but **He** knows it. And there is not a grain in the darkness of the earth and not anything moist or dry but is written in a Clear Record.

60. And **He** is the **One Who** takes your (souls) by night and **He** knows what you have committed by day. Then **He** raises you up therein so that the specified term is fulfilled. Then to **Him** will be your return, then **He** will inform you about what you used to do.

61. And **He** is the Subjugator over **His** slaves, and **He** sends over you guardians (Angels) until, when death comes to one of you, **Our** messengers (i.e., the angels of death) take him, and they do not fail (in their duties).

62. Then they are returned to Allah, their True Protector.

Surah 6: The cattle (v. 58-62) Part - 7

Unquestionably, for **Him** is the judgment. And **He** is the swiftest of the Reckoners.

63. Say, "Who rescues you from the darknesses of the land and sea (when) you call **Him** humbly and secretly (saying), 'If **He** saves us from this, surely we will be among the grateful ones.'"

64. Say, "Allah saves you from it and from every distress, yet you associate partners (with Allah)."

65. Say, "**He** is All-Capable to send upon you punishment from above you or from beneath your feet or to confuse you into sects and make you taste the violence of one another." See how **We** explain the Signs so that you may understand.

66. But your people have denied it, while it is the truth. Say, "I am not a manager over you."

67. For every news is a fixed time, and soon you will know.

68. And when you see those who engage (in vain talks) concerning **Our** Verses, then turn away from them until they engage in a talk other than that. And if Shaitaan causes you to forget, then do not sit after the reminder with the wrongdoing people.

69. And those who fear Allah are not

Surah 6: The cattle (v. 63-69) — Part - 7

70. And leave those who take their religion as play and amusement and deluded them the worldly life. But remind with it, lest a soul be given up to destruction for what it earned, it will not have besides Allah any protector nor any intercessor. And if it offers every ransom, it would not be accepted from it (i.e., the soul). Those are the ones who are given to destruction for what they earned. For them will be a drink of boiling water and a painful punishment because they used to disbelieve.

71. Say, "Shall we invoke besides Allah that which neither benefits us nor harms us, and turn back on our heels after Allah has guided us? Like the one whom Shaitaan enticed in the earth confused, (while) he has companions inviting him to guidance saying, 'Come to us.'" Say, "Indeed, the Guidance of Allah is the (only) Guidance, and we have been commanded to submit to the Lord of the worlds

72. And to establish prayer and fear **Him**. And it is **He** to **Whom**

Surah 6: The cattle (v. 70-72)

73. And it is **He Who** created the heavens and the earth in truth. And the Day **He** says, "Be" and it is, **His** word is the truth. And **His** is the Dominion on the Day the trumpet will be blown. **He** is the All-Knower of the unseen and the seen. And **He** is the All-Wise, the All-Aware.

74. And when Ibrahim said to his father Aazar, "Do you take idols as gods? Indeed, I see you and your people in manifest error."

75. And thus **We** showed Ibrahim the kingdom of the heavens and the earth, so that he would be among those who are certain (in faith).

76. So when the night covered him, he saw a star. He said, "This is my Lord." But when it set, he said, "I do not like the ones that set."

77. When he saw the moon rising, he said, "This is my lord." But when it set, he said, "If my Lord does not guide me, I will surely be among the people who went astray."

78. When he saw the sun rising, he said, "This is my Lord; this is greater." But when it set, he said, "O my people!

Surah 6: The cattle (v. 73-78)

Surah 6: The cattle (v. 79-84)

78. ...Indeed, I am free of what you associate (with Allah)."

79. Indeed, I have turned my face to the One Who created the heavens and the earth as a true monotheist, and I am not of those who associate partners with Allah.

80. And his people argued with him. He said, "Do you argue with me concerning Allah while He has guided me? And I do not fear what you associate with Him, unless my Lord wills something. My Lord encompasses all things in knowledge; then will you not take heed?

81. And how could I fear what you associate with Allah while you do not fear that you have associated with Allah that for which He did not send down to you any authority. So which of the two parties has more right to security, if you know."

82. Those who believe and do not mix their belief with wrong, those will have security, and they are rightly guided.

83. And this is Our argument which We gave Ibrahim against his people. We raise by degrees whom We will. Indeed, your Lord is All-Wise, All-Knowing.

84. And We bestowed to him Ishaq and Yaqub, all (of them) We guided.

84. And Nuh, We guided before; and of his descendents Dawood and Sulaiman and Ayyub and Yusuf and Musa and Harun. And thus We reward the good-doers.

85. And Zakariya and Yahya and Isa and Ilyas - all were of the righteous.

86. And Ismail and Al-Yasaa and Yunus and Lut, all We preferred over the worlds.

87. And from their fathers and their descendents and their brothers - We chose them and We guided them to a straight path.

88. That is the Guidance of Allah by which He guides whom He wills of His slaves. But if they had associated partners with Allah, surely would have become worthless for them what they used to do.

89. Those are the ones whom We gave the Book and the judgment and the Prophethood. But if they disbelieve in it, then indeed, We have entrusted it to a people who are not disbelievers therein.

90. Those are the ones whom Allah has guided, so you follow their guidance. Say, "I do not ask you for it any reward. It is not but a reminder for the worlds."

91. And they did not appraise Allah with His true appraisal,

Surah 6: The cattle (v. 85-91)

when they said, "Allah did not reveal to a human being anything." Say, "Who revealed the Book which Musa brought as light and guidance for the people? You make it into parchments, disclosing (some of it) and concealing much (of it). And you were taught that which you did not know - neither you nor your forefathers." Say, "Allah (revealed it)." Then leave them to play in their (vain) discourse.

92. And this is a Book, which **We** have revealed, blessed and confirming what was before it, so that you may warn the mother of the cities (i.e., Makkah) and those around it. Those who believe in the Hereafter they believe in it, and they guard their prayers.

93. And who is more unjust than one who invents a lie about Allah or says, "It has been inspired to me," while nothing has been inspired to him, and one who says, "I will reveal like what Allah has revealed." And if you could see when the wrongdoers are in the agonies of death while the Angels are stretching their hands (saying), "Discharge your souls! Today you will be recompensed

Surah 6: The cattle (v. 92-93)   Part - 7

with a humiliating punishment because you used to say against Allah other than the truth and you were being arrogant towards **His** Verses."

94. (It will be said to them), "And you have certainly come to **Us** alone as **We** created you the first time, and you have left whatever **We** bestowed upon you behind your backs. And **We** do not see with you your intercessors whom you claimed to be partners with Allah in your matters. Indeed, the bond has been severed between you, and is lost from you what you used to claim."

95. Indeed, Allah is the Cleaver of the grain and the date-seed. **He** brings forth the living from the dead and brings forth the dead from the living. That is Allah, so how are you deluded?

96. **He** is the Cleaver of the daybreak and **He** has made the night for rest and the sun and the moon for reckoning. That is the ordaining of the All-Mighty, the All-Knowing.

97. And **He** is the One Who made for you the stars, so that you may be guided by them in the darkness of the land and the sea. Certainly, **We** have made clear the Signs for a people who know.

Surah 6: The cattle (v. 94-97)

98. And **He** is the **One Who** produced you from a single soul, so there is a place of dwelling and a resting place. Certainly, **We** have made clear the Signs for a people who understand.

99. And **He** is the **One Who** sends down water from the sky, then **We** bring forth with it vegetation of every kind. Then **We** bring forth from it green plants from which **We** bring forth thick cluster of grains. And from the date-palm, from its spathe are clusters of dates hanging low. And gardens of grapes and olives and pomegranates, resembling and yet different. Look at its fruit when it bears fruit and its ripening. Indeed, in these are Signs for a people who believe.

100. And they make the jinn partners with Allah though **He** has created them, and they falsely attribute sons and daughters to **Him** without knowledge. Glorified is **He** and Exalted above what they attribute.

101. Originator of the heavens and the earth. How can **He** have a son when **He** does not have a companion and **He** created everything? And **He** is All-Knower of everything.

Surah 6: The cattle (v. 98-101) — Part - 7

102. That is Allah, your Lord, there is no god except **Him**, the Creator of all things, so worship **Him**. And **He** is the Guardian of everything.

103. No vision can grasp **Him** but **His** grasp is over all vision, and **He** is All-Subtle, All-Aware.

104. Verily, there has come to you enlightenment from your Lord. Then whoever sees does so for his soul, and whoever is blind then it is against himself. And I am not a guardian over you.

105. And thus **We** explain the Signs so that they may say, "You have studied," and that **We** may make it clear for a people who know.

106. Follow what has been inspired to you from your Lord, there is no god except **Him**, and turn away from those who associate partners with Allah.

107. And if Allah had willed, they would not have

Surah 6: The cattle (v. 102-107) Part - 7

associated partners with **Him**. And **We** have not made you a guardian over them nor are you a manager over them.

108. And do not insult those whom they invoke other than Allah, lest they insult Allah in enmity without knowledge. Thus **We** have made fair-seeming to every community their deeds. Then to their Lord is their return, then **He** will inform them about what they used to do.

109. And they swear by Allah their strongest oaths that if a sign came to them, they would surely believe in it. Say, "The signs are only with Allah." And what will make you perceive that even if it (i.e., a sign) came, they will not believe.

110. And **We** will turn their hearts and their sights just as they did not believe in it the first time. And **We** will leave them in their transgression, wandering blindly.

111. And even if We had sent down to them Angels and the dead had spoken to them and We had gathered everything before them, they would not have believed unless Allah willed. But most of them are ignorant.

112. And thus We have made for every Prophet an enemy - devils from mankind and jinn, inspiring one another with decorative speech in deception. But if your Lord had willed, they would not have done it, so leave them and what they invent.

113. And so that the hearts of those who disbelieve in the Hereafter will incline towards it (deceptive speech), and so that they may be pleased with it and so that they may commit that which they are committing.

114. "Then is it other than Allah I should seek as judge while it is He Who has revealed to you the Book explained in detail?" And those to whom We gave the Book know that it is sent down from your Lord in truth, so do not be among the doubters.

115. And the word of your Lord has been fulfilled in truth and justice. None can change His words, and He is the All-Hearer, the All-Knower.

116. And if you obey most of those on the earth, they will mislead you from the way of Allah. They follow nothing except assumption, and they are only guessing.

117. Indeed, your Lord knows best who strays from **His** way, and **He** knows best the guided-ones.

118. So eat of that on which the name of Allah has been mentioned, if you believe in **His** Verses.

119. And why should you not eat of that on which Allah's name has been mentioned, while **He** has explained in detail to you what **He** has forbidden to you, except that to which you are compelled. And indeed, many surely lead astray by their vain desires without knowledge. Indeed, your Lord - **He** is most knowing of the transgressors.

120. Forsake all sins, open and secret. Indeed, those who earn sin, they will be recompensed for what they used to commit.

121. And do not eat of that on which Allah's name has not been mentioned, for indeed, it is grave disobedience. And indeed the devils inspire their friends to dispute with you.

Surah 6: The cattle (v. 116-121)

Part - 8

And if you were to obey them, indeed you would be those who associate partners with **Him**.

122. Is one who was dead and **We** gave him life and made for him light whereby he can walk among people like one who is in darkness, he cannot come out of it? Thus is made fair-seeming to the disbelievers what they were doing.

123. And thus **We** have placed in every city the greatest of its criminals to plot therein. And not they plot except against themselves and they do not perceive.

124. And when a Sign comes to them they say, "We will never believe until we are given the like of that which was given to the Messengers of Allah." Allah knows best where He places His Message. Those who committed crimes will be afflicted by humiliation and a severe punishment from Allah for what they used to plot.

125. So whoever Allah wants to guide, **He** expands his breast to Islam; and whoever **He** wants to let go astray, **He** makes his breast tight and constricted as though he were climbing into the sky. Thus Allah places filth on those who do not believe.

Surah 6: The cattle (v. 122-125)

126. And this is the way of your Lord, straight. Certainly, **We** have detailed the Verses for a people who take heed.

127. For them will be the home of peace (Paradise) with their Lord. And **He** will be their protecting friend because of what they used to do.

128. And the Day **He** will gather them together, (and will say), "O assembly of jinn! Certainly you have (misled) many of mankind." And their friends among men will say, "Our Lord, some of us profited by others, and we have reached our term which **You** appointed for us." He will say, "The Fire is your abode, wherein you will abide forever, except what Allah wills. Indeed, your Lord is All-Wise, All-Knowing.

129. And thus **We** make some of the wrongdoers friends of others because of what they used to earn.

130. O assembly of jinn and men! Did there not come to you Messengers from among you, relating to you **My** Verses and warning you of the meeting of this Day of yours?" They will say, "We bear witness against ourselves." And the life of this world deluded them, and they will bear witness against themselves that they were disbelievers.

Surah 6: The cattle (v. 126-130) — Part - 8

131. That is because your Lord does not destroy the cities for their wrongdoing while their people are unaware.

132. And for all will be degrees for what they did. And your Lord is not unaware of what they do.

133. And your Lord is Self-Sufficient, Owner of Mercy. If **He** wills, **He** can take you away and grant succession after you to whom **He** wills, just as **He** raised you from the descendants of other people.

134. Indeed, what you are promised will surely come, and you cannot escape.

135. Say, "O my people! Work according to your position. Indeed, I am also working. And soon you will know who will have for himself a (good) home in the end. Indeed, the wrongdoers will not succeed."

136. And they assign to Allah out of what **He** produced of the crops and the cattle a share and say, "This is for Allah," by their claim, "And this is for our partners." But what is for their partners does not reach Allah, while what is for Allah reaches

Surah 6: The cattle (v. 131-136)

137. Likewise, to many of those who associate partners with Allah, their partners have made pleasing the killing of their children so that they may ruin them and make confusing to them their religion. And if Allah had willed, they would not have done so. So leave them and what they invent.

138. And they say, "These cattle and crops are forbidden, none can eat them except whom we will," by their claim. And there are cattle whose backs are forbidden; and they do not mention the name of Allah as an invention against **Him**. **He** will recompense them for what they used to invent.

139. And they say, "What is in the wombs of these cattle is exclusively for our males and forbidden to our spouses. But if it is (born) dead, then all of them have a share in it." **He** will punish them for their attribution. Indeed, **He** is All-Wise, All-Knowing.

140. Certainly, are lost those who killed their children in foolishness without knowledge and forbid what Allah has provided them, inventing (lies) against Allah.

Surah 6: The cattle (v. 137-140)

Certainly, they have gone astray and they are not guided.

141. And **He** is the **One Who** produces gardens, trellised and untrellised, and the date-palm and the crops of diverse taste, and olives and pomegranates, similar and dissimilar. Eat of its fruit when it bears fruit and give its due on the day of its harvest. And do not be extravagant. Indeed, **He** does not love those who are extravagant.

142. And of the cattle are some for burden and some for meat. Eat of what Allah has provided you and do not follow the footsteps of Shaitaan. Indeed, he is your open enemy.

143. Eight pairs - of the sheep two and of the goats two. Say, "Is it the two males **He** has forbidden or the two females or that which the wombs of the two females contain? Inform me with knowledge, if you are truthful."

144. And of the camels two and of the cows two. Say, "Is it the two males **He** has forbidden or the two females or that which the wombs

Surah 6: The cattle (v. 141-144)

of the two females contain? Or were you witnesses when Allah enjoined you with this? Then who is more unjust than one who invents a lie against Allah to mislead the people without knowledge? Indeed, Allah does not like the wrongdoing people."

145. Say, "I do not find in what has been revealed to me (anything) forbidden to anyone who would eat it except that it be dead or blood poured forth or the flesh of swine - for indeed, it is filth - or it be (slaughtered in) disobedience, dedicated to other than Allah. But whoever is compelled (by necessity) neither desiring (it) nor transgressing (its limit), then indeed, your Lord is Oft-Forgiving, Most Merciful."

146. And to those who are Jews We forbade every (animal) with claws, and of the cows and the sheep We forbade to them their fat except what adheres to their backs or their entrails or what is joined with the bone. That is their recompense for their rebellion. And indeed, We are truthful.

147. But if they deny you, then say, "Your Lord is the Possessor of Vast Mercy, but His wrath will not be repelled from the people who are criminals."

148. Those who associate partners (with Allah) will say, "If Allah had willed, we would not have associated partners (with Allah) and neither would our forefathers, nor we would have forbidden anything." Likewise had denied those before them until they tasted **Our** wrath. Say, "Do you have any knowledge, then produce it for us? You follow nothing except assumption, and you do nothing but guess."

149. Say, "With Allah is the conclusive argument. Then if **He** had willed, surely **He** would have guided you all."

150. Say, "Bring forward your witnesses who will testify that Allah has prohibited this." Then if they testify, then do not testify with them. And do not follow the desires of those who deny **Our** Signs and those who do not believe in the Hereafter, while they set up equals with their Lord.

151. Say, "Come, I will recite what your Lord has prohibited to you. (**He** commands) that do not associate anything with **Him**, and be good to parents;

Surah 6: The cattle (v. 148-151)

and do not kill your children for fear of poverty, **We** provide for you and for them. And do not approach immoralities whether apparent or concealed. And do not kill the soul, which Allah has forbidden except by (legal) right. This **He** has enjoined on you so that you may use reason."

152. And do not approach the orphan's wealth except in a way that is best until he reaches maturity. And give full measure and weight in justice. **We** do not burden any soul except to its capacity. And when you speak then be just, even if (it concerns) a near relative. And fulfil the Covenant of Allah. This **He** has enjoined on you so that you may remember.

153. And this is **My** straight path, so follow it. And do not follow other paths, lest they will separate you from **His** path. This **He** has enjoined on you, so that you may become righteous.

154. Moreover, **We** gave Musa the Book, completing (**Our** Favor) on the one who did good and an explanation of everything and a guidance and mercy, so that they may

Surah 6: The cattle (v. 152-154)　　　　Part - 8

155. And this is a blessed Book which **We** have revealed, so follow it and fear Allah so that you may receive mercy.

156. (**We** revealed it) lest you say, "The Book was only revealed to the two groups before us, and indeed we were unaware about their study."

157. Or lest you say, "If only the Book had been revealed to us, surely, we would have been better guided than them. So there has come to you clear proofs from your Lord and a Guidance and Mercy. Then who is more unjust than one who denies the Verses of Allah and turns away from them? **We** will recompense those who turn away from **Our** Verses with an evil punishment because they used to turn away.

158. Are they waiting to see if the Angels come to them or your Lord comes to them or some of the Signs of your Lord come to them? On the Day when some of the Signs of your Lord will come, no soul will benefit from its faith if it had not believed before or had earned through its faith some good. Say, "Wait. Indeed, we too are waiting."

Surah 6: The cattle (v. 155-158)

159. Indeed, those who divide their religion and become sects, you (O Muhammad SAWS!) are not (associated) with them in anything. Their affair is only with Allah, then He will inform them about what they used to do.

160. Whoever comes with a good deed will have ten times the like of it. And whoever comes with an evil deed will not be recompensed except the like of it, and they will not be wronged.

161. Say, "Indeed as for me, my Lord has guided me to a straight path - a right religion - the religion of Ibrahim, a true monotheist. And he was not of those who associated partners with Allah.

162. Say, "Indeed my prayer, my rites of sacrifice, my living and my dying are for Allah, Lord of the worlds.

163. He has no partner; and this I have been commanded. And I am the first of those who surrender to Him.

164. Say, "Is it other than Allah I should seek as a Lord, while He is the Lord of everything?" And no soul earns (evil) except against itself, and no bearer of burden will bear the burden of another. Then to your Lord is your return, then He will inform you about what you used to differ.

Surah 6: The cattle (v. 159-164) Part - 8

165. And **He** is the **One Who** has made you successors of the earth and has raised some of you above others in ranks so that **He** may test you in what **He** has given you. Indeed, your Lord is swift in punishing; and certainly, **He** is Oft-Forgiving, Most Merciful.

In the name of Allah, the Most Gracious, the Most Merciful.

1. *Alif Laam Meem Saad.*

2. (This is) a Book revealed to you, so let there not be in your breast an uneasiness therewith, that you warn with it, and (it is) a reminder for the believers.

3. Follow what has been revealed to you from your Lord, and do not follow besides **Him** any allies. Little is what you remember.

4. And how many of a city **We** destroyed, and **Our** punishment came to it at night or while they were sleeping at noon.

5. Then not was their plea when **Our** punishment came to them except that they said, "Indeed, we were wrongdoers."

6. Then **We** will question those to whom (**Our** Messengers) were sent,

Surah 6: The cattle (v. 165); Surah 7: The heights (v. 1-6) Part - 8

7. Then **We** will surely narrate to them with knowledge, and **We** were not absent.

8. And the weighing on that Day will be the true (weighing). So as for those whose scales (of good deeds) will be heavy, they will be the successful ones.

9. And as for those whose scales (of good deeds) will be light, they are the ones who will lose themselves because they were doing injustice to **Our** Verses.

10. And **We** have certainly established you on the earth and **We** have made for you therein (ways of) livelihood. Little are you grateful for.

11. And **We** have certainly created you and **We** fashioned you. Then **We** said to the Angels, "Prostrate to Adam," so they prostrated, except Iblees. He was not of those who prostrated.

12. (Allah) said, "What prevented you from prostrating when I commanded you?" (Shaitaan) said, "I am better than him. You created me from fire and You created him from clay."

13. (Allah) said, "Then go down from it, for it is not for you to be arrogant therein. So get out; indeed, you are of the disgraced."

14. (Shaitaan) said, "Give me respite till the Day they are raised up."

15. (Allah) said, "Indeed you are of those given respite."

16. (Shaitaan) said, "Because You have sent me astray, I will surely sit (in wait) for them on Your straight path.

17. Then I will come to them from before them and from behind them and from their right and from their left, and You will not find most of them grateful."

18. (Allah) said, "Get out from it, disgraced and expelled. Whoever follows you among them, surely, I will fill Hell with all of you.

19. And O Adam! Dwell, you and your wife, in Paradise and eat from wherever you wish but do not approach this tree, lest you be among the wrongdoers."

20. Then Shaitaan whispered to them to make apparent to them that which was concealed to them of their shame. And he said, "Your Lord only forbade you this tree, lest you become Angels or become of the immortals."

21. And he swore to them, "Indeed, I am

Surah 7: The heights (v. 14-21)

22. So he made them fall by deception. Then when they tasted the tree, their shame became apparent to them, and they began to fasten over themselves the leaves of Paradise. And their Lord called out to them, "Did I not forbid you from this tree and tell you that Shaitaan is your open enemy?"

23. Both of them said, "Our Lord, we have wronged ourselves, and if **You** do not forgive us and have mercy on us, we will surely be among the losers."

24. (Allah) said, "Get down as enemies to one another. And for you on the earth is a dwelling place and livelihood for a time."

25. He said, "Therein you will live and therein you will die and from it you will be brought forth."

26. O Children of Adam! **We** have bestowed upon you clothing to cover your shame and as an adornment. And the clothing of righteousness - that is the best. That is from the Signs of Allah so that they may remember.

27. O Children of Adam! Let not Shaitaan tempt you as he drove out

Surah 7: The heights (v. 22-27)   Part - 8

your parents from Paradise, stripping them of their clothing to show them their shame. Indeed, he sees you, he and his tribe, from where you do not see them. Indeed, **We** have made the devils friends of those who do not believe.

28. And when they commit immorality they say, "We found our forefathers doing it, and Allah has ordered us to do it." Say, "Indeed, Allah does not order immorality. Do you say about Allah what you do not know?"

29. Say, "My Lord has ordered justice, and that you set your faces at every masjid and invoke **Him** being sincere to **Him** in religion. Just as **He** originated you, so will you return."

30. A group **He** guided and a group deserved to be in error. Indeed, they take the devils as allies besides Allah while they think that they are guided.

31. O Children of Adam! Take your adornment at every masjid, and eat and drink, but do not be extravagant. Indeed, **He** does not love those who are extravagant.

32. Say, "Who has forbidden the adornment

Surah 7: The heights (v. 28-32)   Part - 8

of	and the pure things	for His slaves,	He has brought forth	which	(from) Allah		
the life	during	believe	(are) for those who	"They	Say,	sustenance?"	
We explain	Thus	(of) Resurrection.	(on the) Day	exclusively (for them)	(of) the world,		
(had) forbidden	"Only	Say,	32	who know."	for (the) people	the Signs	
is concealed,	and what	of it	(is) apparent	what	the shameful deeds	my Lord	
you associate (others)	and that	[the] right,	without	and the oppression	and the sin,		
and that	any authority,	of it	He (has) sent down	not	what	with Allah	
And for every	33	you (do) not know."	what	Allah	about	you say	
seek to delay	(they can) not	their term,	comes	So when	(is a fixed) term.	nation	
(of) Adam!	O Children	34	seek to advance (it).	and not	an hour,		
My Verses,	to you	relating	from you	Messengers	come to you	If	
and not	on them	fear	then no	and reforms,	fears Allah,	then whoever	
Our Verses	deny	But those who	35	will grieve.	they		
(of) the Fire,	(are the) companions	those	towards them	and (are) arrogant			
(is) more unjust	Then who	36	will abide forever.	in it	they		

from Allah which **He** has produced for **His** slaves, and the pure things of sustenance?" Say, "They are for those who believe during the life of this world, (and) exclusively for them on the Day of Resurrection. Thus **We** explain the Signs for a people who know."

33. Say, "My Lord has only forbidden shameful deeds - what is apparent of them and what is concealed - and sin and oppression without right, and that you associate with Allah that for which **He** has not sent down any authority, and that you say about Allah what you do not know."

34. And for every nation is a fixed term. So when their term comes, they will not be able to delay it by an hour nor advance it.

35. O Children of Adam! If there come to you Messengers from among you relating to you **My** Verses, then whoever fears Allah, and reforms, then there will be no fear on them nor will they grieve.

36. But those who deny **Our** Verses and are arrogant towards them, those are the companions of the Fire, they will abide in it forever.

37. Then who is more unjust

Surah 7: The heights (v. 33-37)

than one who invents a lie against Allah or denies **His** Verses? Those will attain their portion from the Book (of decrees), until when **Our** messengers (Angels) come to them to take them in death, they will say, "Where are those whom you used to invoke besides Allah?" They will say, "They have strayed from us," and they will testify against themselves that they were disbelievers.

38. **He** will say, "Enter into the Fire among nations which had passed away before you of jinn and men." Every time a nation enters, it curses its sister nation, until when they have all overtaken one another therein, the last of them will say about the first of them, "Our Lord! These had misled us, so give them double punishment of the Fire." **He** will say, "For each is a double (punishment), but you do not know."

39. And the first of them will say to the last of them, "Then you do not have any superiority over us, so taste the punishment for what you used to earn."

40. Indeed, those who deny **Our** Verses and are arrogant towards them,

Surah 7: The heights (v. 38-40) Part - 8

the doors of heaven will not be opened for them, nor will they enter Paradise until a camel passes through the eye of a needle. And thus **We** recompense the criminals.

41. They will have a bed from Hell and over them will be coverings (of Fire). And thus **We** recompense the wrongdoers.

42. But those who believe and do righteous deeds - **We** do not burden any soul except to its capacity. Those are the companions of Paradise, they will abide in it forever.

43. And **We** will remove whatever malice is within their breasts. Rivers flow beneath them. And they will say, "All the praise is for Allah, the **One Who** guided us to this, and we would not have received guidance if Allah would not have guided us. Certainly, the Messengers of our Lord had come with the truth." And they will be addressed, "This is Paradise, which you have been made to inherit for what you used to do."

44. And the companions of Paradise will call out to the companions of the Fire, "Indeed, we have found what our Lord promised us to be true. So have you found what

your Lord promised to be true?" They will say, "Yes." Then an announcer will announce among them, "The curse of Allah is on the wrongdoers,

45. Those who hinder (people) from the way of Allah and seek crookedness in it while they are, concerning the Hereafter, disbelievers.

46. And between them will be a partition, and on the heights will be men recognizing all by their marks. And they will call out to the companions of Paradise, "Peace be upon you." They have not (yet) entered it, but they hope (to enter it).

47. And when their eyes will be turned towards the companions of the Fire, they will say, "Our Lord! Do not place us with the wrongdoing people."

48. And the companions of the heights will call men whom they recognize by their marks, saying, "Your gathering (of wealth) and your arrogance has not availed you."

49. Are these the ones about whom you swore that Allah will not grant them Mercy? It will be said, "Enter Paradise. You will have no fear nor will you grieve."

50. And the companions of the Fire will call out to the companions

Surah 7: The heights (v. 45-50) Part - 8

اَوْ	الْمَآءِ	مِنْ	عَلَيْنَا	اَفِيْضُوْا	اَنْ		الْجَنَّةِ
or	(some) water	[of]	upon us	"Pour	[that],		(of) Paradise
اللّٰهَ	اِنَّ	قَالُوْا		رَزَقَكُمُ اللّٰهُ			مِمَّا
Allah	"Indeed,	They (will) say,		Allah has provided you."			of what
اتَّخَذُوا	الَّذِيْنَ	۵۰		الْكٰفِرِيْنَ	عَلَى		حَرَّمَهُمَا
took	Those who	50		the disbelievers,	to		has forbidden both
الدُّنْيَا	الْحَيٰوةُ		وَغَرَّتْهُمُ	وَّلَعِبًا	لَهْوًا		دِيْنَهُمْ
(of) the world."	the life		and deluded them	and play	(as) an amusement		their religion
يَوْمِهِمْ هٰذَا		لِقَآءَ	نَسُوْا	كَمَا	نَنْسٰىهُمْ		فَالْيَوْمَ
(of) this Day of theirs,		(the) meeting	they forgot	as	We forget them		So today
وَلَقَدْ		۵۱	بِاٰيٰتِنَا يَجْحَدُوْنَ		كَانُوْا		وَمَا
And certainly		51	reject Our Verses.		(as) they used to		and [what]
عِلْمٍ	عَلٰى		فَصَّلْنٰهُ		بِكِتٰبٍ		جِئْنٰهُمْ
knowledge -	with		which We have explained		a Book		We had brought (to) them
يَنْظُرُوْنَ	هَلْ	۵۲	يُؤْمِنُوْنَ		لِّقَوْمٍ	وَّرَحْمَةً	هُدًى
they wait	Do	52	who believe.		for a people	and mercy	a guidance
الَّذِيْنَ	يَقُوْلُ	تَاْوِيْلَهٗ	يَاْتِيْ		يَوْمَ		اِلَّا
those who	will say	its fulfillment,	(will) come		(The) Day	(for) its fulfillment	except
رَبِّنَا		رُسُلُ	جَآءَتْ	قَدْ	مِنْ قَبْلُ		نَسُوْهُ
(of) our Lord		(the) Messengers	had come	"Verily,	before,		had forgotten it
فَيَشْفَعُوْا		شُفَعَآءَ	مِنْ	لَّنَا	فَهَلْ		بِالْحَقِّ
so (that) they intercede		intercessors	any	for us	so are (there)		with the truth,
الَّذِيْ	غَيْرَ		نَعْمَلَ		نُرَدُّ	اَوْ	لَنَا
that which	other than		so (that) we do (deeds)		we are sent back	or	for us
عَنْهُمْ	وَضَلَّ	اَنْفُسَهُمْ		خَسِرُوْا	قَدْ	نَعْمَلُ	كُنَّا
from them	and strayed	themselves,		they lost	Verily,	do."	we used to
اللّٰهَ		رَبَّكُمُ	اِنَّ	۵۳	يَفْتَرُوْنَ	كَانُوْا	مَا
(is) Allah,		your Lord	Indeed,	53	invent.	they used to	what
اَيَّامٍ	سِتَّةِ	فِيْ		وَالْاَرْضَ	السَّمٰوٰتِ	خَلَقَ	الَّذِيْ
epochs,	six	in		and the earth	the heavens	created	the One Who

Surah 7: The heights (v. 51-54)

of Paradise, "Pour upon us some water or some of what Allah has provided you." They will say, "Allah has forbidden both to the disbelievers,

51. Those who took their religion as an amusement and play and who were deluded by the life of this world." So today **We** forget them just as they forgot the meeting of this Day of theirs and because they used to reject **Our** Verses.

52. And certainly **We** had brought to them a Book which **We** have explained with knowledge - a guidance and mercy for people who believe.

53. Do they await except for its fulfillment? The Day when it is fulfilled, those who had forgotten it before will say, "Verily, the Messengers of our Lord had come with the truth, so are their any intercessors to intercede for us or could we be sent back to do (deeds) other than what we used to do." Verily, they have lost themselves, and has strayed from them what they used to invent.

54. Indeed, your Lord is Allah, the **One Who** created the heavens and the earth in six epochs

and then **He** ascended on the Throne. **He** covers the night with the day chasing it rapidly; and the sun, and the moon and the stars are subjected to **His** command. Unquestionably, **His** is the creation and the command; blessed is Allah, Lord of the worlds.

55. Call upon your Lord humbly and privately. Indeed, **He** does not love the transgressors.

56. And do not cause corruption in the earth after its reformation. And call **Him** in fear and hope. Indeed, the Mercy of Allah is near for the good-doers.

57. And **He** is the One Who sends the winds as glad tidings before **His** Mercy (i.e., rainfall) until, when they have carried heavy clouds, **We** drive them to a dead land and **We** send down rain therein and **We** bring forth from it all kinds of fruits. Thus **We** will raise the dead so that you may take heed.

58. And the pure land - its vegetation comes forth by the permission of its Lord, but that which is bad nothing comes forth from it except with difficulty. Thus **We** explain the Signs for a people who are grateful.

59. **We** had certainly sent Nuh to his people, and he said,

Surah 7: The heights (v. 55-59)

اِلٰهٍ	مِّنْ	لَكُمْ	مَا	اللّٰهَ	اعْبُدُوا	يٰقَوْمِ	
god	any	for you	not	Allah,	Worship	"O my people!	
عَظِيْمٍ	يَوْمٍ	عَذَابَ	عَلَيْكُمْ	اَخَافُ	اِنِّىْٓ	غَيْرُهٗ ۗ	
Great."	(of the) Day	punishment	for you	[I] fear	Indeed, I	other than Him.	
لَنَرٰىكَ	اِنَّا	قَوْمِهٖٓ	مِنْ	الْمَلَاُ	قَالَ		59
surely see you	"Indeed, we	his people,	of	the chiefs	Said		59
لَيْسَ	يٰقَوْمِ	قَالَ		مُّبِيْنٍ	ضَلٰلٍ	فِيْ	
(There is) no	"O my people!	He said,	60	clear error."		in	
الْعٰلَمِيْنَ	رَّبِّ	مِّنْ	رَسُوْلٌ	وَلٰكِنِّيْ	ضَلٰلَةٌ	بِيْ	
(of) the worlds.	(the) Lord	from	a Messenger	but I am	error in me,		
لَكُمْ	وَاَنْصَحُ	رَبِّيْ	رِسٰلٰتِ	اُبَلِّغُكُمْ			61
[to] you,	and [I] advise	(of) my Lord	the Messages	I convey to you			61
	تَعْلَمُوْنَ	لَا	مَا	اللّٰهِ	مِنَ	وَاَعْلَمُ	62
	you (do) not know.		what	Allah	from	and I know	62
اَوَ	مِّنْ	ذِكْرٌ	جَآءَكُمْ	اَنْ	عَجِبْتُمْ	رَّبِّكُمْ	
Do		a reminder	has come to you	that	you wonder	your Lord	
وَلِتَتَّقُوْا	لِيُنْذِرَكُمْ	مِّنْكُمْ	رَجُلٍ	عَلٰى			
and that you may fear,	that he may warn you	among you,	a man	on			
فَاَنْجَيْنٰهُ	فَكَذَّبُوْهُ		تُرْحَمُوْنَ	وَلَعَلَّكُمْ			
so We saved him	But they denied him,	63	receive mercy."	and so that you may			
كَذَّبُوْا	الَّذِيْنَ	وَاَغْرَقْنَا	الْفُلْكِ	فِى	مَعَهٗ	وَالَّذِيْنَ	
denied	those who	And We drowned	the ship.	in	(were) with him	and those who	
وَاِلٰى		عَمِيْنَ	قَوْمًا	كَانُوْا	اِنَّهُمْ	بِاٰيٰتِنَا ۗ	
And to	64	blind.	a people	were	Indeed, they	Our Verses.	
عَادٍ	اَخَاهُمْ	هُوْدًا ۗ	قَالَ	يٰقَوْمِ	اعْبُدُوا	اللّٰهَ	
Aad	(We sent) their brother	Hud.	He said,	"O my people!	Worship	Allah,	
تَتَّقُوْنَ	اَفَلَا	غَيْرُهٗ ۗ	اِلٰهٍ	مِّنْ	لَكُمْ	مَا	
you fear (Allah)?"	Then will not	other than Him.	god	any	for you	not	
اِنَّا	قَوْمِهٖ	مِنْ	كَفَرُوْا	الَّذِيْنَ	الْمَلَاُ	قَالَ	65
"Indeed, we	his people,	from	disbelieved	(of) those who	the chiefs	Said	65

"O my people! Worship Allah, you have no god except **Him**. Indeed, I fear for you the punishment of a Great Day."

60. The chiefs of his people said, "Indeed we see you in clear error."

61. He said, "O my people! There is no error on my part, but I am a Messenger from the Lord of the worlds.

62. I convey to you the Messages of my Lord and I advise you, and I know from Allah what you do not know.

63. Do you wonder that there has come to you a reminder from your Lord on a man from among you, that he may warn you and that you may fear (Allah) so that you may receive mercy."

64. But they denied him, so **We** saved him and those who were with him in the ship. And **We** drowned those who denied **Our** Verses. Indeed, they were a blind people.

65. And to Aad **We** sent their brother Hud. He said, "O my people! Worship Allah, you have no god except **Him**. Then will you not fear Allah?"

66. The chiefs of those who disbelieved among his people said, "Indeed, we

see you in foolishness, and indeed, we think you are of the liars."

67. He said, "O my people! There is no foolishness in me but I am a Messenger from the Lord of the worlds.

68. I convey to you the Messages of my Lord and I am a trustworthy adviser to you.

69. Do you wonder that a reminder has come to you from your Lord on a man from among you, that he may warn you? And remember when He made you successors after the people of Nuh and increased you in stature extensively. So remember the Bounties of Allah so that you may succeed."

70. They said, "Have you come to us that we should worship Allah Alone and forsake what our forefathers used to worship? Then bring to us what you promise us, if you are truthful."

71. He said, "Verily, punishment and anger have fallen upon you from your Lord. Do you dispute with me concerning names which you and your forefathers have devised, for which Allah has not sent down any authority? Then wait, indeed, I am with you among those who wait."

72. So We saved him

Surah 7: The heights (v. 67-72)   Part - 8

and those with him by Mercy from **Us**. And **We** eliminated those who denied **Our** Signs, and they were not believers.

73. And to Thamud (**We** sent) their brother Salih. He said, "O my people! Worship Allah, you have no god other than **Him**. Verily, there has come to you a clear proof from your Lord. This she-camel of Allah is a Sign for you. So leave her to graze on Allah's earth and do not touch her with harm, lest a painful punishment seizes you."

74. And remember when **He** made you successors after Aad, and settled you in the earth, you take for yourselves palaces from its plains and carve from the mountains, homes. So remember the Bounties of Allah and do not act wickedly on the earth spreading corruption.

75. Said the chiefs of those who were arrogant among his people to those who were oppressed - those who believed among them, "Do you know that Salih is the one sent from his Lord?" They said, "Indeed we, in what he has been sent with, are believers."

Surah 7: The heights (v. 73-75)   Part - 8

76. Those who were arrogant said, "Indeed we, in what you believe, are disbelievers."

77. Then they hamstrung the she-camel and were insolent towards the command of their Lord and they said, "O Salih! Bring us what you promise us, if you are of the Messengers."

78. So the earthquake seized them, then they became in their homes fallen prone (dead).

79. So he turned away from them and said, "O my people! Verily, I have conveyed to you the Message of my Lord and advised you, but you do not like the advisers."

80. And when Lut said to his people, "Do you commit such immorality which no one preceding you has committed in the worlds?

81. Indeed, you approach men lustfully instead of women. Nay, you are a people who commit excesses."

82. And the answer of his people was nothing except that they said, "Evict them from your town. Indeed, they are people who keep themselves pure."

83. So **We** saved him and his family except his wife,

Surah 7: The heights (v. 76-83) Part - 8

83. And she was of those who stayed behind.

84. And We showered upon them a rain (of stones). So see how was the end of the criminals.

85. And to Madyan (We sent) his brother Shuaib. He said, "O my people! Worship Allah, you have no god other than Him. Verily, there has come to you clear proof from your Lord. So give full measure and weight and do not deprive people of their dues and do not cause corruption in the earth after its reformation. That is better for you if you are believers.

86. And do not sit on every path threatening and hindering people from the way of Allah, those who believe in Him, seeking to make it crooked. And remember when you were few then He increased you. And see how was the end of the corrupters.

87. And if there is a group among you who has believed in that which I have been sent with and a group that has not believed, then be patient until Allah judges between us. And He is the Best of Judges."

Surah 7: The heights (v. 84-87) — Part - 8

88. The chiefs of his people who were arrogant said, "O Shuaib! We will surely drive you out and those who have believed with you from our city, or you must return to our religion." He said, "Even if we hate it?

89. Verily we would have fabricated a lie against Allah if we returned to your religion after Allah had saved us from it. And it is not for us that we return to it except that Allah, our Lord, wills. Our Lord encompasses everything in knowledge. Upon Allah we put our trust. Our Lord! Decide between us and our people in truth, and You are the Best of those who Decide."

90. The chiefs of those who disbelieved from his people said, "If you follow Shuaib, then certainly you will be losers."

91. So the earthquake seized them, then they became fallen prone (i.e., dead) in their homes.

92. Those who denied Shuaib became as though they had never lived there. Those who denied Shuaib, they were the losers.

93. So he turned away from them and said, "O my people! Verily, I have conveyed to you the Messages

Surah 7: The heights (v. 88-93)

of my Lord and advised you. So how could I grieve for the disbelieving people?"

194. And We did not send to a city any Prophet except that We seized its people with adversity and hardship so that they may become humble.

95. Then We exchanged in place of the bad (condition), good, until they increased and said, "Verily, our forefathers were touched with adversity and ease." So We seized them suddenly, while they did not perceive.

96. And if only the people of the cities had believed and feared Allah, We would have opened upon them blessings from the heaven and the earth, but they denied. So We seized them for what they used to earn.

97. Then did the people of the cities feel secure from Our punishment coming to them at night while they were asleep?

98. Or did the people of the cities feel secure from Our punishment coming to them in daylight while they were at play?

99. Then do they feel secure against the plan of Allah? But no one feels secure from the plan of Allah except the people who are losers.

100. Would it not guide those who inherit the land after

Surah 7: The heights (v. 94-100)   Part - 9

its people that if **We** willed, **We** could afflict them for their sins and put a seal over their hearts so they do not hear?

101. These cities - **We** relate to you some of their news. And certainly their Messengers came to them with clear proofs, but they would not believe in what they had denied before. Thus Allah put a seal on the hearts of the disbelievers.

102. And **We** did not find for most of them (loyalty to) any covenant. But certainly, **We** found most of them defiantly disobedient.

103. Then **We** sent after them Musa with **Our** Signs to Firaun and his chiefs, but they were unjust towards them. So see how was the end of the corrupters.

104. And Musa said, "O Firaun! Indeed, I am a Messenger from the Lord of the worlds

105. Obligated not to say about Allah anything except the truth. Verily, I have come to you with a clear Sign from your Lord, so send with me the Children of Israel."

106. He (Firaun) said, "If you have come with a Sign, then bring it, if you are truthful."

107. So he (Musa) threw his staff, and suddenly it was a serpent, manifest.

108. And he drew out his hand

Surah 7: The heights (v. 101-108)

and suddenly it was white for the observers.

109. The chiefs of the people of Firaun said, "Indeed, this is a learned magician.

110. He wants to drive you out from your land, so what do you instruct?"

111. They said, "Postpone his (matter) and his brother's and send in the cities gatherers.

112. They will bring to you every learned magician."

113. So the magicians came to Firaun. They said, "Indeed, there will be a reward for us if we are the victors."

114. He said, "Yes, and surely you will be of those near (to me)."

115. They said, "O Musa! Whether you throw or we will be the ones to throw."

116. He said, "Throw." Then when they threw, they bewitched the eyes of the people and terrified them, and they came up with a great magic.

117. And We inspired to Musa, "Throw your staff," and suddenly it swallowed what they were falsifying.

118. So the truth was established, and what they used to do became futile.

119. So they were defeated there and returned humiliated.

120. And the magicians fell down prostrate.

121. They said,

Surah 7: The heights (v. 109-121)   Part - 9

"We believe in the Lord of the worlds

122. Lord of Musa and Harun."

123. Firaun said, "You believed in him before I gave you permission. Indeed, this is a plot you have plotted in the city to drive out its people from it. But soon you will know.

124. I will surely cut off your hands and your feet of the opposite side. Then I will surely crucify you all."

125. They said, "Indeed, to our Lord we will return.

126. And you do not take revenge on us except because we have believed in the Signs of our Lord when they came to us, "Our Lord! Pour upon us patience and cause us to die as Muslims."

127. And the chiefs of the people of Firaun said, "Will you leave Musa and his people to cause corruption in the land and forsake you and your gods?" He said, "We will kill their sons and we will let live their women, and indeed, we are subjugators over them."

128. Musa said to his people, "Seek help from Allah and be patient. Indeed, the earth belongs to Allah. He causes to inherit it whom He wills of His servants. And the end is (best) for those who are righteous."

Surah 7: The heights (v. 122-128)

129. They said, "We have been harmed before you came to us and after you have come to us." He said, "Perhaps your Lord will destroy your enemy and make you successors in the earth, and see how you will do."

130. And certainly, **We** seized the people of Firaun with years (of famine) and a deficit of fruits so that they may receive admonition.

131. But when good came to them, they said, "This is for us." And if a bad (condition) afflicted them, they ascribed evil omens to Musa and those with him. Behold! Their evil omens are only with Allah but most of them do not know.

132. And they said, "Whatever sign you bring to bewitch us therewith, we will not believe in you."

133. So **We** sent on them the flood, locusts, lice, frogs and blood as manifest signs, but they showed arrogance and were a criminal people.

134. And when the punishment fell on them, they said, "O Musa! Invoke your Lord for us by what **He** has promised you. If you remove the punishment from us,

Surah 7: The heights (v. 129-134) Part - 9

135. But when We removed the punishment from them for a fixed term which they were to reach, then, they broke the word.

136. So We took retribution from them and We drowned them in the sea because they denied Our Signs, and they were heedless of them.

137. And We made inheritors, the people who were considered weak, of the eastern parts of the land and the western parts, which We blessed. And the best word of your Lord was fulfilled for the Children of Israel because they were patient. And We destroyed what Firaun and his people used to make and what they used to erect.

138. And We led the Children of Israel across the sea. Then they came upon a people devoted to idols they had. They said, "O Musa! Make for us a god just as they have gods. He said, "Indeed, you are an ignorant people.

139. Indeed, these (people) - destroyed is that in which they are (engaged) and vain is what they used to do."

140. He said, "Should

Surah 7: The heights (v. 135-140)

141. And when **We** saved you from the people of Firaun who were afflicting you with the worst torment, killing your sons and letting live your women. And in that was a great trial from your Lord.

142. And **We** appointed for Musa thirty nights and **We** completed them with ten more, so the set term of forty nights by his Lord was completed. And Musa said to his brother Harun, "Take my place among my people, do right, and do not follow the way of the corrupters."

143. And when Musa came to **Our** appointed place and his Lord spoke to him, he said, "O my Lord show me **Yourself** that I may look at **You**." He said, "You cannot see **Me**, but look at the mountain; if it remains in its place, then you will see **Me**." But when his Lord revealed **His** Glory on the mountain, **He** made it crumbled to dust and Musa fell down unconscious. And when he recovered, he said, "Glory be to **You**! I turn to **You** in repentance, and I am the first of the believers."

144. **He** said, "O Musa! Indeed, **I** have chosen you over

Surah 7: The heights (v. 141-144) — Part - 9

the people with **My** Messages and with **My** words. So take what **I** have given you and be among the grateful."

145. And **We** ordained (laws) for him on the tablets regarding everything, an instruction and explanation for everything, "So take them with firmness and order your people to take the best of it. **I** will show you the home of the defiantly disobedient."

146. **I** will turn away from **My** Signs those who are arrogant on the earth without right; and even if they see every sign, they will not believe in it. And if they see the way of righteousness, they will not adopt it as a way, and if they see the way of error, they will adopt it as a way. That is because they denied **Our** Signs and they were heedless of them.

147. Those who denied **Our** Signs and the meeting of the Hereafter, worthless are their deeds. Will they be recompensed except for what they used to do?

148. And the people of Musa made, after his (departure), from their ornaments an image of a calf, which gave a lowing sound. Did they not see that it

Surah 7: The heights (v. 145-148)

149. And when they were regretful and they saw that they had indeed gone astray, they said, "If our Lord does not have Mercy on us and forgive us, we will surely be among the losers."

150. And when Musa returned to his people, angry and grieved, he said, "Evil is what you have done in my place after (I left you). Were you impatient over the matter of your Lord?" And he cast down the tablets and seized his brother by his head dragging him towards himself. He (Harun) said, "O son of my mother! Indeed, the people considered me weak and were about to kill me. So let not the enemies rejoice over me and do not place me among the wrongdoing people."

151. He (Musa) said, "O my Lord! Forgive me and my brother and admit us into **Your** Mercy, for **You** are the Most Merciful of the merciful."

152. Indeed, those who took the calf (for worship) - will reach them the wrath from their Lord and humiliation in the life of this world. And thus **We** recompense the inventors (of falsehood).

153. And those who do

Surah 7: The heights (v. 149-153) Part - 9

evil deeds and repent after that and believe, indeed, after that your Lord is Oft-Forgiving, Most Merciful.

154. And when the anger of Musa calmed down, he took up the tablets, and in their inscription was guidance and mercy for those who are fearful of their Lord.

155. And Musa chose from his people seventy men for Our appointment. Then when the earthquake seized them, he said, "O my Lord! If You had willed, You could have destroyed them before and me (as well). Would You destroy us for what the foolish among us have done? This is not but Your trial by which You let go astray whom You will and guide whom You will. You are our Protector, so forgive us and have mercy upon us, and You are the Best of Forgivers.

156. And ordain for us good in this world and (also) in the Hereafter. Indeed, we have turned to You." He said, "I afflict with My punishment whom I will, but My Mercy encompasses all things. So I will ordain it for those who are righteous and give *zakah* and those who believe in Our Verses.

157. Those who follow the Messenger,

the unlettered Prophet, whom they find written in what they have - the Taurat and the Injeel. He commands them to that which is right and forbids them from that which is wrong and makes lawful for them the pure things and makes unlawful for them the impure things and relieves them of their burden and the fetters which were upon them. So those who believe in him, honor him, and help him and follow the light, which has been sent down with him, those are the successful ones."

158. Say, "O mankind! Indeed I am the Messenger of Allah to you all - to Whom belongs the dominion of the heavens and the earth. There is no god except Him, He gives life and causes death. So believe in Allah and His Messenger, the unlettered Prophet, who believes in Allah and His Words, and follow him so that you may be guided."

159. And among the people of Musa is a community which guides by truth and by it establishes justice.

160. And We divided them into twelve tribes as communities. And We inspired to Musa when his people asked him for water,

Surah 7: The heights (v. 158-160)   Part - 9

"Strike the stone with your staff." Then gushed forth from it twelve springs. Certainly, every tribe knew its drinking place. And **We** shaded them with clouds, and **We** sent down upon them *manna* and quails. "Eat of the good things which **We** have provided you." And they did not wrong **Us** but they were (only) wronging themselves.

161. And when it was said to them, "Live in this city and eat from it wherever you wish and say, 'Repentance,' and enter the gate prostrating, **We** will forgive for you your sins. **We** will increase the (reward) for the good-doers."

162. But those who wronged among them changed the word to other than that which was said to them. So **We** sent upon them torment from the sky because they were doing wrong.

163. And ask them about the town which was by the sea, when they transgressed in the (matter of) Sabbath, when their fish came to them visibly on the day of their Sabbath and the day they had no Sabbath they did not come to them. Thus **We** tested them because they were

Surah 7: The heights (v. 161-164)

مِّنْهُم	أُمَّةٌ	قَالَتْ	وَإِذْ	۱۶۳	يَفْسُقُونَ	
among them,	a community	said	And when	163	defiantly disobeying.	
أَوْ	مُهْلِكُهُمْ	اللَّهُ	قَوْمًا	لِمَ	تَعِظُونَ	
or	(is going to) destroy them	(whom) Allah	a people,	"Why	(do) you preach	
مَعْذِرَةً	قَالُوا	شَدِيدًا	عَذَابًا	مُعَذِّبُهُمْ		
"To be absolved	They said,	severe?"	(with) a punishment	punish them		
فَلَمَّا	۱۶۴	يَتَّقُونَ	وَلَعَلَّهُمْ	رَبِّكُمْ	إِلَىٰ	
So when	164	become righteous."	and that they may	your Lord	before	
يَنْهَوْنَ	الَّذِينَ	أَنْجَيْنَا	بِهِ	ذُكِّرُوا	مَا	نَسُوا
forbade	those who	We saved	with [it],	they had been reminded	what	they forgot
بَئِيسٍ	بِعَذَابٍ	ظَلَمُوا	الَّذِينَ	وَأَخَذْنَا	السُّوءِ	عَنِ
wretched,	with a punishment	wronged	those who	and We seized	the evil,	[from]
عَتَوْا	فَلَمَّا	۱۶۵	يَفْسُقُونَ	كَانُوا	بِمَا	
they exceeded all bounds	So when	165	defiantly disobeying.	they were	because	
قِرَدَةً	كُونُوا	لَهُمْ	قُلْنَا	عَنْهُ	نُهُوا	مَا
apes,	"Be	to them,	We said	from it,	they were forbidden	what	about
لَيَبْعَثَنَّ	رَبُّكَ	تَأَذَّنَ	وَإِذْ	۱۶۶	خَاسِئِينَ	
that He would surely send	your Lord	declared	And when	166	despised."	
يَسُومُهُمْ	مَن	الْقِيَامَةِ	يَوْمِ	إِلَىٰ	عَلَيْهِمْ	
would afflict them	(those) who	(of) the Resurrection	(the) Day	till	upon them	
لَسَرِيعُ	رَبَّكَ	إِنَّ	الْعَذَابِ	سُوءَ		
(is) surely swift	your Lord	Indeed,	[the] punishment.	(with) a grievous		
الْعِقَابِ	رَحِيمٌ	لَغَفُورٌ	وَإِنَّهُ			
167	Most Merciful.	(is) surely Oft-Forgiving,	but indeed, He	(in) the retribution,		
الصَّالِحُونَ	مِنْهُمُ	أُمَمًا	الْأَرْضِ	فِي	وَقَطَّعْنَاهُمْ	
(are) the righteous	Among them	(as) nations.	the earth	in	And We divided them	
بِالْحَسَنَاتِ	ذَٰلِكَ	دُونَ	وَبَلَوْنَاهُم	وَمِنْهُمْ		
with the good	that.	(are) other than	And We tested them	and among them		
مِن بَعْدِهِمْ	فَخَلَفَ	۱۶۸	يَرْجِعُونَ	لَعَلَّهُمْ	وَالسَّيِّئَاتِ	
[after] them	Then succeeded	168	return.	so that they may	and the bad,	

164. And when a community among them said, "Why do you preach a people whom Allah is going to destroy or is going to punish them with a severe punishment?" They said, "To be absolved before your Lord and that they may become righteous."

165. So when they forgot what they had been reminded with, We saved those who had forbidden evil and seized those who wronged with a wretched punishment because they were defiantly disobeying.

166. So when they exceeded all bounds about what they had been forbidden, We said to them, "Be apes, despised."

167. And when your Lord declared that He would surely send upon them until the Day of Resurrection those who would afflict them with a grievous punishment. Indeed, your Lord is swift in retribution, but indeed, He is Oft-Forgiving, Most Merciful.

168. And We divided them in the earth as nations. Among them some are righteous and some are otherwise. And We tested them with good and bad so that they may return (to obedience).

169. Then succeeded them

Surah 7: The heights (v. 164-169)

successors who inherited the Book taking the goods of this lower life (worldly life) and they say, "It will be forgiven for us." And if similar goods come to them, they will take it. Was not the Covenant of the Book taken from them that they would not say about Allah except the truth while they studied what is in it? And the home of the Hereafter is better for those who fear Allah. So will you not use your intellect?

170. And those who hold fast to the Book and establish prayer indeed, We will not let go waste the reward of the reformers.

171. And when We raised the mountain above them as if it was a canopy and they thought that it would fall upon them, (We said), "Hold firmly what We have given you and remember what is in it so that you may fear Allah."

172. And when your Lord took from the Children of Adam - from their loins - their descendents and made them testify over themselves, "Am I not your Lord?" They said, "Yes, we have testified." (This) - lest you say on the Day of Resurrection, "Indeed, we were unaware about this."

173. Or you say, "It was only that our forefathers associated partners (with Allah),

Surah 7: The heights (v. 170-173)　　　　　Part - 9

173. and we are their descendants after them. So will You destroy us for what the falsifiers did?"

174. And thus We explain the Verses so that they may return.

175. And recite to them the story of the one whom We gave Our Signs, but he detached them, so Shaitaan followed him and he became of those gone astray.

176. And if We had willed We could have raised him with these (Signs) but he adhered to the earth and followed his own vain desires. So his example is like that of the dog, if you attack him he lolls out his tongue or if you leave him he (still) lolls out his tongue. That is the example of the people who denied Our Signs. So relate the stories that they may reflect.

177. Evil as an example are the people who denied Our Signs and used to wrong themselves.

178. Whoever Allah guides, he is the guided one while whoever He lets go astray, those are the losers.

179. And certainly We have created many jinn and men for Hell. They have hearts with which they do not

Surah 7: The heights (v. 174-179) — Part - 9

understand, they have eyes with which they do not see, and they have ears with which they do not hear. Those are like cattle; nay, they are more astray. Those are the heedless.

180. And to Allah belong the most beautiful names, so invoke **Him** by them. And leave those who deviate concerning **His** name. They will be recompensed for what they used to do.

181. And among those **We** created is a nation, which guides by truth and thereby establishes justice.

182. But those who deny **Our** Signs, **We** will gradually lead them (to destruction) from where they do not know.

183. And **I** will give respite to them. Indeed, **My** plan is firm.

184. Do they not reflect? There is no madness in their companion. He is only a clear warner.

185. Do they not look in the dominion of the heavens and the earth and everything that Allah has created and that perhaps their term has come near? So in what statement after this will they believe?

186. Whoever Allah lets go astray -

Surah 7: The heights (v. 180-186)

there is no guide for him. And **He** leaves them in their transgression, wandering blindly.

186

187. They ask you about the Hour, when will be its appointed time? Say, "Its knowledge is only with my Lord. None can reveal its time except **Him**. It lays heavily upon the heavens and the earth. It will not come to you but suddenly." They ask you as if you were well informed about it. Say, "Its knowledge is only with Allah, but most of the people do not know."

188. Say, "I have no power for myself to benefit or harm, except what Allah wills. And if I had knowledge of the unseen, I could have multiplied all good and no evil would have touched me. I am not except a warner and a bearer of good tidings to a people who believe."

189. **He** is the **One Who** created you from a single soul and made from it its mate that he might live with her. And when he covers her, she carries a light burden and continues with it. But when she grows heavy, they both invoke Allah, their Lord, "If **You** give us

Surah 7: The heights (v. 187-189)   Part - 9

a righteous (child), we will surely be among the thankful."

190. But when **He** gives them a righteous (child), they ascribe partners to **Him** concerning that which **He** has given them. Exalted is Allah above what they associate with **Him**.

191. Do they associate with **Him** those who create nothing and they are (themselves) created?

192. And they are unable to (give) them any help, nor can they help themselves.

193. And if you call them to guidance, they will not follow you. It is the same for you whether you call them or you remain silent.

194. Indeed, those whom you call upon besides Allah are slaves like you. So invoke them and let them respond to you, if you are truthful.

195. Do they have feet by which they walk? Or do they have hands by which they hold? Or do they have eyes by which they see? Or do they have ears by which they hear? Say, "Call your partners and then scheme against me and give me no respite."

196. Indeed, my protector is Allah, **Who** has revealed the Book

and He protects the righteous.

197. And those whom you invoke besides **Him** are unable to help you, nor can they help themselves.

198. And if you call them to guidance, they do not hear. And you see them looking at you but they do not see.

199. Hold to forgiveness, and enjoin what is good, and turn away from the ignorant.

200. And if an evil suggestion comes to you from Shaitaan, then seek refuge in Allah. Indeed, **He** is All-Hearing, All-Knowing.

201. Indeed, those who fear Allah when an evil thought from Shaitaan touches them, they remember Allah and then they see (aright).

202. But their brothers plunge them in error, then they do not cease.

203. And when you do not bring them a Sign, they say, "Why have you not devised it?" Say, "I only follow what is revealed to me form my Lord. This (Quran) is an enlightenment from your Lord and guidance and mercy for a people who believe."

204. And when the Quran is recited, then listen to it and pay attention

Surah 7: The heights (v. 197-204)

so that you may receive mercy.

205. And remember your Lord within yourself in humility and in fear and without loudness in words in the mornings and evenings. And do not be among the heedless.

206. Indeed, those who are near your Lord do not turn away in pride from His worship, and they glorify Him, and they prostrate to Him.

In the name of Allah, the Most Gracious, the Most Merciful.

1. They ask you concerning the spoils of war. Say, "The spoils of war are for Allah and His Messenger. So fear Allah and set right that which is between you and obey Allah and His Messenger, if you are believers."

2. The believers are only those who feel fear in their hearts when Allah is mentioned, and when His Verses are recited to them, it increases them in faith, and they put their trust in their Lord.

3. Those who establish the prayer and they spend out of what We have provided them.

4. Those are the true believers. For them are ranks with their Lord and forgiveness

رَبُّكَ	أَخْرَجَكَ	كَمَآ	٤	كَرِيمٌ	وَرِزْقٌ	
your Lord	brought you out	As	4	noble.	and a provision	
الْمُؤْمِنِينَ	مِّنَ	فَرِيقًا	وَإِنَّ	بِالْحَقِّ	مِنْ بَيْتِكَ	
the believers	among	a party	while indeed,	in truth,	from your home	
مَا	بَعْدَ	الْحَقِّ	فِي	يُجَادِلُونَكَ	٥	لَكَارِهُونَ
after	what	the truth	concerning	They dispute with you	5	certainly disliked.
يَنظُرُونَ	وَهُمْ	الْمَوْتِ	إِلَى	يُسَاقُونَ	كَأَنَّمَا	تَبَيَّنَ
(were) looking.	while they	[the] death	to	they were driven	as if	was made clear,
أَنَّهَا		الطَّآئِفَتَيْنِ	إِحْدَى	اللَّهُ	يَعِدُكُمُ	وَإِذْ
that it (would be)		(of) the two groups -	one	Allah	promised you	And when
تَكُونُ	ذَاتِ الشَّوْكَةِ	غَيْرَ	أَنَّ	وَتَوَدُّونَ	لَكُمْ	
would be	the armed	(one) other than	that	and you wished	for you -	
وَيَقْطَعَ	بِكَلِمَاتِهِ	الْحَقَّ	أَن يُحِقَّ	اللَّهُ	وَيُرِيدُ	لَكُمْ
and cut off	by His words,	the truth	to justify	But Allah	intended	for you.
الْحَقَّ	لِيُحِقَّ		الْكَافِرِينَ	دَابِرَ		
the truth	That He might justify	7	(of) the disbelievers	(the) roots		
إِذْ	٨	الْمُجْرِمُونَ	كَرِهَ	وَلَوْ	الْبَاطِلَ	وَيُبْطِلَ
When	8	the criminals.	disliked (it)	even if	the falsehood,	and prove false
أَنِّي		لَكُمْ	فَاسْتَجَابَ	رَبَّكُمْ	تَسْتَغِيثُونَ	
"Indeed, I am		[to] you,	and He answered	(of) your Lord	you were seeking help	
مُرْدِفِينَ		الْمَلَائِكَةِ	مِّنَ	بِأَلْفٍ	مُمِدُّكُم	
one after another."		the Angels	of	with a thousand	going to reinforce you	
وَلِتَطْمَئِنَّ		بُشْرَىٰ	إِلَّا	جَعَلَهُ اللَّهُ	وَمَا	٩
and so that might be at rest		good tidings	but	Allah made it	And not	9
اللَّهِ	مِنْ عِندِ	إِلَّا	النَّصْرُ	وَمَا	قُلُوبُكُم	بِهِ
Allah.	from	except	[the] victory	And (there is) no	your hearts.	with it
يُغَشِّيكُمُ	إِذْ		حَكِيمٌ	عَزِيزٌ	اللَّهَ	إِنَّ
He covered you	When	10	All-Wise.	(is) All-Mighty,	Allah	Indeed,
السَّمَآءِ	مِّنَ	عَلَيْكُم	وَيُنَزِّلُ	مِّنْهُ	أَمَنَةً	النُّعَاسَ
the sky	from	upon you	and sent down	from Him,	a security	with [the] slumber,

and a noble provision.

5. Just as your Lord brought you out of your home in truth, while indeed, a party among the believers disliked.

6. They dispute with you concerning the truth after it was made clear, as if they were driven to death while they were looking on.

7. And when Allah promised you that one of the two groups would be yours - and you wished that the unarmed one would be yours. But Allah intended to justify the truth by His words and to eliminate the disbelievers

8. That He might justify the truth and prove false the falsehood, even if the criminals disliked it.

9. When you sought help of your Lord, and He answered you, "Indeed, I will reinforce you with a thousand Angels, following one another."

10. And Allah made it only as good tidings so that your hearts would be at rest thereby. And there is no victory except from Allah. Indeed, Allah is All-Mighty, All-Wise.

11. When He covered you with slumber as a security from Him and sent down upon you water from the sky

Surah 8: The spoils of war (v. 5-11)

to purify you with it and remove from you the evil (suggestions) of Shaitaan and to strengthen your hearts and make firm thereby your feet.

12. When your Lord inspired to the Angels, "I am with you, so strengthen those who believed. I will cast terror in the hearts of those who disbelieved, so strike above their necks and strike from them every fingertip."

13. That is because they opposed Allah and **His** Messenger. And whoever opposes Allah and **His** Messenger, then indeed, Allah is severe in penalty.

14. That (the penalty is yours). "So taste it." And indeed, for the disbelievers is the punishment of the Fire.

15. O you who believe! When you meet those who disbelieve advancing (for battle), do not turn your backs to them.

16. And whoever turns his back to them on that day, except as a strategy of war or to join (his) group, has certainly incurred the wrath of Allah and his abode is Hell, a wretched destination.

17. And you did not kill them, but Allah killed them. And you threw not

Surah 8: The spoils of war (v. 12-17)

رَمٰى	اللّٰهَ	وَلٰكِنَّ	رَمَيْتَ	إِذْ	رَمَيْتَ	وَمَا	
threw	Allah	but	you threw,	when	you threw		
إِنَّ	حَسَنًا	بَلَآءً	مِنْهُ	الْمُؤْمِنِيْنَ	وَلِيُبْلِيَ		
Indeed,	good.	(with) a trial	from Him	the believers	and that He may test		
اللّٰهَ	وَاَنَّ	ذٰلِكُمْ	۱۷	عَلِيْمٌ	سَمِيْعٌ	اللّٰهَ	
Allah (is)	and that,	That (is the case)	17	All-Knowing.	(is) All-Hearing,	Allah	
تَسْتَفْتِحُوْا	إِنْ	۱۸	الْكٰفِرِيْنَ	كَيْدِ	مُوْهِنُ		
you ask for victory	If	18	(of) the disbelievers.	(the) plan	one who makes weak		
فَهُوَ	تَنْتَهُوْا	وَإِنْ	الْفَتْحُ	جَآءَكُمُ	فَقَدْ		
then it (is)	you desist,	And if	the victory.	has come to you	then certainly		
تُغْنِيَ	وَلَنْ	نَعُدْ	تَعُوْدُوْا	وَإِنْ	لَكُمْ	خَيْرٌ	
will avail	And never	We will return (too).	you return,	but if	for you,	good	
اللّٰهَ	وَاَنَّ	كَثُرَتْ	وَلَوْ	شَيْـًٔا	فِئَتُكُمْ	عَنْكُمْ	
Allah	And that	(they are) numerous.	even if	anything,	your forces	you	
اللّٰهَ	اَطِيْعُوا	يٰٓاَيُّهَا الَّذِيْنَ اٰمَنُوْٓا	۱۹	الْمُؤْمِنِيْنَ	مَعَ		
Allah	Obey	O you who believe!	19	the believers.	(is) with		
تَسْمَعُوْنَ	وَاَنْتُمْ	عَنْهُ	تَوَلَّوْا	وَلَا	وَرَسُوْلَهٗ		
hear.	while you	from him	turn away	And (do) not	and His Messenger.		
وَهُمْ	سَمِعْنَا	قَالُوْا	كَالَّذِيْنَ	تَكُوْنُوْا	وَلَا	۲۰	
while they	"We heard,"	say,	like those who	be	And (do) not	20	
عِنْدَ	الدَّوَآبِّ	شَرَّ	إِنَّ	۲۱	يَسْمَعُوْنَ	لَا	
near	(of) the living creatures	worst	Indeed,	21	hear.	(do) not	
۲۲	يَعْقِلُوْنَ	لَا	الَّذِيْنَ	الْبُكْمُ	الصُّمُّ	اللّٰهِ	
22	use (their) intellect.	(do) not	those who	the dumb -	(are) the deaf,	Allah	
لَّاَسْمَعَهُمْ	خَيْرًا	فِيْهِمْ	اللّٰهُ	عَلِمَ	وَلَوْ		
surely, He (would) have made them hear.	any good,	in them	Allah (had) known		And if		
وَّهُمْ	لَّتَوَلَّوْا	اَسْمَعَهُمْ	وَلَوْ				
while they	surely they would have turned away,	He had made them hear,	And if				
لِلّٰهِ	اسْتَجِيْبُوْا	اٰمَنُوا	يٰٓاَيُّهَا الَّذِيْنَ	۲۳	مُعْرِضُوْنَ		
to Allah	Respond		O you who believe!	23	(were) averse.		

when you threw, but it was Allah **Who** threw so that **He** might test the believers with a good trial from **Himself**. Indeed, Allah is All-Hearing, All-Knowing.

18. That (is the case) and (know) that Allah weakens the plan of the disbelievers.

19. If you ask for victory, then certainly the victory has come to you. And if you desist, it is good for you, but if you will return, **We** too will return. And never will your forces avail you anything, even if they are numerous. And Allah is with the believers.

20. O you who believe! Obey Allah and **His** Messenger. And do not turn away from him when you hear (his order).

21. And do not be like those who say, "We hear," while they do not hear.

22. Indeed, worst of the living creatures in the sight of Allah are the deaf and the dumb, those who do not use their intellect.

23. And had Allah known any good in them, **He** would have made them hear. And if **He** had made them hear, they would (still) have turned away, while they were averse.

24. O you who believe! Respond to Allah

Surah 8: The spoils of war (v. 18-24) Part - 9

and **His** Messenger when he calls you to that which gives you life. And know that Allah comes in between a man and his heart and that to **Him** you will be gathered.

25. And fear a trial which will not afflict those who do wrong among you exclusively. And know that Allah is severe in penalty.

26. And remember when you were few and deemed weak in the land fearing that people might do away with you, then **He** sheltered you, strengthened you with **His** help, and provided you with good things, so that you may be thankful.

27. O you who believe! Do not betray Allah and the Messenger nor betray your trusts while you know.

28. And know that your wealth and your children are a trial. And that, with Allah is a great reward.

29. O you who believe! If you fear Allah, **He** will grant you a criterion and will remove your evil deeds and forgive you. And Allah is the Possessor of Great Bounty.

30. And when those who disbelieved plotted against you to restrain you

Surah 8: The spoils of war (v. 25-30)   Part - 9

Surah 8: The spoils of war (v. 31-36)

31. And when **Our** Verses are recited to them, they say, "Verily, we have heard. If we wished, we could also say like this. This is not but the tales of the former people."

32. And when they said, "O Allah! If this is the truth from **You**, then send rain of stones upon us from the sky or bring upon us a painful punishment."

33. But Allah would not punish them while you are among them, and Allah would not punish them while they seek forgiveness.

34. But why should Allah not punish them while they hinder (people) from Al-Masjid Al-Haraam while they are not its guardians? None can be its guardian except those who fear Allah, but most of them do not know.

35. And their prayer at the House was nothing but whistling and clapping. So taste the punishment because you used to disbelieve.

36. Indeed, those who

37. That Allah may distinguish the wicked from the good, and place the wicked over one another and heap them all together and put them into Hell. It is they who are the losers.

38. Say to those who disbelieve, if they cease, their past will be forgiven. But if they return, then the practice of the former people has already preceded (as a warning).

39. And fight them until there is no oppression and the religion is all for Allah. But if they desist, then indeed, Allah is All-Seer of what they do.

40. And if they turn away, then know that Allah is your Protector, an Excellent Protector, and an Excellent Helper.

Surah 8: The spoils of war (v. 37-40)

فَأَنَّ	مِّن شَيْءٍ	غَنِمْتُم	أَنَّمَا	وَاعْلَمُوٓا۟
then that,	anything,	of	you obtain (as) spoils of war	that what	And know

وَلِذِى الْقُرْبَىٰ	وَلِلرَّسُولِ	خُمُسَهُ	لِلَّهِ
and for the near relatives,	and for the Messenger	(is) one fifth of it	for Allah

ءَامَنتُم	إِن كُنتُمْ	وَابْنِ السَّبِيلِ	وَالْمَسَٰكِينِ	وَالْيَتَٰمَىٰ
believe	you	if	and the wayfarer,	and the needy	and the orphans

الْفُرْقَانِ	يَوْمَ	عَلَىٰ عَبْدِنَا	وَمَآ أَنزَلْنَا	بِٱللَّهِ
(of) the criterion,	(on the) day	Our slave	to	We sent down	and (in) what	in Allah,

شَىْءٍ	كُلِّ	عَلَىٰ	وَٱللَّهُ	ٱلْجَمْعَانِ	ٱلْتَقَى	يَوْمَ
thing	every	(is) on	And Allah	the two forces.	(when) met	(the) day

وَهُم	بِٱلْعُدْوَةِ ٱلدُّنْيَا	إِذْ أَنتُم	٤١	قَدِيرٌ
and they	on the nearer side of the valley	you (were)	When	41	All-Powerful.

وَلَوْ	مِنكُمْ	أَسْفَلَ	وَٱلرَّكْبُ	بِٱلْعُدْوَةِ ٱلْقُصْوَىٰ
And if	than you.	(was) lower	and the caravan	(were) on the farther side

فِى ٱلْمِيعَٰدِ	لَٱخْتَلَفْتُمْ	تَوَاعَدتُّمْ
the appointment.	in	certainly you would have failed	you (had) made an appointment

مَفْعُولًا	كَانَ	أَمْرًا	لِّيَقْضِىَ ٱللَّهُ	وَلَٰكِن
destined,	(that) was	a matter	that Allah might accomplish	But

بَيِّنَةٍ	عَن	هَلَكَ	مَن	لِّيَهْلِكَ
a clear evidence	on	(were to be) destroyed	(those) who	that (might be) destroyed

ٱللَّهَ	وَإِنَّ	بَيِّنَةٍ	عَنْ	حَىَّ	مَنْ	وَيَحْيَىٰ
Allah	And indeed,	a clear evidence.	on	(were to) live	(those) who	and (might) live

فِى	يُرِيكَهُمُ ٱللَّهُ	إِذْ	٤٢	عَلِيمٌ	لَسَمِيعٌ
in	Allah showed them to you	When	42	All-Knowing.	(is) All-Hearing,

كَثِيرًا	أَرَىٰكَهُمْ	وَلَوْ	قَلِيلًا	مَنَامِكَ
(as) many	He had shown them to you	and if	(as) few,	your dream

فِى ٱلْأَمْرِ	وَلَتَنَٰزَعْتُمْ	لَّفَشِلْتُمْ
the matter,	in	and surely you would have disputed	surely you would have lost courage

وَلَٰكِنَّ	بِذَاتِ ٱلصُّدُورِ	عَلِيمٌۢ	إِنَّهُۥ	سَلَّمَ	ٱللَّهَ
of what is in the breasts.	(is) All-Knower	Indeed, He	saved (you).	Allah	but

41. And know that anything you obtain as spoils of war, then indeed, one fifth of it is for Allah, and for the Messenger, and for the near relatives and the orphans, the needy, and the wayfarer, if you believe in Allah and in what **We** sent down to **Our** slave on the day of the criterion, the day when the two forces met. And Allah has power over everything.

42. When you were on the nearer side of the valley and they were on the farther side, and the caravan was lower (in position) than you. And if you had made an appointment (to meet), certainly, you would have missed the appointment. But (it was) so that Allah might accomplish a matter already destined, that might be destroyed those who were to be destroyed upon clear evidence and might live those who were to live upon a clear evidence. And indeed, Allah is All-Hearing, All-Knowing.

43. When Allah showed them to you in your dream as few, and if **He** had shown them to you as many, surely you would have lost courage and surely you would have disputed in the matter, but Allah saved you. Indeed, **He** is All-Knower of what is in the breasts.

Surah 8: The spoils of war (v. 41-43)

44. And when **He** showed them to you, when you met, as few in your eyes, and **He** made you (appear) as few in their eyes so that Allah might accomplish a matter that was already destined. And to Allah return (all) the matters.

45. O you who believe! When you meet a force, then be firm and remember Allah much, so that you may be successful.

46. And obey Allah and **His** Messenger, and do not dispute lest you lose courage and your strength would depart, and be patient. Indeed, Allah is with the patient ones.

47. And do not be like those who came forth from their homes boastfully and showing off to people and hindering them from the way of Allah. And Allah is All-Encompassing of what they do.

48. And when Shaitaan made their deeds fair-seeming to them and said, "No one can overcome you today from among the people, and indeed, I am your neighbor (for each and every help)." But when the two forces sighted each other, he turned away on his heels and said, "Indeed, I am free of you. Indeed, I see what you do not see, indeed, I

Surah 8: The spoils of war (v. 44-48)   **Part - 10**

fear Allah. And Allah is severe in penalty."

49. When the hypocrites and those in whose hearts was a disease said, "Their religion has deluded these (people)." But whoever puts his trust in Allah then indeed, Allah is All-Mighty, All Wise.

50. And if you could see when the Angels take away souls of those who disbelieve, striking their faces and their backs (saying), "Taste the punishment of the Blazing Fire."

51. That is because of what your hands have sent forth. And indeed, Allah is not unjust to **His** slaves.

52. Like the way of the people of Firaun and those who were before them. They disbelieved in the Signs of Allah, so Allah seized them for their sins. Indeed, Allah is All-Strong and severe in penalty.

53. That is because Allah will not change a favor, which **He** had bestowed on a people until they change what is within themselves. And indeed, Allah is All-Hearing, All-Knowing.

54. Like the way of the people of Firaun and those who were before them. They denied the Signs of their Lord, so **We** destroyed them for their sins and **We** drowned

the people of Firaun and all of them were wrongdoers.

55. Indeed, the worst of living creatures in the sight of Allah are those who disbelieve, and they will not believe.

56. The ones with whom you made a covenant, then they break their covenant every time, and they do not fear Allah.

57. So if you gain dominance over them in war, disperse by (means of) them those who are behind them, so that they may take heed.

58. And if you fear betrayal from a people, throw back to them on equal terms. Indeed, Allah does not love the traitors.

59. And let not those who disbelieve think that they can outstrip (Allah's plan). Indeed, they cannot escape.

60. And prepare against them whatever you are able to of force and cavalry to terrify therewith the enemy of Allah and your enemy and others besides them whom you do not know, but Allah knows them. And whatever you spend in the way of Allah will be fully repaid to you, and you will not be wronged.

61. And if they incline to peace,

then you also incline to it and put your trust in Allah. Indeed, **He** is All-Hearer, All-Knower.

62. But if they intend to deceive you, then indeed, Allah is sufficient for you. **He** is the **One Who** supported you with **His** help and with the believers

63. And **He** has put affection between their hearts. If you had spent all that is in the earth, you could not have put affection between their hearts, but Allah has put affection between them. Indeed, **He** is All-Mighty, All-Wise.

64. O Prophet! Allah is sufficient for you and those who follow you of the believers.

65. O Prophet! Urge the believers to fight. If there are twenty among you (who are) steadfast, they will overcome two hundred. And if there are one hundred among you (who are steadfast), they will overcome one thousand of those who disbelieve because they are a people who do not understand.

66. Now Allah has lightened for you, and **He** knows that there is weakness in you. So if there are among you one hundred (who are) steadfast, they will overcome two hundred. And if there are among you a thousand,

Surah 8: The spoils of war (v. 62-66)   Part - 10

they will overcome two thousand with Allah's permission. And Allah is with the steadfast.

67. It is not for a Prophet that he should have prisoners of war until he has battled strenuously in the land. You desire the commodities of this world but Allah desires (for you) the Hereafter. And Allah is All-Mighty, All-Wise.

68. Had it not been an ordainment from Allah that preceded, you would have been touched by a great punishment for what you took.

69. So consume what you got as war booty, lawful and good, and fear Allah. Indeed, Allah is Oft-Forgiving, Most Merciful.

70. O Prophet! Say to those who are captives in your hands, "If Allah knows any good in your hearts, He will give you better than what was taken from you, and He will forgive you. And Allah is Oft-Forgiving, Most Merciful."

71. But if they intend to betray you, certainly they have betrayed Allah before. So He gave you power over them. And Allah is All-Knower, All-Wise.

72. Indeed, those who believed and emigrated and strove hard in the way of Allah with their wealth and lives and those who gave shelter

Surah 8: The spoils of war (v. 67-72)   **Part - 10**

Surah Al-Taubah

73. And those who disbelieve are allies of one another. If you do not do so there will be oppression in the earth and great corruption.

74. And those who believed and emigrated and strove hard in the way of Allah and those who gave shelter and helped them, those are the believers in truth. For them is forgiveness and a noble provision.

75. And those who believed afterwards, and emigrated and strove hard with you then those are of you. But those of blood relationship are nearer to one another in the Book of Allah. Indeed, Allah is All-Knower of everything.

Surah Al-Taubah

1. Freedom from obligations from Allah and His Messenger

Surah 8: The spoils of war (v.73-75); Surah 9: The repentance (v.1)   Part - 10

to those with whom you made a treaty from the polytheists.

2. So move about in the land during four months but know that you cannot escape Allah and that Allah will disgrace the disbelievers.

3. And an announcement from Allah and His Messenger to the people on the day of the greater Pilgrimage that Allah is free from all obligations to the polytheists, and (so is) His Messenger. So if you repent, it is best for you. But if you turn away, then know that you cannot escape Allah. And give glad tidings to those who disbelieve of a painful punishment.

4. Except those with whom you have a treaty among the polytheists and they have not failed you in anything and they have not supported anyone against you, so fulfil their treaty until their term (has ended). Indeed, Allah loves the righteous.

5. Then, when the sacred months have passed, then kill the polytheists wherever you find them and seize them and besiege them and sit in wait for them at every place of ambush. But if they repent and establish prayer and give zakah, then leave their way. Indeed, Allah

Surah 9: The repentance (v. 2-5) Part - 10

is Oft-Forgiving, Most Merciful.

6. And if anyone of the polytheists seek your protection then grant him protection so that he may hear the Words of Allah. Then escort him to his place of safety. That is because they are a people who do not know.

7. How can there be a covenant with Allah and **His** Messenger for the polytheists, except those with whom you made a treaty near Al-Masjid Al-Haraam? So long as they are upright to you, be upright to them. Indeed, Allah loves those who are righteous.

8. How (can there be a treaty) while, if they gain dominance over you, they do not regard the ties of kinship with you or covenant of protection? They satisfy you with their mouths, but their hearts refuse, and most of them are defiantly disobedient.

9. They exchange the Verses of Allah for a little price, and they hinder (people) from **His** way. Evil indeed is what they used to do.

10. With regard to a believer, they do not respect the ties of kinship or covenant of protection. And it is they who are the transgressors.

11. But if they repent, establish prayer and give *zakah*,

Surah 9: The repentance (v. 6-11)   Part - 10

12. And if they break their oaths after their treaty and defame your religion, then fight the leaders of disbelief - indeed their oaths are nothing to them - so that they may cease.

13. Will you not fight a people who broke their oaths and determined to expel the Messenger and they began (the attack upon) you the first time? Do you fear them? Allah has more right that you should fear **Him**, if you are believers.

14. Fight them; Allah will punish them by your hands and disgrace them and give you victory over them and will heal the breasts of the believers.

15. And remove the anger of their hearts. And Allah accepts repentance of whom **He** wills. And Allah is All-Knower, All-Wise.

16. Or do you think that you would be left while Allah has not yet made evident those who strive (in **His** way) among you and do not take other than Allah, **His** Messenger and the believers as intimates? And Allah is All-Aware

Surah 9: The repentance (v. 12-16)   **Part - 10**

17. It is not for the polytheists to maintain the masajid of Allah, bearing witness against themselves of disbelief. For those, their deeds are worthless, and they will abide forever in the Fire.

18. The masajid of Allah are only to be maintained by those who believe in Allah and the Last Day and establish prayer and give *zakah* and fear none except Allah. Then perhaps they are the guided ones.

19. Do you make the providing of water for the pilgrims and the maintenance of Al-Masjid Al-Haraam equal to (the deeds of) one who believes in Allah and the Last Day and strives in the way of Allah? They are not equal in the sight of Allah. And Allah does not guide the wrongdoing people.

20. Those who believe, emigrate and strive in the way of Allah with their wealth and their lives are greater in rank in the sight of Allah. And they are the successful.

21. Their Lord gives them glad tidings of Mercy from **Him** and Pleasure, and Gardens wherein is enduring bliss for them.

22. They will abide in it forever. Indeed, with Allah is a great reward.

23. O you who

Surah 9: The repentance (v. 17-23) Part - 10

believe! Do not take your fathers and your brothers as allies if they prefer disbelief over belief. And whoever of you takes them as allies, then they are the wrongdoers.

24. Say, "If your fathers, your sons, your brothers, your spouses, your relatives, wealth which you have acquired, commerce wherein you fear a decline and dwellings in which you delight are more beloved to you than Allah and **His** Messenger and striving in **His** way, then wait until Allah brings **His** Command. And Allah does not guide the defiantly disobedient people."

25. Verily, Allah helped you in many regions, and on the day of Hunain, when pleased you your multitude, but it did not avail you at all, and the earth in spite of its vastness was straitened for you, then you turned back fleeing.

26. Then Allah sent down **His** tranquility on **His** Messenger, and on the believers and sent down forces (Angels), which you did not see and **He** punished those who disbelieved. And that is the recompense of the disbelievers.

27. Then Allah accepts repentance

Surah 9: The repentance (v. 24-27)   **Part - 10**

after that for whom **He** wills. And Allah is Oft-Forgiving, Most Merciful.

28. O you who believe! Indeed, the polytheists are unclean, so let them not come near Al-Masjid Al-Haraam after this, their (final) year. And if you fear poverty, then soon Allah will enrich you from **His** Bounty, if **He** wills. And Allah is All-Knower, All-Wise.

29. Fight those who do not believe in Allah and in the Last Day, and they do not make unlawful what Allah and **His** Messenger have made unlawful, and they do not acknowledge the true religion (Islam) from those who were given the Scripture, until they pay the *Jizyah* willingly while they are subdued.

30. And the Jews say, "Uzair is the son of Allah." And the Christians say, "Messiah is the son of Allah." That is their saying with their mouths, they imitate the saying of those who disbelieved before them. May Allah destroy them. How deluded are they!

31. They have taken their rabbis and their monks and the Messiah, son of Maryam, as Lords besides Allah. And they were not

Surah 9: The repentance (v. 28-31)   Part - 10

commanded except to worship the One God. There is no god except Him. Glory be to Him from all that they associate with Him.

32. They want to extinguish Allah's light with their mouths, but Allah refuses except to perfect His Light, although the disbelievers dislike it.

33. He is the One Who has sent His Messenger with guidance and the religion of truth (Islam) to manifest it over all religions, although the polytheists dislike it.

34. O you who believe! Indeed, many of the rabbis and the monks devour the wealth of people in falsehood and hinder (them) from the way of Allah. And those who hoard the gold and silver and do not spend it in the way of Allah, give them tidings of a painful punishment.

35. The Day when it (the gold and silver) will be heated in the Fire of Hell and their foreheads, flanks and their backs will be branded with it (it will be said), "This is what you hoarded for yourselves, so taste what you used to hoard."

36. Indeed, the number of months with Allah is twelve months in

the ordinance of Allah (from) the Day **He** created the heavens and the earth; of them four are sacred. That is the right religion, so do not wrong yourselves therein. And fight all the polytheists as they fight against you all together. And know that Allah is with the righteous.

37. Indeed, the postponing (of a Sacred month) is only an increase in disbelief by which are led astray those who disbelieve. They make it lawful one year and make it unlawful another year to adjust the number Allah has made unlawful and making lawful what Allah has made unlawful. The evil of their deeds is made fair-seeming to them. And Allah (does) not guide the disbelieving people.

38. O you who believe! What (is the matter) with you when it is said to you go forth in the way of Allah, you cling heavily to the earth? Are you pleased with the life of this world rather than the Hereafter? But what is the enjoyment of the life of this world compared to the Hereafter except a little.

39. If you do not go forth, He will punish you with a painful punishment and will replace you with another people,

Surah 9: The repentance (v. 36-39)

and you cannot harm **Him** at all. And Allah is on everything All-Powerful.

40. If you do not help him (Prophet Muhammad SAWS), certainly, Allah helped him when those who disbelieved drove him out (of Makkah), the second of two, when they both were in the cave, he said to his companion, "Do not grieve, indeed, Allah is with us." Then Allah sent down **His** tranquility upon him and supported him with forces (Angels) which you did not see and made the word of those who disbelieved the lowest, while the Word of Allah is the highest. And Allah is All-Mighty, All-Wise.

41. Go forth, whether light or heavy, and strive in the way of Allah with your wealth and your lives. That is better for you, if you only knew.

42. If it had been a near gain and an easy journey, surely they would have followed you, but the distance was long for them. And they will swear by Allah, "If we were able, certainly, we would have come forth with you." They destroy their own selves and Allah knows that indeed, they are liars.

43. May Allah forgive you! Why did you grant them leave until became evident to you those who

Surah 9: The repentance (v. 40-43)

43. ...were truthful and you knew who were the liars?

44. Those who believe in Allah and the Last Day would not ask your permission for striving with their wealth and their lives. And Allah is All-Knower of the righteous.

45. Only those ask your permission who do not believe in Allah and the Last Day and whose hearts are in doubt, so they waver in their doubts.

46. And if they had wished to go forth, surely they would have prepared for it some preparation. But Allah disliked their being sent, so He made them lag behind and it was said, "Sit with those who sit."

47. If they had gone forth with you, they would not have increased you except in confusion, and they would have been active in your midst seeking to cause dissension among you. And among you are some who would have listened to them. And Allah is All-Knower of the wrongdoers.

48. Verily, they had sought dissension before and had upset matters for you until the truth came and the Order of Allah became manifest, while they disliked it.

49. And among them is he who says, "Grant me leave and do not put me to trial."

Surah 9: The repentance (v. 44-49)

Surely, they have fallen into trial. And indeed, Hell will surround the disbelievers.

(will) surely surround	Hell	And indeed,	they have fallen.	the trial	in	Surely,

it distresses them,	good,	befalls you	If	49	the disbelievers.

50. If good befalls you, it distresses them; but if a calamity befalls you, they say, "Verily, we took care of our matter before." And they turn away while they are rejoicing.

our matter	we took	"Verily,	they say,	a calamity	befalls you	but if

Say,	50	(are) rejoicing.	while they	And they turn away	before."

51. Say, "Never will befall us (a calamity) except what Allah has decreed for us, **He** is our protector." And on Allah let the believers put their trust.

for us,	Allah has decreed	what	except	will befall us	"Never

[so] let the believers put (their) trust.	Allah	And on	(is) our Protector."	He

except	for us	you await	"Do	Say,	51

52. Say, "Do you await for us except one of the two best things (martyrdom or victory) while we await for you that Allah will afflict you with a punishment from **Himself** or at our hands? So wait, indeed we, along with you, are waiting."

for you	[we] await	while we	(of) the two best (things)	one

or	[near] **Him,**	from	with a punishment	Allah will afflict you	that

52	(are) waiting."	with you	indeed, we	So wait,	by our hands?

53. Say, "Spend willingly or unwillingly; never will it be accepted from you. Indeed, you are a defiantly disobedient people."

from you.	will be accepted	never	unwillingly;	or	willingly	"Spend	Say,

And not	53	defiantly disobedient."	a people	[you] are	Indeed, you

54. And nothing prevents their contributions from being accepted from them, except that they disbelieve in Allah and in His Messenger and that they come not to prayer except being lazy and that they do not spend except

that they	except	their contributions	from them	is accepted	that	prevents them

(to) the prayer	they come	and not	and in **His** Messenger,	in Allah	disbelieve

while they	except	they spend	and not	(are) lazy,	while they	except

Surah 9: The repentance (v. 50-54)

55. So let not their wealth and their children impress you. Allah only intends to punish them with it in the life of this world and their souls should depart while they are disbelievers.

56. And they swear by Allah that they indeed are of you while they are not of you, but they are a people who are afraid.

57. If they could find a refuge or some caves or a place to enter, surely they would turn to it and they run wild.

58. And among them are some who criticize you concerning the (distribution of) charities. If they are given from it, they are pleased; but if they are not given from it then they are enraged.

59. And if they were satisfied with what Allah and **His** Messenger gave them, and had said, "Sufficient for us is Allah, Allah will give us of **His** Bounty and (so will) **His** Messenger. Indeed, we turn our hopes to Allah."

60. The charities are only for the poor, the needy, those who collect them, and for those whose hearts are inclined (to the truth), and for the freeing of the slaves, and for those in debt and in the way of Allah and for the wayfarer - an obligation (imposed) by Allah. And Allah

61. And among them are those who hurt the Prophet (SAWS) and say, "He is (all) ears." Say, "An ear of goodness for you, he believes in Allah and believes the believers and is a mercy to those who believe among you." And those who hurt the Messenger of Allah, for them is a painful punishment.

62. They swear by Allah to you (Muslims) to please you. And Allah and **His** Messenger have more right that they should please **Him**, if they are believers.

63. Do they not know that whoever opposes Allah and **His** Messenger, that for him is the Fire of Hell, wherein he will abide forever? That is the great disgrace.

64. The hypocrites fear lest a Surah be revealed about them, informing them of what is in their hearts. Say, "Mock, indeed, Allah will bring forth what you fear."

65. And if you ask them, they will surely say, "We were only conversing and playing." Say, "Is it Allah and **His** Verses and **His** Messenger that you were mocking?"

66. Make no excuse; verily,

Surah 9: The repentance (v. 61-66)

عَنْ	نَعْفُ	إِنْ	إِيْمَانِكُمْ	بَعْدَ	كَفَرْتُمْ		
[on]	We pardon	If	your belief.	after	you have disbelieved		
طَآئِفَةٍ	مِّنْكُمْ	نُعَذِّبْ	بِأَنَّهُمْ	طَآئِفَةً	كَانُوْا	مُجْرِمِيْنَ	
criminals.	were	because they	a party,	We will punish	of you	a party	
مِّنْ	بَعْضُهُمْ	وَالْمُنٰفِقٰتُ			اَلْمُنٰفِقُوْنَ	66	
(are) of	some of them	and the hypocrite women,			The hypocrite men	66	
الْمَعْرُوْفِ	عَنِ	وَيَنْهَوْنَ	بِالْمُنْكَرِ	يَأْمُرُوْنَ	بَعْضٍ		
(is) the right,	what	and forbid	the wrong	They enjoin	others.		
فَنَسِيَهُمْ		اللّٰهَ	نَسُوْا	أَيْدِيَهُمْ	وَيَقْبِضُوْنَ		
so He has forgotten them.		Allah,	They forget	their hands.	and they close		
	الْفٰسِقُوْنَ	هُمُ	الْمُنٰفِقِيْنَ	إِنَّ			
67	the defiantly disobedient.	they (are)	the hypocrites,	Indeed,			
وَالْكُفَّارَ		وَالْمُنٰفِقٰتِ	الْمُنٰفِقِيْنَ	وَعَدَ اللّٰهُ			
and the disbelievers,		and the hypocrite women	the hypocrite men,	Allah has promised			
حَسْبُهُمْ		هِيَ	فِيْهَا	خٰلِدِيْنَ	جَهَنَّمَ	نَارَ	
sufficient for them.		It (is)	in it.	they (will) abide forever	(of) Hell,	Fire	
مُّقِيْمٌ		عَذَابٌ	وَلَهُمْ	وَلَعَنَهُمُ اللّٰهُ			
enduring.		(is) a punishment	and for them	And Allah has cursed them,			
مِّنْكُمْ	أَشَدَّ		كَانُوْا	مِنْ قَبْلِكُمْ	كَالَّذِيْنَ	68	
than you	mightier		they were	before you	Like those	68	
فَاسْتَمْتَعُوْا	وَّأَوْلَادًا		أَمْوَالًا	وَأَكْثَرَ	قُوَّةً		
So they enjoyed	and children.		(in) wealth	and more abundant	(in) strength,		
الَّذِيْنَ	اسْتَمْتَعَ	كَمَا	بِخَلَاقِكُمْ	فَاسْتَمْتَعْتُمْ	بِخَلَاقِهِمْ		
those	enjoyed	like	your portion	and you have enjoyed	their portion,		
كَالَّذِيْ		وَخُضْتُمْ	بِخَلَاقِهِمْ	مِنْ قَبْلِكُمْ			
like the one who		and you indulge (in idle talk)	their portion,	before you			
فِي الدُّنْيَا		أَعْمَالُهُمْ	حَبِطَتْ	أُولٰۤئِكَ	خَاضُوْا		
the world	in	(are) their deeds	worthless,	Those,	indulges (in idle talk)		
الْخٰسِرُوْنَ		هُمُ	وَأُولٰۤئِكَ	وَالْاٰخِرَةِ			
69	(are) the losers.	they	And those,	and (in) the Hereafter.			

you have disbelieved after your belief. If **We** pardon a party of you, **We** will punish a party because they were criminals.

67. The hypocrite men and the hypocrite women are of one another. They enjoin what is wrong and forbid what is right and close their hands. They forget Allah, so Allah has forgotten them. Indeed, the hypocrites, they are the defiantly disobedient.

68. Allah has promised the hypocrite men and the hypocrite women and the disbelievers the Fire of Hell, wherein they will abide forever. It is sufficient for them. And Allah has cursed them, and for them is an enduring punishment.

69. Like those before you, they were mightier than you in strength, and more abundant in wealth and children. So they enjoyed their portion and you have enjoyed your portion like those before you enjoyed their portion, and you indulge in idle talk like that in which they indulged. Those, their deeds are worthless in this world and in the Hereafter, and it is they who are the losers.

70. Has not come to them the news of those who were before them, the people of Nuh, and Aad, and Thamud, and the people of Ibrahim and the companions (i.e., dwellers) of Madyan, and the towns overturned? Their Messengers came to them with clear proofs. And Allah did not wrong them but they wronged themselves.

71. And the believing men and the believing women are allies of one another. They enjoin what is right and forbid what is wrong and establish prayer and give *zakah* and obey Allah and **His** Messenger. Those, Allah will have mercy on them. Indeed, Allah is All-Mighty, All-Wise.

72. Allah has promised to the believing men and the believing women Gardens underneath which rivers flow, wherein they will abide forever, and blessed dwellings in Gardens of everlasting bliss. But the pleasure of Allah is (far) greater. That is a great success.

73. O Prophet! Strive against the disbelievers and the hypocrites and be stern with them. And their abode is Hell, and wretched is the destination.

Surah 9: The repentance (v. 70-73)

Surah 9: The repentance (v. 74-78)

74. They swear by Allah that they said nothing (wrong) while certainly they had said the word of disbelief and disbelieved after their (pretense of) Islam and planned that which they could not attain. And they were not resentful except (for the fact that) Allah and **His** Messenger had enriched them of **His** bounty. So if they repent, it is better for them, and if they turn away, Allah will punish them with a painful punishment in this world and in the Hereafter. And they have none on the earth as a protector or a helper.

75. And among them is he who made a covenant with Allah (saying), "If **He** gives us out of **His** bounty, surely we will give charity and surely we will be among the righteous."

76. But when **He** gave them of **His** bounty, they became stingy with it and turned away while they were averse.

77. So **He** penalized them with hypocrisy in their hearts until the day when they will meet **Him**, because they broke their covenant with Allah which they had promised **Him** and because they used to lie.

78. Do they not know that Allah knows their secrets and their secret conversations and that Allah is All-Knower

79. Those who criticize the contributors among the believers concerning their charities and (criticize) those who find nothing (to spend) except their effort, so they ridicule them - Allah will ridicule them, and for them is a painful punishment.

80. Ask forgiveness for them or do not ask forgiveness for them. If you ask forgiveness for them seventy times, Allah will never forgive them. That is because they disbelieved in Allah and **His** Messenger, and Allah does not guide the defiantly disobedient people.

81. Those who remained behind rejoiced in their staying (at home) behind the Messenger of Allah and they disliked to strive with their wealth and their lives in the way of Allah and said, "Do not go forth in the heat." Say, "The Fire of Hell is more intense in heat," if only they could understand.

82. So let them laugh a little and they will weep much as a recompense for what they used to earn.

83. Then if Allah returns you to a group of them and they ask you permission to go out, then say, "You will never come out with me, ever, and you will not fight with me any enemy. Indeed, you were satisfied

with sitting (at home) the first time, so sit with those who stay behind."

84. And never pray for any of them who dies or stand by his grave. Indeed, they disbelieved in Allah and His Messenger and died while they were defiantly disobedient.

85. And let not their wealth and their children impress you. Allah only intends to punish them through these (things) in this world and that their souls will depart while they are disbelievers.

86. And when a Surah was revealed to believe in Allah and strive with His Messenger, men of wealth among them asked your permission (to stay back) and said, "Leave us to be with those who sit (at home)."

87. They were satisfied to be with those who stayed behind, and their hearts were sealed so they do not understand.

88. But the Messenger and those who believed with him strove with their wealth and their lives. For them are the good things, and those - they are the successful ones.

89. Allah has prepared for them Gardens underneath which rivers flow, wherein they will abide forever. That is the great success.

Surah 9: The repentance (v. 84-89) Part - 10

90. And those who made excuses among the bedouins came asking permission (to stay behind), and those who had lied to Allah and **His** Messenger sat (at home). A painful punishment will strike those who disbelieved among them.

91. There is not on the weak or on the sick or on those who do not find anything to spend any blame if they are sincere to Allah and **His** Messenger. There is not on the good-doers any way (for blame). And Allah is Oft-Forgiving, Most Merciful.

92. Nor (is their blame) on those who, when they came to you that you provide them with mounts, you said, "I can find no mounts for you." They turned back with their eyes flowing with tears of sorrow that they could not find something to spend.

93. The way (for blame) is only on those who ask your permission while they are rich. They are satisfied to be with those who stay behind, and Allah has sealed their hearts, so they do not know.

Surah 9: The repentance (v. 90-93)